The Vietnam War

BLOOMSBURY TOPICS IN CONTEMPORARY
NORTH AMERICAN LITERATURE

Series Editor: Sarah Graham

Bloomsbury's Topics in Contemporary North American Literature series offers authoritative guides to major themes in recent American writing. With chapters written by leading scholars in their field, each book surveys a wide range of writing in a variety of genres.

These informative and accessible volumes are essential reading for advanced undergraduate and graduate students, facilitating discussion and supporting close analysis of the texts covered.

Also available in the *Bloomsbury Studies in Contemporary North American Fiction* series:

Bret Easton Ellis, edited by Naomi Mandel
Chuck Palahniuk, edited by Francisco Collado-Rodriguez
Cormac McCarthy, edited by Sara Spurgeon
Don DeLillo, edited by Stacey Olster
Leslie Marmon Silko, edited by David L. Moore
Louise Erdrich, edited by Deborah L. Madsen
Margaret Atwood, edited by J. Brooks Bouson
Philip Roth, edited by Debra Shostak
Toni Morrison, edited by Lucille P. Fultz

The Vietnam War

Topics in Contemporary North American Literature

Edited by
Brenda M. Boyle

Bloomsbury Academic
An imprint of Bloomsbury Publishing Plc

B L O O M S B U R Y
LONDON • NEW DELHI • NEW YORK • SYDNEY

Bloomsbury Academic
An imprint of Bloomsbury Publishing Plc

50 Bedford Square	1385 Broadway
London	New York
WC1B 3DP	NY 10018
UK	USA

www.bloomsbury.com

BLOOMSBURY and the Diana logo are trademarks of Bloomsbury Publishing Plc

First published 2015

© Brenda Boyle and Contributors, 2015

All rights reserved. No part of this publication may be reproduced or transmitted in any form or by any means, electronic or mechanical, including photocopying, recording, or any information storage or retrieval system, without prior permission in writing from the publishers.

No responsibility for loss caused to any individual or organization acting on or refraining from action as a result of the material in this publication can be accepted by Bloomsbury or the author.

British Library Cataloguing-in-Publication Data
A catalogue record for this book is available from the British Library.

ISBN: HB: 978-1-4725-1204-8
PB: 978-1-4725-0626-9
ePDF: 978-1-4725-1017-4
ePub: 978-1-4725-1077-8

Library of Congress Cataloging-in-Publication Data
A catalog record for this book is available from the Library of Congress.

Typeset by Newgen Knowledge Works (P) Ltd., Chennai, India

CONTENTS

Map vii
Chronology viii

Introduction: The war stories we tell
  Brenda M. Boyle 1

1 Michael Herr's traumatic New Journalism:
   Dispatches Mark Heberle 27

2 Dương Thu Hương's *Paradise of the Blind*
   and *Novel Without a Name*, and Bảo Ninh's
   The Sorrow of War: Corrective, politically
   incorrect, and challenging Michele Janette 47

3 "Ten years burning down the road":
   Trauma, mourning, and postmemory in
   Bobbie Ann Mason's *In Country* Joanna Price 71

4 War, gender, and race in le thi diem thuy's
   The Gangster We Are All Looking For
   Isabelle Thuy Pelaud 95

5 The home front and the front lines in
   the war novels of Tim O'Brien Susan Farrell 115

6 The ghost that won't be exorcised:
   Larry Heinemann's *Paco's Story*
   Stacey Peebles 137

7 American totem society in the twenty-first
   century: Denis Johnson's *Tree of Smoke*,
   Karl Marlantes's *Matterhorn*, and Tatjana Solis's
   The Lotus Eaters Brenda M. Boyle 159

Further reading 183
Works cited 187
Index 203

MAP

A 1960s map of Viet Nam given to all US service people.

CHRONOLOGY

1897	After decades of colonizing and warring, France makes itself the government of the Indochina Union.
1917	In "Fourteen Points," US President Woodrow Wilson insists all nations should be self-determining.
1919	Nguyen Ai Quoc (aka Ho Chi Minh) petitions the WWI Versailles Peace Conference for Vietnamese independence.
1930	The Vietnamese Nationalist Party, founded in 1927, is suppressed by the French colonial government. Subsequently, Ho Chi Minh founds the Indochinese Communist Party.
1940	Japan occupies Viet Nam, retaining the French Vichy administration.
1941	The Indochinese Communist Party creates its military arm, the Viet Minh. US President Franklin D. Roosevelt insists in "Atlantic Charter" that all nations should be self-determining.
1944	Roosevelt advocates a "trusteeship" for Viet Nam in preparation for its freedom from French governance.
1945	Japan expels French officials from Viet Nam and recognizes Emperor Bao Dai as the head of Viet Nam's government. Roosevelt dies; Vice President Harry S. Truman becomes President. Ho Chi Minh declares the independence of the "Democratic Republic of Viet Nam" and asks for President Truman's acknowledgment.
1946	The First Indochina War begins: France versus the Viet Minh.

1947	In the "Truman Doctrine," Truman promises to support people seeking independence from outsiders.
1948	The US indirectly supports the French in Viet Nam financially.
1949	France recognizes Emperor Bao Dai as the head of the new State of Vietnam, and grants Viet Nam independence only within the French Union.
1950	The Soviet Union and the People's Republic of China recognize the (northern) Democratic Republic of Vietnam as the legitimate state of Viet Nam; the United States and Great Britain recognize as legitimate the (southern) State of Vietnam, headed by Bao Dai. The United States directly provides economic and military aid to France in its war with the Viet Minh. US military personnel: about 60.
1953	US President Dwight D. Eisenhower grants financial aid to the French war effort, totaling 80% of the French war costs.
1954	Eisenhower formulates the "domino theory"; France surrenders to the Viet Minh at Dien Bien Phu, ending the First Indochina War. Emperor Bao Dai appoints Ngo Dinh Diem as prime minister of the (southern) State of Vietnam. The Geneva Peace Agreement temporarily partitions Viet Nam into north and south, guarantees elections in 1956, and facilitates moving hundreds of thousands of (mostly Catholic) refugees from north to south.
1955–1956	Graham Greene publishes his novel *The Quiet American*.
1957	Diem visits the United States, where he is hailed by *Life* magazine as the "Tough Miracle Man of Vietnam." As a Catholic, Diem especially is lauded by US Catholics, including Cardinal Spellman.
1958	With US help, Ngo Dinh Diem deposes Bao Dai, creates the (southern) Republic of Vietnam, and becomes President. Eugene Burdick and William Lederer publish their novel, *The Ugly American*.

1959	The Democratic Republic of Vietnam begins building the Ho Chi Minh Trail through Laos. Two US advisers become the first US casualties of the Second Indochina War, part of which is known to Americans later as the Vietnam War.
1960	The National Liberation Front (NLF) is formed in southern Viet Nam by the Communist Party of northern Viet Nam. The NLF's military arm is referred to derogatorily as "Viet Cong." US military personnel: about 900.
1961	US President John F. Kennedy refuses to send US combat units to Viet Nam. Bernard Fall publishes his account of the French in Viet Nam, *Street Without Joy*. US military personnel: about 3200.
1962	US Military Assistance Command (MACV) is established in South Vietnam. US military personnel: 11,300.
1963	In January, South Vietnamese military forces are soundly defeated at Ap Bac. In June, protesting Diem's oppression of Buddhists, Buddhist monk Thich Quang Duc immolates himself on a Saigon street. In early November, the US supports a coup against Diem that ends in the deaths of Diem and his brother, Ngo Dinh Nhu. Three weeks after the coup and deaths, US President John F. Kennedy is assassinated and Vice President Lyndon Baines Johnson becomes President. US military personnel: 16,300.
1964	North Vietnamese allegedly attack US Navy destroyers in the Gulf of Tonkin. With the Gulf of Tonkin Resolution, the US Congress authorizes President Johnson to use armed force in Viet Nam. US military personnel: 23,300.
1965	In March, after an attack on US forces at Pleiku, Johnson authorizes "Operation Rolling Thunder," the bombing of North Vietnam that persists for 3.5 years. Johnson also authorizes the use of combat units in South Vietnam: an American Marine

brigade lands at Da Nang in March. Anti-War activities begin at the University of Michigan and in a Washington, DC protest organized by Students for a Democratic Society (SDS). In November, the first meeting of US and North Vietnamese military forces occurs in the Battle of Ia Drang. Robin Moore publishes his novel *The Green Berets*. US military personnel: 184,300.

1966   Buddhists lead anti-government demonstrations in cities all over South Vietnam. The US Senate Foreign Relations Committee begins public hearings about the War. Barry Sadler and Robin Moore's song, "The Ballad of the Green Berets" becomes a hit; Bernard Fall publishes *Hell In a Very Small Place*, his account of the Dien Bien Phu siege of the French in 1954. US military personnel: 385,300.

1967   In early April, Martin Luther King, Jr. delivers "A Time to Break Silence." Weeks later, US-wide anti-War demonstrations are held, including a rally of 300,000 in New York City. In October, 50,000 anti-War protestors march on the Pentagon. In November, the commander of US forces in Viet Nam, General William Westmoreland, declares the end of the War is near. David Halberstam publishes his novel *One Very Hot Day*. US military personnel: 485,600.

1968   In January, the siege at Khe Sanh begins simultaneous to the Tet Offensive. Following the Offensive's conclusion in February, respected journalist Walter Cronkite opines the United States should negotiate an end to the War. The massacre at My Lai occurs in March but is kept from the US public until November, 1969. Johnson announces in March he will not seek re-election, and days later, Martin Luther King, Jr. is assassinated. On the November day when Robert F. Kennedy wins the Democratic presidential primary, he, too, is assassinated. Just before the elections that make

	Richard M. Nixon President, Johnson ends "Rolling Thunder," 3.5 years after it began. The Doors release "The Unknown Soldier." Film adaptation of *The Green Berets* is released, featuring John Wayne. US military personnel: 536,100.
1969	Secret US bombing of Cambodia begins, as does "Vietnamization" of the War. In the "Nixon Doctrine," President Nixon announces that while the United States will support allies, they must defend themselves. Ho Chi Minh dies, massive anti-War demonstrations occur across the United States, the My Lai massacre is publicly revealed, and the US Selective Service begins a draft lottery. David Rabe's play, "Sticks and Bones," is premiered; Creedence Clearwater Revival releases single "Fortunate Son." US military personnel: 475,200.
1970	A draw-down of US forces in Viet Nam is planned. US military actions in Cambodia spur widespread protests. Protesting students at Kent State and Jackson State are killed by National Guardsmen and police. The US Senate repeals the 1964 Gulf of Tonkin Resolution. Edwin Starr releases his single "War"; Crosby, Stills, Nash, and Young release their singles, "Ohio" and "Find the Cost of Freedom." US military personnel: 334,600.
1971	1LT William Calley is found guilty of murder in the My Lai massacre. Vietnam Veterans Against the War (VVAW) stage the Winter Soldier Investigations in Detroit and, in "Dewey Canyon III," throw their medals on the steps of the US Capitol Building. More nationwide anti-War protests gather hundreds of thousands of people. Daniel Ellsberg leaks the "Pentagon Papers" to *The New York Times*. Plans for more US troop reductions in South Vietnam. David Rabe's play, "The Basic Training of Pavlo Hummel," is premiered; Marvin Gaye releases album "What's Going On"; Ronald J. Glasser publishes his memoir as a US Army doctor in Vietnam, *365 Days*. US military personnel: 156,800.

1972	Nixon meets separately with leaders of the Soviet Union and the People's Republic of China. National Security Advisor (and, in 1973, also the Secretary of State) Henry Kissinger announces "peace is at hand"; months later, peace talks break down and the US bombs the North Vietnamese cities Hanoi and Haiphong. US military personnel: 24,200.
1973	Peace talks resume, resulting in the Paris Peace Accords of January 27, 1973. The US draft lottery ends, American POWs are released, US military personnel leave Viet Nam by the end of March, and Congress ends the President's unilateral authority to send US forces into combat. The "Vietnam War" is over. US Vice President Spiro T. Agnew resigns and President Nixon appoints Gerald Ford. Congress blocks further funding of the war in Viet Nam. Tim O'Brien publishes his memoir *If I Die in a Combat Zone*. US military personnel: 240.
1974	The South Vietnamese military—the Army of the Republic of Viet Nam (ARVN)—continues to war against the (northern) People's Army of Viet Nam (PAVN), but without US military aid. Although Calley was sentenced to life in prison for his part in the My Lai massacre, President Nixon pardons him. In August, Nixon resigns as a result of the Watergate Scandal and Vice President Gerald Ford becomes President. Robert Stone publishes *Dog Soldiers*, which shares the 1975 National Book Award.
1975	In early March, the PAVN begins its Spring Offensive in the South, quickly overcoming city after city. The US Congress rejects Ford's request for emergency military aid to ARVN. As PAVN and Viet Cong troops enter Saigon, the remaining Americans and some Vietnamese allies evacuate the city by helicopter. Saigon is renamed Ho Chi Minh City; the country is reunified as the Socialist Republic of Vietnam; and the Second Indochina War ends. The US cuts all ties to Viet Nam.

1976	Jimmy Carter is elected as President of the United States; he extends amnesty to Vietnam War draft resisters. US bicentennial celebrations occur nationwide. Ron Kovic publishes his memoir, *Born on the Fourth of July*.
1977	The Socialist Republic of Vietnam is admitted to the United Nations. Philip Caputo publishes his memoir, *A Rumor of War*, and Michael Herr publishes his journalism in *Dispatches*.
1978	Dire conditions and oppression force many Vietnamese to flee Viet Nam by boat. Their hazardous flights and squalid conditions in refugee camps across Southeast Asia call attention to the plight of the "Boat People." People's Republic of China discontinues aid to Viet Nam because of its discrimination against ethnic Chinese people living in Viet Nam. The Socialist Republic of Vietnam and the Union of Soviet Socialist Republics (USSR) form an alliance. Viet Nam invades Cambodia. James Webb publishes *Fields of Fire* and Tim O'Brien publishes *Going After Cacciato*, which wins the 1979 National Book Award. The films *The Deer Hunter*, *Coming Home*, and *Go Tell the Spartans* are released.
1979	The United States and the People's Republic of China establish diplomatic relations. China attacks Viet Nam, remaining there for a month. The film *Apocalypse Now* is released.
1980	Ronald Reagan is elected President of the United States. During the campaign, he coins the term "Vietnam Syndrome" and argues that the War was "a noble cause." In response to symptoms displayed by veterans of the war, Post-Traumatic Stress Disorder is added to the *Diagnostic and Statistical Manual of Mental Disorders* (DSM III). Charles Coleman publishes the first novel about PTSD, *Sergeant Back Again*.

1982	The Vietnam Veterans Memorial in Washington, DC is dedicated. John Del Vecchio publishes *The 13th Valley*.
1983	Stephen Wright publishes a novel, *Meditations in Green*. Lynda Van Devanter publishes her memoir, *Home Before Morning*.
1984	Vietnam War veterans win a settlement against Dow Chemical for its manufacture of Agent Orange. Louise Erdrich publishes a novel, *Love Medicine*.
1985	Bobbie Ann Mason publishes a novel, *In Country*.
1986	Larry Heinemann publishes his novel, *Paco's Story*, which wins the 1987 National Book Award. The film *Platoon* is released and is awarded Best Picture and Director in the 1987 Oscars.
1987	The film *Full Metal Jacket* is released.
1988	Dương Thu Hương publishes her novel, *Paradise of the Blind* in Vietnamese; its English translation is published in 1993.
1989	The Socialist Republic of Vietnam withdraws its military from Cambodia after 11 years. Le Ly Hayslip publishes her memoir, *When Heaven and Earth Changed Places*. The film adaptation of *Born on the Fourth of July* is released and wins the 1990 Oscar for Best Director.
1990	Tim O'Brien publishes his novel, *The Things They Carried*. Bảo Ninh publishes his novel, *The Sorrow of War* in Vietnamese; its English translation is published in 1994. Dương Thu Hương publishes *Novel Without a Name* in Vietnamese; its French translation is published in 1994, and its English translation in 1995.
1991	Before launching the Persian Gulf War, President George H. W. Bush pledges "it will not be another Vietnam." At the 5-week-long war's conclusion, Bush exalts "By God, we've kicked the Vietnam syndrome once and for all!"
1993	The Vietnam Women's Memorial is dedicated in Washington, DC.

1994	US President Bill Clinton ends the decades-long US embargo against the Socialist Republic of Vietnam. Tim O'Brien publishes his novel, *In the Lake of the Woods*.
1995	Dương Thu Hương publishes *Novel Without a Name* in English. The United States normalizes diplomatic relations with the Socialist Republic of Vietnam.
1997	Lan Cao publishes *Monkey Bridge*, the first "Vietnamese American" novel.
1998	President Clinton signs the Iraq Liberation Act, authorizing the removal of the Saddam Hussein regime in Iraq.
2001	In an attack by Al Qaeda operatives on September 11, two passenger planes crash into the World Trade Center towers in NYC, one crashes into the Pentagon, and a fourth crashes into a Pennsylvania field. The US invades Afghanistan in October; plans to invade Iraq begin in November. Critics worry that war in Iraq will be another Vietnam War.
2003–2011	In March 2003, United States and allied forces invade Iraq. In early 2004, reports surface of prisoner abuse by US military police at the Abu Ghraib prison in Iraq. In November 2004, a plaque is added to the Vietnam Veteran's Memorial, commemorating veterans who die after the War; an education center has been authorized for the Memorial site. Allied forces remain in Iraq until 2011; US forces plan to leave Afghanistan in 2014. Estimates for costs of the three wars (including Pakistan, which the US funds) run up to US$4.4 trillion and the deaths of 330,000 people directly from war violence. In 2007, Denis Johnson publishes his Vietnam War novel, *Tree of Smoke*, which wins the 2007 National Book Award. Early in 2010, Karl Marlantes publishes *Matterhorn* and Tatjana Solis publishes *The Lotus Eaters*.

Introduction: The war stories we tell

Brenda M. Boyle

(Hi)stories about the Vietnamese

Westerners have been telling stories about the country and the people of Viet Nam[1] for a long time. Well before March, 1965—when "the Vietnam War" officially began with American Marines storming the shores at Da Nang—stories were told that might have encouraged or incited the willingness to escalate American involvement in Viet Nam's conflict.[2] In his discussion of Vietnamese characters featured in Hollywood films produced between 1929 and 1964, for instance, historian Scott Laderman asserts that post-World War II films likened the contemporary threat posed by Viet Minh "reds" to ordinary Vietnamese, to the threat posed by "redskins" to frontier Americans. This parallel cast ordinary Vietnamese as children and females needing rescue. In films throughout the 1950s, Laderman explains, Vietnamese characters were signified as helpless:

> This symbolic infantilization (and perhaps feminization) of Vietnam, as well as the familiar American Indian context in which it appeared, were instrumental in constructing Vietnam as a childlike place in need of tutelage and instruction—such as the trusteeship system contemplated by Franklin D. Roosevelt during World War II—before genuine independence could be allowed. ("Hollywood's Vietnam" 579)

Films have didactic effects and so these were not simply "entertainment"; they "began to script an interventionist narrative for U.S. involvement in Southeast Asia at a time when U.S. military interest in the region was still in its infancy" Laderman continues (581). He deduces that "Vietnamese people, as portrayed by Hollywood, were exceedingly vulnerable to the international communist menace, leaving Americans with a solemn obligation to aid in their rescue" (607).

These filmic stories were told against a backdrop of nineteenth and twentieth-century racialized "reportage literature" written by journalists, scholars, missionaries, hunters, and travel writers who cast the Vietnamese as "'primitive,' 'lazy,' 'cowardly,' 'vain,' 'dishonest,' 'unclean,' and 'somnolent'" (Bradley, *Imagining* 46). "Embedded in these harsh judgments of colonial Vietnam was a broader interwar discourse on the relationship between what was seen as the backward character of nonwhite peoples and the more progressive West," explains historian Mark Philip Bradley. "American images of Vietnamese society and nationalism reflected a fundamental belief in racialized cultural hierarchies that had underlain the American encounter with nonwhite people at home and abroad since the mid-nineteenth century" Bradley continues, a belief echoing those of European colonialists, especially the French in regard to Viet Nam. "Americans relied almost exclusively [for their opinions about Viet Nam and Vietnamese people] on the writings of French scholars, colonial officials, and journalists" whose "deprecating assessments" were "part of a wider Orientalist discourse on the non-Western 'other' through which European colonial powers used a culturally constructed conception of the negative essence of colonized peoples to denote Western superiority and reinforce colonial military and economic dominance" (47). In short, for the Western cultures to look good, they had to make the Vietnamese look bad.

As Bradley makes clear earlier, American storytellers were not the first Westerners to cast the Vietnamese in this way. During the long era of French colonialism in Indochina, French culture producers also cast the Vietnamese in demeaning ways. Karl Ashoka Britto points out how France maintained its ethos as a benevolent colonizer, not a tyrannical occupier: "The crucial difference between the French and their colonial 'others' was articulated and reinforced through discursive forms and material strategies that included legal codes, urban planning, and pseudo-scientific race theory, as well as travel narratives and literary texts that trafficked in racial and cultural stereotypes" (4). Dana

S. Hale investigates some late-nineteenth and early-twentieth-century discursive forms, commercial trademarks, and French cultural expositions, concluding that these venues promoted the Vietnamese as docile and skilled workers appreciative of their colonial overlords' guidance (82) and as the empire's "gifted children" requiring France's protection (141).

Viet Nam has a long history of resisting such "protection," the "French War" and the "American War" being two of its most recent independence movements.[3] What follows are the broad strokes of a debatable, complex, and confusing situation, as alliances shift and groups assume or are assigned new and different names.[4] Viet Nam was colonized and dubbed part of "Indochine" by the French in the nineteenth century, and ceded by France's World War II Vichy government to Japanese control.[5] Vietnamese communists known as the Viet Minh (supported by, among others, the United States) resisted the Vichy French and then the Japanese; after World War II, when France militarily tried to recolonize Viet Nam, the Viet Minh (supported by the People's Republic of China) resisted France's efforts (supported by the United States).[6] This 8-year-long "First Indochina War," or "French War," concluded in May 1954 after the defeat of the French at Dien Bien Phu, with the 1954 Geneva peace agreement temporarily dividing the country into two parts while promising reunification and elections in 1956.[7] In the meantime, the United States increased its political and financial support of Ngo Dinh Diem, the southern half's anticommunist government leader, while the Soviet Union and People's Republic of China continued their support for the communist north, the Democratic Republic of Viet Nam, and its leader, Ho Chi Minh. Subsequently, the promised 1956 reunification did not happen and elections were not held. "Instead," says historian Mark Philip Bradley, "the growing clash between communist insurgency ['Viet Cong'] and the US-backed Ngo Dinh Diem in the late 1950s and early 1960s would bring another war" (*Vietnam* 68).[8] By 1955, American military advisors were sent by President Eisenhower to assist the fledgling military of the Republic of Viet Nam (South Vietnam) in its battle with insurgents; by 1960, the United States was subsidizing most of South Vietnam's governmental budget (84); and from 1961 to 1963, President Kennedy increased the number of advisors sevenfold, from 3,200 to 23,000. "These advisors were directly involved in ARVN [Army of the Republic of Viet Nam] combat operations, flying Diem's troops into battle zones . . . and advising on tactics and strategy in the field" (103). Thus, while August 1964's Gulf of Tonkin episode commonly is regarded as igniting the 1965–1968 US bombing campaign against the north ("Rolling Thunder") and initiating the 1965 open-ended deployment of American combat troops, the United States already had been involved in Viet Nam for nearly 20 years. However, March 1965 is generally agreed upon as the outset of what is known as the "Second Indochina War" to Western historians, the "American War" to Vietnamese, and the "Vietnam War" to Americans and their allies.[9]

Why does this historical record matter to the study of Vietnam War literature? What do the political origins of US involvement in Viet Nam have to do with its fictional representations? The answer to both questions is that fiction has an important role in teaching readers how to think of and about the war and its outcome, especially because fiction—prose and film—often is the only exposure to the war many Americans now have.[10] American fictions, like all of the stories told about Viet Nam and about the Vietnam War, do not simply reflect what "happened"; moreover, they configure readers' understandings of the war, sometimes establishing, sometimes confirming, and sometimes challenging the national narrative, or what war correspondent Chris Hedges calls "the myth of war." "The potency of myth," Hedges alerts readers, "is that it allows us to make sense of mayhem and violent death. It gives a justification to what is often nothing more than gross human cruelty and stupidity" (23). When myth does not prevail, "war is exposed for what it is—organized murder" (21). Hedges cautions readers to pay attention to how stories are told and to the elements included and excluded in that storytelling, as the "lie of omission" is often at the heart of myth-making (22).

American storytelling

Two early-1960s US publications can illustrate history's relevance to the study of Vietnam War literature, as the two texts frame a narrative, a myth, or tell a story about American involvement in Viet Nam that persists to this day. The first, a pamphlet published in 1962 by the US Department of Defense for American military advisors being sent to South Vietnam, states: "The Vietnamese have paid a heavy price in suffering for their long fight against the Communists. We military men are in Vietnam now because *their government has asked us to help* its soldiers and people in winning their struggle" (Department iii; emphasis added). First, these sentences frame Americans as dutifully and charitably aiding the hapless Vietnamese; had the United States not been invited to Viet Nam, it would not be there. Second, the sentences dichotomize "Vietnamese" and "Communists." That is, these identities are mutually exclusive: "Vietnamese" cannot be "Communists"; "Communists" cannot be "Vietnamese"; and the country of "Vietnam" includes only the southern half, the Republic of Viet Nam. What is implied is that the recipients of United States aid, *because* they are receiving aid from an authenticating source, are the authentic and legitimate citizens of the country of Viet Nam; despite the southern, nationalist origins of the Viet Cong, "Communists" are other, outsiders, invalid Vietnamese. Later, in a passage about Viet Nam's recent history, the pamphlet situates the French as a benign presence in the region: "The French *assumed control* over the province of Cochin China in 1863. Before another decade has [*sic*] passed, the other two regions, Tonkin and Annam, also *went under* French rule" (13; emphasis added). The passage's rhetoric casts the citizens of Cochin China, Tonkin, and Annam as passive (and implies willing) beneficiaries of French "control" and "rule." According to the pamphlet, then, the American and French interventions are well-meaning and ingenuous responses to what must be Vietnamese needs or requests. The French did not "colonize," "invade," "occupy," or subjugate the Vietnamese; instead, the French mysteriously found themselves controlling and ruling, as though they had been thrust into the situation unwittingly. Furthermore, "When the French tried to regain a foothold in Vietnam in 1946, Viet Minh forces attacked them on a wide front" (14). Again, the French are innocent of imperial intents; trying to "regain a foothold" is far less belligerent than the Viet Minh's "attacking." Finally, the pamphlet's rhetoric casts the United States in an especially positive light: although the Vietnamese passively accept the friendly generosity of the French controllers, they actively request the Americans' helping hand.[11]

The second US document, "Why Vietnam," was published by the US Congress in August 1965 ("US Government"). Intended to justify publicly why the United States is involved in Viet Nam, the document includes letters by past American presidents (Eisenhower and Kennedy) and speeches by the then-current president (Lyndon Baines Johnson), Secretary of State (Dean Rusk), and Secretary of Defense (Robert McNamara). Johnson's texts employ rhetoric similar to that in the advisor's pamphlet. In the document's Foreword, Johnson concludes that the "tragic conflict in Vietnam" is one "we did not seek" and "we do not desire." In a July 1965 press conference announcing sending another 50,000 military personnel to South Vietnam, he says "We did not choose to be the guardians at the gate, but there is no one else" (5), "We cannot now dishonor our word or abandon our commitment" (6), and the United States has "obligations of justice toward our fellow men" (8). In a May 1965 address to the Association of American Editorial Cartoonists, Johnson reiterates that "[t]his task is commanded to us by the moral values of our civilization" (29). His rhetoric emphasizes that American intervention in Viet Nam is a moral duty, an obligation, a burden to be carried, albeit reluctantly, by the world's "guardians." Like Johnson, Secretary of State Rusk depicts the United States as the blameless victim of "aggression by the other side" (13). "Our military forces are there," Rusk insists, "because of the North Vietnamese aggression against South Vietnam and for no other reason" (15), and only in response to "the aggressive appetites of others" (20). Ultimately, though, to Rusk engagement in Viet Nam is not a question of morality: "much more is at stake than preserving the independence of the peoples of Southeast Asia," he asserts; "our security is involved" (9–10). Secretary of Defense, Robert McNamara, agrees with Rusk's security concerns. Notorious for his "body count" method of waging the Vietnam War and his 1995 memoir, *In Retrospect*, lamenting "we were wrong, terribly wrong" (xx), McNamara claims that if the spread of "militant Asian communism" is not halted, "our strategic position in the world will be weakened and our national security directly endangered" (22). What readers can see in this second document, then, are two strains of argument for the US intervention in Viet Nam: (i) it is a moral duty that only the United States can fulfill and (ii) it is in the geopolitical interests of the United States to intervene. The first strain reveals a theme of American exceptionalism, the second, of American power.

Elements of American Vietnam War literature

The point of identifying these strains in the early, public discourse about American relations with Viet Nam is because they echo in the fiction labeled "Vietnam War Literature," whether set in Viet Nam or the United States.[12] Although Westerners previously needed the Vietnamese as a bad to their good, in most American Vietnam War representations the Vietnamese are not even supporting characters as they disappear and the Americans take center stage.[13] Whether motivated by moral selflessness or strategic protection of the United States, the depiction of US citizens in American literature focuses largely on the trauma of their personal disappointment. Disabused of the myths perpetrated about war generally and the Vietnam War specifically, about American exceptionalism and power, in-country American warrior characters typically are angry, lonely, and miserable.[14] They may be angry that war has not turned out to be the glorious, ennobling, and morally satisfying experience they were led to expect, or they may be angry that someone or something—higher-ranking US military members, war correspondents, ARVN incompetence, American antiwar protestors, and politicians—prevents their winning. If the warrior characters are not angry, they are mystified by the conduct of war, by its boredom, untidiness, and complexity. As combatants, they do not understand the purpose of their unit's military tactics and they are confused by the (usually racial and socioeconomic) conflicts among American military personnel. Sometimes the combatants show symptoms of Post-Traumatic Stress Disorder and, other times, of Moral Injury, but rarely are these conditions named.[15] Combat narratives set in Viet Nam sometimes problematize the national myth and at other times they sanctify it, striving to assert the morality of the US mission.

Stateside narratives featuring mainstream American characters, some of whom are veterans of the war, explore the effects of a conflict not fought on American soil. Veterans often are confused by the wide spectrum of attitudes toward the war—the energy of the antiwar movement and the apathy of the populace—and, feeling out of place in the United States, often long to return to war, where they felt purposeful as part of a collective effort, no matter how misguided or fruitless. Non-warrior characters have some connection to the war, usually via a family member's participation, and are equally confused by the war and its lingering effect on their loved one. Narratives about the experiences of Americans of Vietnamese descent vary depending on a number of factors, including time and conditions of arrival, but most often deal with questions of home and exile.[16]

Readers will notice that the anguish experienced by the individual American combatant usually is the focus in American Vietnam War literature; readers may also notice that published authors often are Vietnam War veterans, a condition often used to guarantee the veracity of the literature. Note how critics almost always mention an author is a veteran, shorthand for truth-teller. The logic is that because a veteran author—as it happens, usually an officer or a war correspondent, almost always a male—had the experience of being at war, of being an eyewitness, he knows best about the conduct of war; better than anyone, he can articulate the conditions of war in Vietnam.[17] The premise of this logic is that being at war means being in combat. What the logic does not acknowledge, though, is how at most only one-half to one-third of the American armed forces sent to Vietnam were in combat units, with the remaining half or two-thirds engaged in supporting and commanding those combat units (McGrath 28–32). Going to war does not ensure participation in combat; "veteran" does not signify "combatant." Moreover, if the veteran author knows the "truth" about the war, then there would only need to be one novel, memoir, play, film, or history, these representations being interchangeable and all following the first, redundant. With thousands of these publications in existence, clearly a single perspective is insufficient to representing the war. It seems there are many "truths" about a single war, even a single skirmish.

Narrative omissions and inclusions

Furthermore, mindful of Chris Hedges's caution that myth's prevalence relies on omissions from the stories told, many war occurrences represented in histories rarely appear in fiction. This omission is apparent in regard to historical context, especially in relation to the US post-World War II support for the Viet Minh and then the French. But rape, murder, atrocity, and homosexuality, occurrences more common in the historical record than the fiction, also seldom are represented.[18] This line of thought is not to argue that fiction must be faithful to the historical record or that history holds the ultimate truth, as the two are different genres with different conventions of storytelling. Moreover, contrary to the popular belief that history is static and always told in the same way, history's storytelling is a process rather than a state: it is only the currently most informed interpretation of the past. History, then, is always only partial and contingent and politically influenced if not motivated.

Consider, for instance, the case of the 1968 My Lai massacre, when hundreds of Vietnamese civilians were systematically killed over many hours and only one person, a junior officer, 1LT William Calley, was found responsible. How has this event been recorded in history? As sociologists Joachim J. Savelsberg and Ryan D. King note, the event's public airing "did not affect the telling of American history and the public esteem of the American military as profoundly as some had expected at the onset of the 1970s ... powerful social actors have an interest in the untarnished reputation of the American military . . . [resulting in] a cleansing of American memory of atrocities" (52–53). In *Kill Anything That Moves*, journalist and historian Nick Turse contends, after a decade of archival and ethnographic research in the United States and Viet Nam, that the My Lai massacre was not an anomaly or the result of crazed, rogue soldiers, but the outcome of US military strategy:

> Most [atrocities] weren't photographed, and many were not documented in any way. The great majority were never known outside the offending unit, and most investigations that did result were closed, quashed, or abandoned. Even on the rare occasions when the allegations were seriously investigated within the military, the reports were soon buried in classified files without ever seeing the light of day. (5)[19]

Turse concludes with a warning similar to Hedges's about myth-making and echoes the conclusions of Savelsberg and King: "The true history of Vietnamese civilian suffering does not fit comfortably into America's preferred postwar narrative—the tale of a conflict nobly fought by responsible commanders and good American boys, who should not be tainted by the occasional mistakes of a few 'bad apples' in their midst" (262).

What does it mean that occurrences unpalatable to popular taste do not appear in fictional story lines? As Turse points out, although US military actions in Viet Nam were felt direly by millions of Vietnamese people, their stories did not fit into the preferred American narrative. Neither, it seems, did the stories of Vietnamese people who actively supported the American intervention and, following North Vietnam's victory in April 1975, under duress left Viet Nam for the United States.[20] Not only were most Americans hostile to these immigrants, because Vietnamese and Vietnamese Americans were seen as signifying the lost war, but also their stories were deemed invalid. In 1995's *The Viet Nam War/The American War*, Renny Christopher condemns this conflation of the war with the people:

> By identifying Viet Nam, the country, with the war in Viet Nam, U.S. representations collapse all distinctions between enemy and ally and among Vietnamese individuals, leaving only one distinction: "The World" of the West, being desirable, homey, and "good," versus "Vietnam," an entity composed of country and war together where only evil resides. (5)

Such an attitude, Christopher argues, deeply impacts the formation of a literary canon, privileging the homogenizing voices of US veteran authors and denying those of other war participants, notably Vietnamese and Vietnamese Americans.[21] By 1990, she claims, of the "seven thousand or so books published" in the United States dealing with the Vietnam War, only about 12 were by "Vietnamese exile writers" (25). Even those few were ignored or were not widely known, published and distributed as they were by small presses. Christopher concludes that, because these writers "seriously challenge the bases and scope of that [nationalistic and ethnocentric definition of American experience] perspective," they have been marginalized (28).

By 2008, the situation had not changed markedly, at least according to Maureen Ryan's *The Other Side of Grief*: "Of all the narratives of the legacy of America's Vietnam War, perhaps none promises to teach and challenge *us*—to bring the war home, to chronicle its other side—*in the coming years* as much as the collective story of the refugees and their descendants" (254; emphasis added). Notice Ryan's rhetoric: "us" does not include "the refugees and their descendants," and she refers to future literature, not present. Of course, it was not until 1997 that the first novel written by an American of Vietnamese descent, Lan Cao's *Monkey Bridge*, was widely published, and others have followed. Still, this literature is not typically part of the American Vietnam War literary canon, something this volume attempts to remedy.[22]

Others telling stories of the war through fiction include people from the former North Vietnam. With changed policies ("doi moi," or "Renovation") in the Socialist Republic of Viet Nam in 1986 and the opening of diplomatic relations between Viet Nam and the United States in 1994, some literary voices emerged, impacting the English-speaking literary canon. There still are few texts available in English, and much of that was translated first from Vietnamese to French and then to English. Understandably, meaning could have been lost in translation. Literature published later, from the mid-1990s on, has been translated directly from Vietnamese to English.[23]

Chris Hedges asserts that national war mythologies rely on omission. Critics earlier have argued that omitting the voices of Vietnamese and Vietnamese Americans from the American literary canon and excluding some of the more atrocious elements of the war sustain the postwar narrative. Readers, therefore, should ask themselves how the fiction is impacted by these absences. But they should also consider what elements of the war appear in the literature, and how those inclusions impact the stories told. Fictions set stateside usually concern themselves with the reintegration of the veteran, including discourses about war-engendered disabilities, conflict between veterans and civilians on the conduct of the war, the challenges of finding and keeping employment and housing, and sometimes Post-Traumatic Stress Disorder (if the fiction was published after the disorder's inclusion in the 1980 *Diagnostic and Statistical Manual of Mental Disorders*). Elements common to most Vietnam War combat fiction, in addition to the violence of combat, are: the tedium of waiting for combat and of running patrols; drug use, mostly by enlisted men; racial conflict, mostly among enlisted men; fraggings, mostly by enlisted men; and men, mostly enlisted, constantly seeking sexual outlets. What narratives, readers should ask, do these inclusions and exclusions or omissions enable?

The literary canon and criticism

Fiction about the war written by Americans has been published at least since the mid-1950s. In this early period, the best-known novels published in the United States by American authors include Eugene Burdick and William Lederer's *The Ugly American* (1958), Robin Moore's *The Green Berets* (1965), Daniel Ford's *Incident at Muc Wa* (1967), and David Halberstam's *One Very Hot Day* (1967). All are set in Viet Nam during armed conflict. English author Graham Greene's novel, *The Quiet American* (1955), often is included in the canon for its prescience by a non-American, as are Bernard Fall's book-length reports about the French in Viet Nam, *Street Without Joy* (1961) and *Hell In a Very Small Place* (1966). Most American canonical texts, including memoirs and histories, were published after the United States withdrew in 1973 and after South Vietnam lost its war with the North in April 1975. Literary criticism of the war's narratives began in the late 1970s, mostly aimed at legitimizing as literature the fictional work produced by veteran authors.[24] For instance, Jerome Klinkowitz and John Somer's 1978 publication is an anthology of short stories written about the war by veterans whom, the editors claim, "unlike their counterparts from World War II, seem to feel a need to talk about their 'tour of duty'" (1). Klinkowitz and Somers's introduction sets out other themes that resurface in criticism subsequently: the search for "authenticity" and lost American innocence (2), a war that made no sense (8), "moral dislocation" (13), "the ambiguities of Vietnam" (14), and the ontological basis for storytelling. "[T]hese stories," the editors assert, "argue that literature is man's private weapon against lies and hypocrisy, that a precise and concrete use of language is a moral act" (18). This postwar rhetoric echoes President Johnson's 1965 claim that the United States was morally obligated to intervene militarily in Viet Nam. Just as the US armed forces were sent to counter moral turpitude, so, too, do the authors of this fiction. The presupposition that veterans would and should be the only Americans writing fiction about the war goes unexamined by the editors, a presupposition persisting in the critical history.

Most American critics of Vietnam War fiction agree that as a mode of cultural memory fiction must be understood in some kind of historical context, but they diverge into two camps on this issue of veteran authors.[25] Following Klinkowitz and Somer's lead, critics in one camp think that the (usually white, male, officer or war correspondent) American veteran author is most qualified to commemorate the war in fiction. Although his fiction may not always be realistic—realism being the preferred mode of war fiction—his having been in Viet Nam (or in the US military) during the war era warrants his authority to represent the war, and what he says in his fiction should be accepted by readers.[26] This authority extends to some of the critics as well, many of whom claim or are granted authority (by reviewers and publishers) to critique based on their Vietnam War veteran status. Just as veterans often claim "you had to be there" to understand the Vietnam War, having been there is also regarded as an asset if not a prerequisite to literary analysis of the war's fiction. A reader's only job with this approach is to discern the veteran author's intentions for the literature. In this critical vein, the veteran's voice is central in both the fiction and the literary criticism; biography takes greatest priority. These biography-privileging methodologies dominate the early critical works and have rematerialized in the decades since.

In the other camp, critics regard the veteran voice as one among many, attempting to treat with equal weight those fictions written by veteran authors and those by authors without firsthand connections to the war. For critics in this vein, the biographical "truth-telling" power of the veteran is not privileged over those authors or characters unauthorized by veteran status: women, children, non-European Americans, Vietnamese people (Southerners, Northerners, and Viet Cong), and Americans of Vietnamese descent. Furthermore, these critics often are compelled overtly by rhetorical and theoretical concerns that are not biographical, methodologies that reveal in the literature many "truths."

Critics who privilege the veteran voice include Vietnam veterans Philip Beidler and Tobey Herzog. In one of Vietnam War fiction's earliest critical works, *American Literature and the Experience of Vietnam* (1982), Beidler aims to legitimize Vietnam War fiction as literature by establishing its place in a centuries-long US mythic narrative of manifest destiny:

> [O]ur classic inheritance of native expression has prophesied much of what we now know of Vietnam, made it by self-engendering symbolic fiat part of our collective mythology long before it existed in fact . . . For all their terrible, urgent strangeness, they [Vietnam War stories] also possess an older, almost ritualized quality of iconographic permanence. (19, 25)

In line with the book's title, Beidler invokes experience as the basis for literary "sense-making": "the experience of the war can now be made to signify" (xiii); "the experience of Vietnam is in certain uncanny ways already there, already there, perhaps, 350 years down a dim, beckoning path of discovery" (21); the literature "has told about an experience more 'real,' finally, than any one that ever existed in fact" (26). With references like the war's being a "game . . . of cowboys versus gooks" (15), Beidler strongly implies that this experience is the combat veteran's. Although over the decades Beidler has maintained his attitude about the veteran author, given the still precariously ignoble social status of the veteran in the early 1980s, it might have been all Beidler could do to imply rather than state that the veteran's fiction is laudable.

In the decade between Beidler's early foray and Tobey Herzog's *Vietnam Stories: Innocence Lost* (1992), the status of Vietnam War veterans was rehabilitated during the Reagan administration,[27] enabling Tobey Herzog's explicit examination of "American soldier-authors' narratives" (2). Herzog invokes Beidler's "sense-making," asserting that, because soldier authors gleaned "crucial insights about human nature" and joined the "timeless brotherhood of warriors" (4), their renditions "counterbalanc[e] the views of media, historians, the military hierarchy, government, and people at home" (5). Herzog contends that a reader will develop "sympathy for the combat soldier" and an understanding of the "universality among wars" (3). Like Beidler, Herzog champions firsthand witness: "These stories . . . have the feel of experiential truth as their authors recreate for readers the sights, sounds, smells, feelings, language, and strategies of war" (5). Collections of essays, like Philip Jason's *Fourteen Landing Zones* (1991), also privilege the veteran voice and discourage (theoretical) methodologies that detract from "what literary works express" (xviii).

Other critical works echoing Beidler and Herzog's partiality for the experienced, veteran voice, but moving away from it somewhat include John Hellmann's *American Myth and the Legacy of Vietnam* (1986) and Don Ringnalda's *Fighting and Writing the Vietnam War* (1994). Hellmann's work counters Beidler's assertion that Vietnam War literature is part of the US mythic heritage, saying that the war experience deconstructed rather than confirmed that association. "Vietnam," he claims, "is an experience that has severely called into question American myth" (ix), so that despite President Reagan's efforts to achieve a national "renewal of spirit . . . [it] feels more like bravado" (222). Ringnalda directly confronts Beidler's "sense-making," arguing "the last thing America needs to do with the Vietnam experience is make sense of it" (ix). Ringnalda reverses the privileging of the veteran voice, saying "the fighter-writer" is weakened by his "memories of Vietnam's complexities," and that the fighter-writer's "tough-minded realism (I-was-there-you weren't-so-listen-up machismo)" is the same way of thinking that took the United States to war in Viet Nam (x). Ty Hawkins's 2012 monograph, *Reading Vietnam Amid the War on Terror*, calls on American myth to create community among readers of Vietnam War fiction and the experience of the War on Terror. American myth, he argues, is the metanarrative that binds citizens, and fiction aids in that binding process across wars: "It is precisely toward the creation of a community of memory . . . that the best American narratives of the Vietnam War toil. Because they do so, these narratives demand to be read with renewed urgency as contributors to the recasting of American myth and America itself" (24).

American President Ronald Reagan's aims in the 1980s to rehabilitate the status of the Vietnam War veteran led to one of the first critical works to depart from the Beidler lead, and to a slew of similarly departing approaches since. Susan Jeffords's *The Remasculinization of America* (1989) examines what she says is the Reagan rehabilitation's foundation, masculinity, and "remasculinization" of veterans as "the large-scale renegotiation and regeneration of the interests, value, and projects of patriarchy now taking place in U.S. social relations" (ix). Jeffords's work has had remarkable influence since its publication, hastening skepticism about many master narratives, not just those of patriarchy. Thus, Milton Bates claims in *The Wars We Took to Vietnam* (1996) that the American war in Viet Nam was not a single war but many, originating not in Viet Nam's communism but in American culture. Furthermore, Bates acknowledges the veteran's powerful voice but does not privilege it: "Look for evidence of authority in the war stories themselves," he insists, "rather than pursuing the elusive 'real' authors into the thickets of biography" (222). Parallel to Bates's argument is Katherine Kinney's assertion in *Friendly Fire* (2000) that in Vietnam War fiction Americans are "portrayed as the victims of their own ideals, practices, and beliefs, while the ostensible enemy... remains shadowy figures glimpsed only occasionally" (4). This "friendly fire" "retelling of Vietnam as a domestic American war" enables a triumphalist narrative of the war (8). To Kinney, the responsibility for the war's narrative has been ceded to veterans, a responsibility that needs to be more broadly assumed. "At stake," she stresses, "is a demystification of the Vietnam War as a truth known only to veterans" (10).

Other American literature and culture critics have built on those preceding them without presupposing the authority of the veteran voice. Many of these critics also use theoretical methodologies explicitly to inform their "against the grain" readings of Vietnam War literature. In *Warring Fictions* (1998), Jim Neilson employs a materialist methodology to investigate the publishing of Vietnam War literature, concluding that literary culture has helped to rewrite the war in accord with the needs of capital. "[T]he most consistently praised narrative prose of the Vietnam War, though critical of U.S. policy and graphic in its depictions of American atrocities," Neilson avers, "makes only a modest critique that fits well within an elite-sanctioned doctrinal framework" (7). He indicts 1990s feminist and postcolonialist critics for overlooking "the political economy of the Vietnam War, the connections between America's (and the West's) economic interests and an anticommunist war in Indochina" (218), and condemns all of American literary culture for ignoring American imperialism. "Indeed," Neilson declares, "for American literary culture it is as if there were no such thing as U.S. imperialism" (219). Mark Taylor insists in *The Vietnam*

War in History, Literature and Film (2003) that the war cannot be understood except interdisciplinarily, from the perspectives of film, history, and fiction. Using multiple perspectives exposes the hazards of single-voiced, veteran "authenticity" (27). In *Masculinity in Vietnam War Narratives* (2009), Brenda Boyle complicates Jeffords's assertion by identifying in the literature not single but multiple versions of masculinities, versions predicated on interactions among identities of sexuality, race, and able-bodiedness. This study uses an array of masculinity, race, queer, and disability theories to pluralize approaches to the literature. Finally, collections like *Thirty Years After* (Heberle 2009) and *Four Decades On* (Laderman and Martini 2013) include essays that read with theory and against the grain.

Publications of the last decade introduce critical approaches to literature written by allies of the United States in the War and Americans of Vietnamese descent. Jinim Park's analysis of novels written by Koreans about Korean military personnel in Viet Nam's war, *Narratives of the Vietnam War by Korean and American Writers* (2007), brings to light some of the stories not usually considered under the heading "Vietnam War literature." Isabelle Thuy Pelaud's monograph, *this is all I choose to tell* (2011), outlines the publishing history of fiction written by Americans of Vietnamese descent. Thirty years after Philip Beidler's lauding of experience, Pelaud returns to it. Instead of claiming a monolithic experience for Vietnamese refugees leaving for the United States, she focuses on the variations in experience based on "time of arrival, socio-economic class, race, gender, sexuality, and exposure to trauma" (1). In *Four Decades On* (2013), a multidisciplinary consideration of the four decades since the 1975 conclusion of the Second Indochina War, literary critic Viet Thanh Nguyen advocates in "Remembering War, Dreaming Peace" for a wider array of protagonists in the stories told about the Vietnam War. The stories already told "are melodramas of traumatized white manhood," stories that limit, by way of "compulsory empathy" for the beleaguered American soldier, compassion available for others who felt the effects of the War (147). "Cosmopolitanism" is called for in American literature about the War, he claims, a practice that creates in readers empathy for the ignored others, enabling a dream of peace.

The chapters in this collection

The last 13 years of United States forays into the Middle East, the invasion and occupation of Iraq in particular, have evoked comparisons to the decades spent in Viet Nam. That evocation has produced a renewed interest in the Vietnam conflict, resulting in the reprinting of older War narratives and the publication of new ones. To cover fully such an array of genres or multitude of texts is impossible in a single collection. Therefore, the seven chapters in this volume provide analytical frameworks for those cultural texts that elucidate American and Vietnamese sensibilities about the war: a number of the standard American-centered texts; texts written about and by Vietnamese war participants; texts by and about Americans of Vietnamese descent; and acclaimed novels concerning the war published in the last decade.

This collection of chapters adds to the critical canon both in terms of new analytical frameworks applied to some of the standards in Vietnam War literature, and also in its critical approaches to literary works not yet included in the canon. The canonical standards include Michael Herr's *Dispatches* (1977), Bobbie Ann Mason's *In Country* (1985), Larry Heinemann's *Paco's Story* (1986), and Tim O'Brien's Vietnam War trilogy, *Going After Cacciato* (1978), *The Things They Carried* (1990), and *In the Lake of the Woods* (1994). Nonstandard narratives addressed in this collection include novels about the northern experience of war, written by Vietnamese northerners; narratives by and about Americans of Vietnamese descent who came to the United States after 1975; and best-selling novels about the War published in the United States in the last decade. Each of the seven chapters takes a theoretical stance in reading its text, the approaches sometimes more implied than explicit, but the primary methodology for all is close-reading of the primary texts.

Once Post-Traumatic Stress Disorder was formulated in 1980 as a diagnosis of many of the symptoms Vietnam War veterans were experiencing, the effects of trauma became visible in many of the war's fictional representations. Three of the chapters in this volume approach their texts using a trauma lens. The first of these analyses appears in Chapter 1, "Michael Herr's traumatic New Journalism: *Dispatches*," where Mark Heberle reads Herr's work not only as fiction but also as a trauma narrative. The trauma is multileveled, applying not only to the combatants who journalist Michael Herr reports about in his "dispatches," but also to himself as an observer-participant in war. Heberle investigates both levels, exploring additionally how *Dispatches*' form—of multiple vignettes and scenarios over the course of a year—exposes a traumatized Herr.

In Chapter 2, "Dương Thu Hương's *Paradise of the Blind* and *Novel Without a Name*, and Bảo Ninh's *Sorrow of War*: Corrective, politically incorrect, and challenging," Michele Janette analyzes three novels written about the North Vietnamese experience of the "American War." Janette argues that, contrary to many US criticisms of these novels, they do not mirror the antiwar sentiments of many American texts nor do they fill in the gaps between American renditions of the war. Instead, with a clear understanding of the novelists' daunting publishing contexts these novels can be read as "provocations" to the dominant American representations of the Vietnam War. According to Janette, the novels provoke in two important ways: first, they challenge the value of war outright and second, they focus entirely on Vietnamese characters and rarely feature Americans. "Rather than supplying what is missing," Janette contends, "they challenge rather than complement the American literary canon of Vietnam War books."

The second of this volume's trauma approaches appears in Chapter 3, Joanna Price's "'Ten years burning down the road': Trauma, mourning, and postmemory in Bobbie Ann Mason's *In Country*." Employing Marianne Hirsch's theory of "postmemory," Price examines how the novel's adolescent focal character, Sam, navigates to her own sense of self via the war memories of her hometown's Vietnam War veterans and of those about her father, who died in Viet Nam before her birth. Although her ability to empathize about a war in which she did not participate might overwhelm the development of her personal identity, Sam's case instead illustrates how mourning occurs collectively. This guide for "ethical mourning" resonates during the violence of the early twenty-first century, Price urges, with *In Country* anticipating "contemporary questions about what constitutes an ethical response to mourning arising from the large-scale loss of life through acts of military or other aggression."

Susan Jeffords's *The Remasculinization of America* facilitated the use of gender lenses, specifically masculinity, to critique Vietnam War narratives. Three of this volume's remaining four chapters use gender to critique individual or groups of texts. In Chapter 4, "War, gender, and race in le thi diem thuy's *The Gangster We Are All Looking For*," Isabelle Thuy Pelaud examines how gender, race, and refugee status together function for Vietnamese American women writers and their characters. Pelaud's objective is to challenge a common misapprehension about the sameness of all Vietnamese American people and their stories. She finds not only that le thi diem thuy's novel often is willfully misread as autobiographical because people of Vietnamese descent are expected to tell their personal stories of the War, but also that le's female character carries the "*triple burden* of being a refugee and a woman, but also a [racial] minority."

In the second of the gendered approaches, Chapter 5, "The home front and the front lines in the war novels of Tim O'Brien," Susan Farrell contemplates the typical dichotomy in US Vietnam War narratives of (feminine) home and (masculine) war. To Farrell, O'Brien's three war novels—*Going After Cacciato*, *The Things They Carried*, and *In The Lake of the Woods*—query this clean divide "between a domestic life that is associated with literature and ideas and that is characterized largely as feminine and a more traditionally masculine experience of war." Instead, the novels demonstrate the inextricability of "the world" and "Nam," and the equally mistaken notion that one man can have both "a war self and a domestic self." Farrell concludes that O'Brien's novels examine specifically the Vietnam War but more generally the moral dilemma of behaving ethically in (unjust) war.

Chapter 6, "The ghost that won't be exorcised: The legacy of Larry Heinemann's *Paco's Story*," is this volume's third chapter using a trauma approach. Stacey Peebles's analysis differs, though, as she contextualizes *Paco's Story* in relation to two other texts: Toni Morrison's *Beloved*, which also encounters the literal and figurative traces of violence, and the 2003–2004 incidents of torture and humiliation by Americans at Abu Ghraib prison during the war in Iraq. Peebles concludes that, although *Beloved* promises restitution and recovery from the wounds of slavery through communal action, *Paco's Story* offers no such redemption when the "wounds" are self-inflicted. The novel is "a portrait of Vietnam as irrecuperable trauma, a ghost that can't be exorcised—and one that has, in turn, haunted Americans' more recent wars," claims Peebles.

In the final chapter, "American totem society in the twenty-first century: Denis Johnson's *Tree of Smoke*, Karl Marlantes's *Matterhorn*, and Tatjana Solis's *The Lotus Eaters*," Brenda M. Boyle uses masculinity theories and the historical context of American culture in the last decade to analyze three novels recently published in the United States: *Tree of Smoke* (2007), *Matterhorn* (2010), and *The Lotus Eaters* (2010). Like Price and Peebles, Boyle connects these novels about the Vietnam War to the early twenty-first century US war in Iraq, especially to what she terms the "Support the Troops Syndrome." Like so many representations of the War, these three novels appear to challenge the war's purpose. In their endings, however, as part of the Syndrome the novels pacify potential antiwar activity as they make readers feel good about sending others to war.

The approaches to these texts are not the only ones available. Most of these primary texts have been ably critiqued through other theoretical lenses: historicist, postcolonial, queer, disability, New Critical, reader response, semiotic, materialist, and feminist, among others. The critiques featured in this volume, moreover, are not strict about adhering to one set of tenets or another: they cross theoretical boundaries, and without always naming the theories, blend genre with trauma (Heberle), literary critical with comparative (Janette), historicist and new historicist with trauma and memory (Price), race with gender and materialist (Pelaud), biographical with gender (Farrell), postcolonial with trauma (Peebles), or queer with masculinity (Boyle). Theory is useful as a flexible tool to pluralize textual readings, not as a rigid prescription limiting possible readings. In fact, one might argue that the difference between critics of Vietnam War literature who focus primarily on the author and critics who do not is theoretical, as theoretical tacks shape what readers notice and how they respond to each of these stories. Students of fiction in the twenty-first century read with theoretical lenses, knowingly or not, and the theoretical frames matter.

In addition to considering the usefulness of theory, readers might also ask why read fiction, especially about times long past? There are as many reasons for reading literature as there are different combinations of theory. Some advocates for reading literature will say it develops in readers empathy for others; others insist that it helps readers develop their own selves; some advocates might argue that, as a cultural artifact, literature can reveal and sometimes create the sensibilities of a time or a place or a people; still others insist that one should read literature to take pleasure in the fluency and aesthetics of the written word. In her book about Vietnam War literature, *Friendly Fire* (2000), Katherine Kinney persuasively maintains that understanding the War requires reading its literature for all of the sociological, historical, and aesthetic reasons. "[L]iterature," she claims, "is an important, even an essential place to study the Vietnam War" as the literature compels the reader to cross disciplinary and theoretical boundaries. In reading critically "the reader is forced to negotiate narratives of history, categories of identity, and the limits of narrative possibility." Fictions, Kinney concludes, graciously "offer us the space to imagine and interpret as well as remember" (191). Now more than ever, as the United States recovers from its long venture in Iraq and an even longer one in Afghanistan, and as it prepares to commemorate in 2015 the end of the Second Indochina War, it is vital to do this hard work of imagination, interpretation, and remembrance.

NOTA BENE: Names in this book sometimes may appear unfamiliar.

The name of the country in which the United States warred during the 1954–1975 Second Indochina War is variously spelled in this book. The 1965–1973 war fought by the United States is the "Vietnam War." "War" is implied when only "Vietnam" is written. Similarly, "North Vietnam" and "South Vietnam" are used to indicate the two parts of the country designated by the 1954 Geneva Peace Agreement and ended with the 1975 conclusion of the Second Indochina War. "Viet Nam" is used in reference to the geographical entirety of the country, north or south.

Names of Vietnamese people also may seem unfamiliar. Most in their original language appear with diacritical marks; in this book, diacritical marks appear only in Chapter 2. Vietnamese names also begin with what Western readers think of as the surname, but that convention is followed only in Chapter 2. Most references in this book to Vietnamese names follow the Western convention of putting the surname last in a string of names.

Notes

1 This book refers to the country as "Viet Nam," and to the war as "the Vietnam War."
2 Although the Constitution of the United States requires a formal declaration before going to war, US intervention in Viet Nam was never officially declared. Technically, it was not a "war."
3 For Vietnamese history from a Vietnamese perspective, written in English, see Tran and Reid.
4 Histories of the wars continue to be published, especially as more archives around the world are opened to scholars. For scholarship on the war's historiography, see Bradley and Young, and Wiest and Doidge.
5 The concept of "Indochina" was created by the French. See Norindr.
6 Mark Philip Bradley says: "At the [French] war's end in 1954, the United States had paid as much as 80 per cent of its cost, some $1 billion" (*Vietnam* 56).
7 For more about the French and Viet Nam, see Norindr, and Cooper; about the relationship between France and the United States, see Blang, Statler, and Dommen.
8 The Viet Minh fought against the French through the length of Viet Nam. The "Viet Cong" were the military arm of the National Liberation Front, a group formed after the partitioning of the country, and fought in South Vietnam against the South Vietnamese government and its ally, the United States. See Truong.
9 There are innumerable histories of these events. For recent publications, see Bradley and Young, Bradley (2009), Logevall (1999, 2012), Lien-Han Nguyen, Prados, and Hess. Allies included Australia, Canada, New Zealand, Philippines, and South Korea, in addition to South Vietnam and the indigenous people, named by the French, "Montagnards."
10 In *Inventing Vietnam* (1991), editor Michael Anderegg says: "Cinematic representations, in short, seem to have supplanted even so-called factual analyses as *the* discourse of the war, as the place where some kind of reckoning will need to be made and tested. Even those for whom film can only be a tendentious and cynical product of American capitalism respond passionately to whatever they feel Hollywood seems to be saying about the war" (1). In his survey of US high school history books, James Loewen asserts that the Vietnam War is rarely tackled in meaningful ways (245), and those books that do sanitize the American involvement in the war (247–258). To see how the Vietnam War is treated in French, Vietnamese, and Canadian high school history books, see Lindaman and Ward, 310–317.

11 The French and Americans notoriously were at odds with one another. As Bradley puts it, "Despite the fact that non-communist alternatives to the Ho Chi Minh government remained as weak after 1954 as they had been in the late colonial and French war periods, the US policy makers came out of the French war sure that they could do better" (*Vietnam* 73). This antipathy between allies might explain the substitution of an American claymore (as written in the script) with a mine from the French War in *Tropic Thunder*, a satire of Vietnam War films. See Combe and Boyle, chapter 4 for a discussion of the substitution.
12 This essay collection distinguishes between literary fiction and what critic Philip Beidler refers to as "Viet pulp" ("Thirty" 15).
13 Viet Thanh Nguyen categorizes Vietnam War literature in two ways: the "major writing" whose authors "thought the war was a major screw-up and who wanted their writing to express that in both content and form" and the "minor writing" that is "realistic," "straightforward," and depicts US combatants as "good guys on a bad mission" ("Grunts vs. Gooks"). In an expansive taxonomy, *The Other Side of Grief*, Maureen Ryan largely categorizes Vietnam War narratives—including memoirs—by author identity: veteran writers, women, prisoners of war, antiwar activists, and Vietnamese "exiles."
14 Focal characters in Viet Nam almost always are depicted as combatants, not as support to the combatants.
15 For PTSD, see *PTSD*. For Moral Injury, see Maguen and Litz.
16 See Pelaud.
17 Some critics insist that the veteran voice should be privileged because the war notoriously was conducted by men who did not fight, except from afar, and so could not understand the plight of the ground troop. The voices of the higher-ups prevailed during the failed war, goes the argument, and so the lowers should have the last word. This privilege persists in the narratives of subsequent wars. See Gibson 461–476.
18 For American males' rape of American and Vietnamese women, see Weaver. For murder and atrocity, see Turse. For homosexuality, see Shilts, Scott and Stanley, and *Homosexuality*.
19 Turse found files at the US National Archives documenting "300 allegations of massacres, murders, rapes, torture, assaults, mutilations, and other atrocities that were substantiated by army investigators. They [the War Crimes Working Group files, begun after the My Lai trials] detailed the deaths of 137 civilians in mass killings, and 78 smaller-scale attacks in which Vietnamese civilians were killed, wounded, and sexually assaulted. They identified 141 instances in which U.S. troops used fists, sticks, bats, water torture, and electrical torture on noncombatants. The files also contained 500 allegations

that weren't proven at the time—like the murders of scores, perhaps hundreds, of Vietnamese civilians by the 101st Airborne Division's Tiger Force, which would be confirmed and made public only in 2003" (14–15).
20 See Boyle, "At Home" for a discussion of Vietnamese "resettlement."
21 Also notably absent are focal characters who are Americans not of European descent. Fiction about the war has also been published in countries whose military forces and war correspondents participated in the war. See Park, Kaiko, and Doyle et al.
22 Nor should it always have to do with the war, anyway. See Pelaud for analysis of Vietnamese American literature, and Tran, B. et al.; see Janette for a recent anthology of Vietnamese American literature.
23 See Dinh, "Introduction," ix–xvii.
24 Although the John Wayne vehicle, *The Green Berets*, was produced in 1968, the late 1970s is also when the war's film canon began: *Coming Home* (1978), *The Deer Hunter* (1978), *Go tell the Spartans* (1978; based on Ford's 1967 novel), and *Apocalypse Now* (1979).
25 A similar divide occurs in the field of History: veterans want to control the story told, but historians find in their research evidence that challenges the veteran's story. See "Vietnam Veterans to Correct the Myths" and "Boston Manifesto."
26 See Martini, chapter 4, "I Am Reality."
27 See Hixson.

1

Michael Herr's traumatic New Journalism: *Dispatches*

Mark Heberle

Mapping the terrain

Michael Herr opens his account of the Vietnam War in *Dispatches* (1977) with an exercise in mapmaking that extends itself to include the principles and practice of New Journalism as well the effects of trauma:

> There was a map of Vietnam on the wall of my apartment in Saigon and some nights, coming back late to the city, I'd lie out on my bed and look at it, too tired to do anything more than just get my boots off. That map was a marvel, especially now that it wasn't real anymore. For one thing, it was very old. It had been left there years before by another tenant, probably a Frenchman, since the map had been made in Paris. The paper had buckled in its frame after years in the wet Saigon heat, laying a kind of veil over the countries it depicted. (3)

The veil is historical and ideological as well as physical, since it represents French Indochina, a 100-year-old fiction that had attempted to efface the 1,000-year-old Vietnamese nation that had outlasted the rule of those who had made the map, which would still have been real in the eyes of its fabricators more than a decade before Herr marveled at it. What is most astonishing, therefore, is not the age of the map, but the misreading and misrepresentation of its subject until the dispersal of the veil at Geneva in July 1954.

Uncannily, however, the maps that replaced this one did not correct it, but laid their own veil over reality: "It was late '67 now, even the most detailed maps didn't reveal much anymore; reading them was like trying to read the faces of the Vietnamese, and that was like trying to read the wind. We knew that the uses of most information were flexible, different pieces of ground told different stories to different people" (3). Herr's ethnocentrism at least acknowledges its own ignorance of the Vietnamese. It also questions another fiction that had passed away by the time *Dispatches* was published in 1977. The Republic of Viet Nam, like French Indochina, was a name on maps between 1955 and 1975 that turned out to be as unreal as the ones on Herr's Saigon map in 1967: "We also knew that for years now there had been no country here but the war."

But who are the "we" who distrust the official maps, who recognize that mapmaking is necessarily ideologically self-interested, contingent, and errant, and who defined Viet Nam in 1967 as a war rather than a country? The answer is most directly addressed in the fifth section of *Dispatches*, "Colleagues," where the "we" introduced at the beginning of *Dispatches* turn out to be a subset of a much larger professional collective, a "brotherhood" (223) of journalist colleagues with whom Herr associates himself, who see the War more clearly than the "normals," disabled by ideological blinkers or investments that cover up the truth, whether through reporting that evades contact with it or the official maps that guide such misreading. Covering one's subject intimately, reflecting it authentically, and rendering it as resonantly as possible are hallmarks of the self-styled New Journalism of the 1960s; in Viet Nam, and throughout *Dispatches*, it marks itself off from the passive reproduction of officially sanctioned misrepresentation that calls itself objective journalism.

As an alternative to the two official maps at the beginning of *Dispatches*, Herr offers his own: "If dead ground could come back and haunt you the way dead people do, they'd have been able to mark my map CURRENT and burn the ones they'd been using since '64, but count on it, nothing like that was going to happen" (3). While the final phrase opens Herr's critique of official maps and conventional journalism in *Dispatches*, the initial simile transposes a posttraumatic reality into a physical impossibility: "dead ground" cannot normally return and disturb one's mind, but the people who died on that ground can. The "you" invokes anyone who has looked at a soldier killed in action. But the sentence hypothesizes a more personal map, what Herr experienced in Viet Nam and what he would perhaps reexperience, a trauma that is (re)current. Herr's bad dreams or bad memories have been produced by actual experiences and are true, although products of his imagination. But "ground" itself is not what is haunting him, nor can the dead be turned into ground, at least for him (although that is where they have been ultimately buried, whether in Viet Nam or in America). Moreover, "they" (a reference that comprises the American political and military planners and implementers of the war as well as the journalists who reproduced their view of it) are interested in ground that they can map, not those who have died on it (American OR Vietnamese). Even if Herr's posttraumatic visitations could challenge the operational and ideological maps that brought American forces into Viet Nam after the 1964 Tonkin Gulf Incident, they would be ignored or discarded. That Herr's internal map is only hypothetical suggests, metaphorically, one of the most pervasive features of trauma: it is fundamentally incommunicable to anyone else, or at least not to those who are "normal." Herr cannot identify, even to us, "the dead" or what actually happened to them.

Later attempts to map the Vietnam War provide similar conjunctions of the ethos of New Journalism and the elements of traumatization. Section II of "Khe Sanh" situates that battle in the Vietnamese Central Highlands, which run continuously for 700 miles along the Vietnamese and Laotian border as part of the Annamese Cordillera, the major mountain range of both countries, which divides rivers draining into the Mekong basin from those flowing into the South China Sea. Herr begins this section by questioning the American military mapping of South Vietnam and reporting that was oriented by the assumptions that lay behind that framework. The post-1955 division of Viet Nam into two warring republics, a result of America's support for Ngo Dinh Diem's rejection of the Geneva Accord framework for national elections, created a politically and militarily divided Viet Nam that had not existed even on the French maps. The American military command (MACV) then divided South Vietnam into four Corp Tactical Zones that misrepresented the real geography of Viet Nam. The distinction between IV Corps (the area south of Saigon) and III Corps (Saigon and its surroundings) cut the northernmost parts of the Mekong Delta from the rest of it. The division between II Corps (the Central Highlands) and I Corps (the northernmost battle zone, from the Demilitarized Zone south to Chu Lai) ignored the continuous sweep of the highlands from Pleiku north into Laos and into the rest of Viet Nam that lay beyond the DMZ. The result was another artificial mapping that literally defined the Republic of Viet Nam as a war divided into four parts. Herr suggests that bad maps reinforce ignorance and produce bad reporting: "it would be as impossible to know what Vietnam looked like from reading most newspaper stories as it would be to know how it smelled" (93). Here, as throughout *Dispatches*, Herr's biting satire distinguishes his role and his goals in covering the War from those of the "normal" journalist, whose affiliations tie him inevitably to the role and goals of political, military, and economic policymakers.

Moving toward the conclusion of *Dispatches*, Herr presents a final personal map of the War. As he leaves Viet Nam, he takes "a *National Geographic* map of Indochina" on which he has marked in pencil every place that he has been during his time in country: "Real places, then real only in the distance behind me, faces and places sustaining serious dislocation, mind slip and memory play. When the map fell apart along the fold lines its spirit held together, it landed in safe but shaky hands and one mark was enough, the one at LZ Loon" (255). The pun on "dislocation" prepares us for the flashback that follows, a brief account of the terrifying first night at Landing Zone (LZ) Loon after the Marines have completed the perimeter wire, reinforced the guard, and sent half the men out on night patrols, an account dislocated almost immediately by a memory of later building LZ Loon out of sand on China Beach with other colleagues: "we laughed so hard we couldn't sit up" (255). An earlier account appears near the end of "Colleagues." Here the place that was actually experienced and then playfully reproduced by Herr and his comrades hovers uncertainly between what was real and what was later reimagined: "we'd talk about LZ Loon, the mythical place where it got dark so fast that by the time you realized that there wouldn't be another chopper in until morning, you'd already picked a place to sleep for the night. Loon was the ultimate Vietnam movie location, where all of the mad colonels and death-spaced grunts we'd ever known showed up all at once" (234–235). The mark on the map and the details of Herr's first night there suggest actuality, but the "ultimate Vietnam movie location," such as the sand castle, suggests something made up, again and again, after the actual experience. Like the map, which has fallen apart, LZ Loon lives on in "spirit" in the writing of *Dispatches*. Herr ends up "safe"—he gets out of LZ Loon and Viet Nam alive—but "shaky": the hands that have produced these accounts have done so at least partly as an exorcism of a haunting, recreated stylishly and permanently in words rather than in sand. Herr's posttraumatic account(s) of LZ Loon are symptomatic of what makes *Dispatches* the greatest work of American Vietnam War fiction for many readers. Circumstantially the work of a Vietnam War correspondent, classified as a "personal narrative" on the copyright page of my edition, excerpted in all the anthologies of American New Journalism after 1971, Herr's book is also a work of posttraumatic literature. That feature, together with its transformation of personal narrative into collective vision, distinguishes *Dispatches* from nearly all the canonical works of New Journalism, an American literary movement of enduring importance and vitality that began just before Herr went to Viet Nam and that he carried with him when he went there.

New Journalism

New Journalism emerged from the America of the 1960s, an age of extraordinary and transformative and also violent and counterproductive social, cultural, and political upheaval that included the Civil Rights Movement; the Women's movement; a vibrant countercultural youth movement; a golden age of popular music that fueled and reflected America's youth culture; widespread use and celebration of illegal drugs; loosening of conventional, quasi-puritanical sexual mores; as well as a strident conservative counter-movement in support of "traditional values"; assassinations and attempted assassinations of American political leaders, beginning with the murder of John F. Kennedy in 1963; and the Vietnam War, which began in the early 1960s and occasioned a massive popular antiwar movement, as well as a smaller pro-war reaction. All of these issues were given often spectacular public attention through television. They were also covered by conventional journalism, but to many younger journalists of the period, these events and movements were epochal harbingers of critical changes in American society, prompted by the emergence of the enormous baby-boomer generation into young adulthood in the 1960s. To many, conventional reporting was incapable of coming to terms with what was happening.

The first writer and the first work usually identified with the emergence of New Journalism is Tom Wolfe's long article, "There Goes (Varoom! Varoom!) That Kandy-Kolored Tangerine-Flake Streamline Baby," a report to his editor Byron Dobell on the hot rod and custom car culture of Los Angeles, where Wolfe was sent by *Esquire* magazine in 1963 and where he interviewed everyone connected with the phenomenon. As Marc Weingarten notes, Wolfe regarded everything he saw in Los Angeles as only part of an extraordinary American youth culture that was rewriting the history of Western art and architecture (93–95). The essay was later extended into a book in 1965 (*The Kandy-Kolored Tangerine-Flake Streamline Baby*), and the work of other writers for *Esquire* and *New York* (the Sunday supplement of the *New York Herald Tribune*) such as Gay Talese, Jimmy Breslin, Gail Sheehy, and Gloria Steinem extended New Journalism in other directions. While Wolfe eventually became a novelist in the late 1980s, writers like Truman Capote (*In Cold Blood*, 1965) and Norman Mailer (*The Armies of the Night* and *Miami and the Siege of Chicago*, both 1968) were moving from writing novels to nonfiction works that employed the techniques of literary fiction. Wolfe and E. W. Johnson's 1973 anthology, *The New Journalism*, widens the scope of what Wolfe denies was ever a "movement," but simply "some sort of artistic excitement in journalism" (23). Ultimately, however, the new literary journalism not only transcended and exposed the limits of conventional journalism but also displaced and usurped the traditional literary supremacy of the novel itself, at least according to Wolfe's tendentious account in "Seizing the Power" (23).

Wolfe's definition of New Journalism identifies four distinctive elements: scene-by-scene reconstruction that eliminates external, historical narrative as much as possible; full, realistic dialogue within those scenes; intimate third person point of view that presents every scene through the eyes and feelings of a particular character; and symbolic details of what Wolfe calls people's *status life* (32), the everyday gestures and external habits and customs that express their sense of selfhood. All four were drastically truncated or simply omitted from conventional journalism, but for Wolfe they enabled the literary journalist to reenergize the power of social realism that had been displaced and replaced in the contemporary novel by postmodern fabulism and metafictional exercises. As a result, he claims, "The—New Journalists—Parajournalists—had the whole crazed obscene uproarious Mammon-faced, drug-soaked mau–mau lust-oozing Sixties in America all to themselves" (31).

A fifth element of what we might also call neorealism is what sets New Journalism radically apart from Balzac as well as from Robbe-Grillet: everything we are reading actually occurred—factuality and actuality have been transmuted into a work that has the structure, style, and resonance of fiction but is completely authentic. The foundation of this transformative power is saturation journalism: typically, living with one's subjects for long periods of time, getting to know them perhaps even better than they know themselves, exhaustive or at least significantly extended interviews transcribed in full and then revised, and, whatever the time period of research or direct experience, recording and recalling minute circumstantial details, including self-presentation of those who are involved. Wolfe rightly claims that the great social realists of the nineteenth century did extensive and exhaustive research in Paris, London, Moscow, or wherever their subjects lived, dined, presented themselves to others, and died. That research was turned into fiction by Zola, or Dickens, or Turgenev, however, while the literary journalist/New Journalist/documentary novelist represents his subjects in their actuality. Saturation journalism requires that the writer accompanies his subjects in their activities, as Wolfe did with Ken Kesey and the Merry Pranksters (*The Electric Kool-Aid Acid Test*, 1968) or Thompson did with the Hell's Angels (*Hell's Angels: A Strange and Terrible Saga*, 1966). Gaining their trust and validating one's credibility so that they allow full public exposure in print are essential, and it sometimes involves rites of passage that help the writer understand his subjects as intimately as possible. Wolfe could not publish the Kesey book without finally taking LSD himself (Weingarten 115), and Thompson was beaten to within an inch of his life by gang members after calling a drunken and drugged-out Angel gang member a "punk" for hitting his own girlfriend in the face. The testimony of Thompson's Random House editor could be applied to other New Journalists: "I told Hunter,

'Your method of research is to tie yourself to a railroad track when you know a train is coming to it, and see what happens'" (quoted in Weingarten 141).

Wolfe's characterization of New Journalism (as well as his disparagement of the postmodern novel) has been found "self-serving" by Thomas Connery (*Sourcebook* xi) and other critics, but it provides a framework within which and against which to consider Herr's work. Primarily stylistic, it deemphasizes or omits other characteristics of New Journalism that are just as significant. As Stacey Olster notes, although New Journalists seem almost obsessive in providing minute factual detail, they have typically chosen subjects that could be treated as synecdoches for larger issues or problems within modern and postmodern American society and culture: "subjects possessing traits with deeper historical and cultural resonance enabled writers to turn them into the kind of national emblems that novelists had, out of despair, relinquished" (45–46). Thus, *In Cold Blood* is not simply or even primarily the story of a multiple murder in the middle of Nebraska: "Its brilliance derives instead from Capote's use of that murder to portray the decline of the American West, the death of the small town, and the ease with which American dreams can turn into American nightmares" (46). *Slouching Towards Bethlehem*, Joan Didion's account of Lucille Miller's murder of her husband in their flaming Volkswagen, provides the same sort of resonance, beginning with its title ("Some Dreamers of the Golden Dream") and first sentences: "This is a story about love and death in the golden land, and begins with the country. The San Bernardino Valley lies only an hour east of Los Angeles by the San Bernardino Freeway but is in certain ways an alien place . . ." (304). In Didion's meticulously reconstructed story of the marriage, what seems initially an incident from a horror movie turns out to be a not uncommon story of lower middle-class hopes and desires gone awry. Like Didion's, Hunter Thompson's titles expose tarnished American dreams and icons: "The Kentucky Derby Is Decadent and Depraved" (for *Scanlan's Monthly*, June 1970); *Fear and Loathing in Las Vegas: A Savage Journey to the Heart of the American Dream* (1971).

Finally, although documentary novels like *In Cold Blood* and Mailer's *The Executioner's Song* efface the journalist/researcher/writer who has created them and present the characteristics, actions, and thoughts of the subjects whom he or she has reproduced, much New Journalism is characterized by the very visible and audible presence of the writer himself or herself. In *Fear and Loathing in Las Vegas* as well as some earlier shorter pieces, Thompson appears as a persona, Raoul Duke, accompanied by Dr Gonzo, the persona of his Chicano friend and civil rights attorney, Oscar Acosta. The two figures spend much of their time together taking drugs, with the alternative names thin covers for their actual identities and activities on the literal and figurative trip. Mailer is of course the main character in both of his 1968 works of New Journalism, showing up drunk to give his pre-March speech to assembled activists in *The Armies of the Night* and otherwise replicating his own role as participant and, more importantly, observer, but under his own name. His later remarks in "Superman Comes to the Supermarket," his analysis of John F. Kennedy's nomination for President at the 1960 Democratic Convention in Los Angeles, sum up both the journalistic and moral credo behind the blatant subjectivism of much New Journalism, an "enormously personalized journalism in which the character of the narrator was one of the elements in the way the reader would finally assess the experience. I had felt that I had some dim intuitive feeling that what was wrong with all journalism is that the reporter tended to be objective and that that was one of the great lies of all time" (Weingarten 55).

New Journalism and *Dispatches*

Whatever label we might attach to *Dispatches*—New Journalism, literary journalism, personal narrative, history as a novel—the anthologies of New Journalism published after 1974, including Tom Wolfe's, have identified it with that movement. *Dispatches* occupies the sixth and final chapter of John Hellmann's *Fables of Fact: The New Journalism as New Fiction* (1981), and Don Ringnalda contributed a chapter on Herr to Thomas Connery's *Sourcebook of American Literary Journalism: Representing Writers in an Emerging Genre* (1992). Herr appears quite late in both these books, after Capote, Wolfe, Talese, and Thompson. Herr's relative belatedness as a New Journalist is a product of chronology in two senses. His correspondent's tour of the Vietnam War began in

November of 1967 and ended in August 1968, several years after *In Cold Blood* and the initial articles of Talese, Breslin, and Wolfe, and Herr's initial articles for *Esquire* and *New American Review* appeared in 1968, 1969, and 1970. More importantly, *Dispatches* was not published as a whole until 1977, half a decade after both of Thompson's *Fear and Loathing* volumes. The contrast with other New Journalist icons is striking. For example, Mailer covered the March on the Pentagon in October 1967 and published *The Armies of the Night* in 1968, the year it received the Pulitzer Prize. John Sack's *M*, based on his experiences in 1965–1966 with an army company from infantry training through its year in the War, was published in 1967. Herr's delay in completing *Dispatches* is a symptom of the posttraumatic focus of the book, for it is nearly a requirement of all journalism (including New Journalism) that its subjects be covered, reported on, and published as soon as possible to sustain the interest of its audience and to insure maximum impact of the information that it provides.

Nonetheless, Herr's work is characteristic of many typical aspects of New Journalism. He was sent as a correspondent to Viet Nam by *Esquire*, one of the founding publications of the movement, and four of the six portions of what became a longer book *were* published close in time to the events they represent. "Hell Sucks," the first of the *Esquire* pieces, was published in the August 1968 edition, only 6 months after the end of the Battle of Hué, which Herr covered in February, about a week after the beginning of this longest and most destructive American battle in the Tet Offensive. Herr's original account of Hué is closer to conventional, on-site, objective reporting than the other six sections of *Dispatches*. "Khe Sanh" and "Conclusion at Khe Sanh," Herr's second and third pieces for *Esquire*, cover the longest single American operation, the costly defense of the embattled Marine base just below the DMZ from late 1967 until the lifting of the siege in April 1968. Originally published in two parts in the September and October 1969 editions, "Khe Sanh" is the third and longest of the six sections of *Dispatches*, appearing just after "Hell Sucks," the second piece. "Illumination Rounds," a metaphor that fuses the howitzer-propelled parachute flares used to help locate targets for high-explosive projectiles with Herr's own brief illuminations of the war, appeared in *New American Review* in 1969. A series of 21 brief, unconnected scenes and character portraits presented without introductions, transitions, or connections from one to the next, these vivid spotlights on the War exemplify the direct scene-by-scene representation of reality characteristic of New Journalism even as they evade any sense of narrative structure. In *Dispatches*, four of the original illuminations were transposed to "Hell Sucks," perhaps because all four scenes occurred during the battle for Hué. Herr's revision of his first reporting of the War thus makes it more consonant with New Journalism practices. The fifth *Esquire* piece, which would be largely reproduced in 1977 as "Colleagues," was published in April 1970, less than 2 years after Herr had left the War, and was initially titled "The War Correspondent: A Reappraisal." The original title more explicitly addresses Herr's critique of conventional journalism in the Vietnam War, which he contrasts unfavorably with the "brotherhood" of freelance writers and photographers whose practices and purposes constitute or complement New Journalism. "Colleagues" is the only section of *Dispatches* that dramatically represents and names actual persons throughout, from Herr's comrades Dana Stone, Sean Flynn, and Tim Page to General Westmoreland, and photographs of a dozen colleagues appeared with the original long article in *Esquire*.

Wolfe chose to excerpt the first half of "Khe Sanh" in his 1973 anthology. In many ways, the three earliest pieces in *Dispatches* are its closest in method, form, and/or purpose to conventional reporting, as well as to New Journalism. Thus, "Hell Sucks," with its play on Sherman's fundamental definition of war, is a relatively conventional account of what Herr observed of the terrible battle in Hué, with its carnage among the civilian population and combination of exhaustion and loss of hope among the Marines. Herr occupies the observer function throughout "Hell Sucks," the telling anecdote, observation, or comment speaking volumes about the overwhelming firepower and devastation visited upon the former imperial capital of Viet Nam by and upon both sides. Arranged in loose chronological order, Herr's account ends when he accompanies a South Vietnamese field officer and his English-speaking driver to the Imperial Palace, damaged beyond restoration and filled with corpses only 3 weeks earlier. The experience is the last of the original "Illumination Rounds" transferred to "Hell Sucks" in 1977. Herr's conventional but irrelevant questions to the driver about the former line of Vietnamese emperors are abruptly cut off by his guide in Herr's last sentence: "'Major Trong is emperor now,' he said, and gunned the jeep into the Palace grounds" (85). Like "Hell Sucks," "Khe Sanh" is a largely chronological account of a single operation from beginning to end. Herr sets the battle in a much larger political, military, and physical context, however, including the geography of the Highlands and the uncanny resemblances to Dien Bien Phu that haunted Lyndon Johnson, the commanders in the field, and the American press corps, and he introduces two Marines that he met during his three trips (and 12 days and nights) to the worst place in the world, a dwarfish white teenager from Kansas whom Herr renames "Mayhew" and "Daytripper," his large, mustachioed African-American buddy from Detroit. As in "Hell Sucks," Herr subordinates himself by taking on an observer role but also uses second person ("you") and third plural ("we") pronouns to particularize Khe Sanh as an experience shared by everyone else confined to that particular hell. Wolfe praises Herr's technique of transforming personal experiences into quasi-fictional scenes in "Khe Sanh" and thus avoiding mere autobiography: "he attempted the far more difficult feat of penetrating the psyches, the points of view, of the line troops themselves, using the third as well as the first person" (*The New Journalism* 85). Throughout *Dispatches*, as in the passages earlier, Herr sustains a middle perspective between the self-aggrandizing self-dramatization of a Mailer or Thompson and the self-denying disappearance and replacement of the documentary novelist or fiction writer, like Capote or Didion, by his or her intimate or omniscient third-person narrative. Herr's presence in the scenes that he recreates not only ensures authenticity and deconstructs conventional objectivity but also often acknowledges the writer's ethical obligations to those whom he is representing for his own purposes:

> I went to cover the war and the war covered me; an old story, unless you've never heard it. I went there behind the crude but serious belief that you had to be able to look at anything, serious because I acted on it and went, crude because I didn't know, it took the war to teach it, that you were as responsible for everything you saw as you were for everything you did. (20)

Within *Dispatches* as a whole, however, Herr's reproduction in "Khe Sanh" of whole scenes and complete dialogues involving

Mayhew and Day Tripper is unusual. His subjects are always the actual soldiers whom he covered, but they are seldom given even pseudonyms by Herr, beginning with the "4th Division Lurp who took his pills by the fistful" (5) and ending with "IGOR FROM THE NORTH" at China Beach, "who spoke twice an hour in a spooky clipped language of his own like slow rounds, . . . 'Got to go Dong Ha kill more'" (258). Herr's use of generic, unspecific identifiers for his subjects and second and first person plural pronouns for his own activities has the effect of making *Dispatches* a collective and paradigmatic account of the War rather than either the personal testimony or detached omniscience typical of New Journalism. Frequent references to soldiers through third person plural pronouns, nearly unheard of in New Journalism, also give Herr's subjects emblematic resonance, while constantly reminding us that "they" have experienced things that their interviewers cannot even imagine.

Herr's own method of saturation journalism ruled out embedding himself in particular units and following individuals and their narratives continuously, in any case. As a freelance writer, he could travel wherever there was space for him on a vehicle or helicopter, and his ability to fly in and out of the War is an important theme in *Dispatches*, one that also has ethical implications. Although Herr arrived in scores of combat bases and encountered the War nearly as intensely as the G.I.s or Marines who shared their quarters, their experiences, and their stories with him for a day or a week, he and his colleagues always had the option and opportunity of leaving the combat zone, and such decisions typically removed them from the shared threat of being killed in, or at least by, action. Thus, their flight into a camp at Soc Trang begins with an inviting but unsettling welcome from the young captain in command: "If you come looking for a story this is your lucky day, we got Condition Red here, . . . That's affirmative, . . . we are *definitely* expecting rain." The visit lasts one quiet but harrowing night: "Ten minutes before daybreak I was down at the lz asking about choppers" (12).

Herr addresses the issue of journalistic parasitism more fully and more frankly in Section II of "Colleagues," including the hatred—not admiration—some G.I.s and Marines felt for journalists who were not forced to remain in combat zones, as they were, but freely chose to be there with them. But the more common reaction, from a typically unnamed subject imprisoned in combat who watches Herr escape from Hué on a helicopter, points to the most important focus and principle of Herr's New Journalism:

> We knew each other by now, and when he caught up with me he grabbed my sleeve so violently that I thought he was going to accuse me, or worse, try to stop me from going. His face was all but blank with exhaustion, but he had enough feeling left to say, "Okay, man, you go on, you go on out of here you cocksucker, but I mean it, you tell it! You tell it, man. If you don't tell it...." (207)

For Herr, the real war is the grunt experience, and the stories that tell it most brutally, and most honestly, are theirs.

Herr's close observations of the soldiers and Marines are without false pieties: "I stood as close to them as I could without actually being one of them, and then I stood as far back as I could without leaving the planet. Disgust doesn't begin to describe what they made me feel, they threw people out of helicopters, tied people up and put the dogs on them. Brutality was just a word in my mouth before that" (67). Nonetheless, for Herr, only those who did the fighting, the killing, and the dying had the authority and the moral right to speak of the War, partly because they lacked the privileged ignorance, obligation, or mendacity to justify it.

Trauma and *Dispatches*

Although Herr's critique of the war and its coverage by conventional journalism begins in the first section of *Dispatches*, it is supplemented and expanded in "Colleagues," the fifth section, where he recalls the "brotherhood" of reporters who questioned and critiqued what John Paul Vann identified as "the bright shining lie" (Sheehan 342) propagated by the Administration, the Command, and the Mission, and reproduced by most reporting. Those colleagues ("we [un]happy few," in Herr's viewpoint) may or may not have saturated themselves in the grunts' experience as Herr did, but they all shared his view of one undeniable but often ignored truth: "that in back of every column of print you read about Vietnam there was a dripping, laughing death-face; it hid there in the newspapers and magazines and held to your television screens for hours after the set was turned off for the night, an after-image that simply wanted to tell you at last what somehow had not been told" (218). Here, as at the end of his account of Pacification, Herr switches from self-referential description to the vocative: the "you" being addressed is the American public, which has been given a picture of the War that ignores, evades, or subordinates death. In its final form, *Dispatches* highlights that truth, which had been present as an after-image in the four sections of the book that had been published in earlier versions between 1968 and 1970. For Herr, the faces of the dead began to accumulate and would eventually overwhelm him when the Tet Offensive broke on January 30, 1968, 2 months after he had arrived in country. Tet was politically, ethically, and professionally a turning point for the author: in a letter to his *Esquire* editor Harold Hayes, Herr saw the War as lost and "ignoble," and his previous writing on the Vietnam War not worth keeping, because "It is not the same war, not in any way" (Weingarten 164).

His personal experience of the Communist offensive was even more transformative. The Viet Cong attack on Can Tho, where Herr was billeted that first night of Tet, led to what he labels "one last war story" (67) near the end of the first section of *Dispatches* that recalls his first direct experience of killing as well as survival, and that continues his account of both intimacy with and repulsion from the grunts that was quoted earlier:

> We covered each other, an exchange of services that worked all right until one night when I slid over to the wrong end of the story, propped up behind some sandbags at an airstrip in Can Tho with a .30-caliber automatic in my hands, firing cover for a four-man reaction team trying to get back. (67)

The "reporter" has become a "shooter" (68), and in the morning the corpses of 12 dead Vietnamese are picked up; Herr remembers "looking at the empty clips about my feet behind the berm, telling myself that there would never be any way to know for sure" (even before the morning revealed the Vietnamese K.I.A.): "I couldn't remember ever feeling so tired, so changed, so happy" (68). He works on the badly wounded as an "unskilled and scared" medic in the Can Tho American compound, and then recalls how the experience of seeing the dead was to reemerge 6 years later in a nightmare: "New York City, 1975, when I got up the next morning I was laughing" (68–69). Herr ends the first part of *Dispatches* here, 2 years after the intrusive dream, after a final subsection that has taken us from his reflections on the bloody killers whom he has covered so intimately to that terrible but exhilarating night in Can Tho and its aftermath, the bloody fatigues, the 6 years of hauntings, the Dantesque nightmare that forces him to look at the faces of the dead that he initially turned away from (and may have killed), to waking up cleansed and laughing, probably happier than that night, 7 years earlier, when he was still alive and the enemy were dead.

"If dead ground could come back and haunt you the way dead people do"—Herr's impossible conditional at the beginning of *Dispatches* has nearly been realized here as he looks at the faces of the dead, but the *traumwerk* is therapeutic, allowing the writer to revisit and face a site of wounding that was collective as well as personal (68). If the shooter helped Herr and others to save their lives that night, perhaps we readers can imagine that the "unaccustomed mercy" (157) of the clumsy and frightened therapist may have helped the shooter to recover.

Death ultimately has dominion in *Dispatches*, and trauma is the sign of its extended power. From its origin as the Greek word for battlefield wounds (implicating war at the origin of Western literary culture), since World War I trauma has become primarily identified with the psychosomatic and psychological effects of life-threatening or life-destroying bodily desecration of any kind, both for victims and for those who observe them. Trauma and its posttraumatic effects on victims and observers are not limited to war, of course: natural and manmade accidents and catastrophes, rape, incest, childhood sexual abuse; domestic violence; and terrorism as well as combat trauma have been recognized, in clinical studies like Judith Herman's *Trauma and Recovery*, as equally if differently destructive of an individual's sense of security, integrity, and value. The symptoms of combat trauma, including intrusion and flashbacks, constriction and repression, hyperarousal and berserking, anomie and suicide, have been traced in literary works from Homer to the American Vietnam War poet and memoirist W. D. Ehrhardt, in studies by Kalí Tal, Jonathan Shay, and others. When Herr becomes the direct subject of *Dispatches*, often via the "I" who has seen the dead but cannot face them again in words, he represents himself as traumatized by that experience.

But *Dispatches* also represents what Tal has called "other people's trauma" in a way that is not simply metaphoric, since Herr has shared that experience, though less continuously, with the grunts who never leave the combat zone ("Speaking" 246). However brutal Herr's subjects have become, they have also been scourged by the War: "I think that those people who used to say that they only wept for the Vietnamese never really wept for anyone at all if they couldn't squeeze out at least one for these men and boys when they died or had their lives cracked open for them" (67). The survivor whose life has been cracked open has been traumatized, and *Dispatches* offers numerous portraits of such figures, from Herr's first subject in *Dispatches*, the fourth Division Lurp, "a good killer" who "slept with his eyes open" (6) to a battalion of soldiers just returned from the Battle of Dak To, who looked like "a colony of stroke victims, a thousand men on a cold rainy airfield after too much of something I'd never really know" (22), to the young Marine at Khe Sanh whose tour in the Vietnam War has ended but is so paralyzed by "acute environmental reaction" (91) that he can't bring himself to board the daily flights waiting to take him away.

Most of the trauma scenes and traumatized figures in *Dispatches*, including Herr himself, appear in the first and final sections of the book, which were first published in 1977 as "High on War" in *Esquire* and "LZ Loon" in *Rolling Stone*, just before the publication of *Dispatches* in the same year, 7–10 years after the original versions of the middle four parts of the book. As Herr explained to Eric James Schroeder in an interview published in 1992, he had gone to Viet Nam for *Esquire* expecting to write a book, and two-thirds of it (the middle four sections) had been written by 1970. But what Herr calls "post-Vietnam syndrome" (35) disabled his efforts for 5 or 6 years, "trying to write a first chapter and a last chapter that would be a circle to draw around the rest of the pieces and somehow make it a book" (41). In the end, Herr's post-Vietnam War anomie is integrated with the other traumatized subjects of the first and concluding portions, titled "Breathing In" and "Breathing Out" in *Dispatches*, as if the book were an inspiration, culled from memory, which needed to be recalled but then expelled. The "circle" that enabled Herr to introduce and conclude *Dispatches* is literally posttraumatic writing, including Herr's personal maps of Viet Nam. Death-saturated in the way that Herr had found so irresponsibly absent in media coverage when he wrote "The War Correspondent: A Reappraisal" in 1970, the early scenes in "Breathing In" include a Lurp who cannot go home again after three tours of killing; a ride on a chopper full of G.I. corpses; a helmet "more alive now than the man who'd worn it," abandoned by Herr when he realizes where and who it has come from; and a savage parody of the dehumanizing metonym, "boots on the ground," at a solemn ceremony by the 173d Airborne Division after the Dak To campaign in honor of their K.I.A., each represented by "a company's worth of jump boots in the dust taking benediction" (23). Finally, Herr's title for the material—*Dispatches*—that it took him 10 years to write and reshape into a book is not just a term from journalism but resonates with the sense of a verb that has also meant "to kill" since 1530, according to the O.E.D.

What distinguishes Herr's New Journalism, formally and qualitatively, from that of other unconventional as well as conventional journalists' writing on the war is his resonant focus on death and, even more significantly, trauma, the psychological residue of combat that can destroy soldiers without killing them. "Breathing Out," the final and shortest section of *Dispatches*, focuses almost exclusively on Herr himself—his return to America, his continuing memories of the War, and—most importantly—its end. The section includes the final two LZ Loon memories as well as some events that postdated the account of "Colleagues," most significantly the disappearance of Sean Flynn and Dana Stone in Cambodia and their deaths, probably in 1971. Riddled with post-Vietnam War apparitions and memories of the dead, "Breathing Out" prompts Herr's most painful confession ("I was once in such a bad head about it that I thought the dead had only been spared a great deal of pain") as well as his most poignant: "Debriefed by dreams, friends coming in from the other side to see that I was still alive" (259). Commentators who have critiqued the sometimes celebratory tone of Herr's love/hate attitude toward the War (e.g. "I think that Vietnam was what we had instead of happy childhoods" [244]) seem to have ignored the astringent posttraumatic wisdom articulated by the survivor in 1977 near the end of *Dispatches*: "If you can't find your courage in a war, you have to keep looking for it anyway, and not in another war either;

in where it's old and jammed until the rocks start moving around, a little light and air, long time no see. Another frequency, another information, and death no deterrent to receiving it" (259).

Since *Dispatches* concludes with the end of the Second Indochina War in 1975, it suggests that Herr's personal recovery—including the writing of the book and its publication more than 10 years after his arrival in Viet Nam—needed political and historical closure: "The war ended, and then it really ended, the cities 'fell,' I watched the choppers I'd loved dropping into the South China Sea as their Vietnamese pilots jumped clear, and one last chopper revved it up, lifted off, and flew out of my chest" (259–260). The conclusion of *Dispatches* has a therapeutic tone, and perhaps even a therapeutic purpose, even though for most Americans in 1977 the reunification of Viet Nam was likely to have been painful, shameful, and tragic. Unlike Tim O'Brien, whose career has never sought or never been able to leave the War behind, Herr's "dispersion" (260) from the Vietnam War has been complete, despite later postwar excursions in helping to write War screen plays for Francis Ford Coppola in 1977 and Stanley Kubrick in 1987. Ultimately, like all of the canonical works of New Journalism, *Dispatches* was a one-time project, not to be repeated or continued. But none of the other works took 10 years to complete, and none of them focus so eloquently on traumatization, a subject that gives Herr's masterpiece its coherence and also much of its resonance and power.

2

Dương Thu Hương's *Paradise of the Blind* and *Novel Without a Name*, and Bảo Ninh's *The Sorrow of War*: Corrective, politically incorrect, and challenging

Michele Janette

Paradise of the Blind, *Novel Without a Name*, and *The Sorrow of War* are frequently turned to by Western readers seeking to "balance out the troubling impact of the canonical . . . Vietnam war story" or to "[fill] in the fissures of political knowledge about Vietnam" (Liparulo, "Beyond" 215; Lan Duong 103). Such readings understandably seek correctives for incomplete knowledge about the war the United States fought in Viet Nam. But the demand for corrective is at once both urgent and impossible. It is urgent that Americans in particular attempt to overcome the historic myopia with which, as Bruce Franklin has argued, America has viewed Vietnam as "something that happened to us, an event that divided, wounded, and victimized America" rather than as a nation with its own history that long predated US involvement, its own postwar reconstructions and rebirths, its own narratives about the wars on its soil, and an identity beyond those wars (28).[1] It is impossible, in that no book (or even three) or author (or even a pair) can provide completion, coherence, or "answers," as if this global conflict were a puzzle for which we have simply been missing the "Vietnamese piece."

This chapter takes as its impetus the challenge of corrective, and corrective as challenge. Not seeking completion or closure, I read these three novels, *Paradise of the Blind* (Dương Thu Hương, 1988, hereafter *Paradise*), *Novel Without a Name* (Dương Thu Hương, 1990, hereafter *Novel*), and *The Sorrow of War* (Bảo Ninh, 1990, hereafter *Sorrow*) as instead staging particular provocations. Rather than supplying what is missing, these works suggest avenues to rethink the entire picture; they challenge rather than complement the American literary canon of Vietnam War books. They answer Nguyen-Vo Thu-Huong's call for attention to "radical alterity, irreducible to ourselves" (171). Nguyen-Vo urges us to "be hospitable to all the dead of [the Vietnam] war and its aftermath if we are to form our memory of that war without cannibalizing all of these histories into the single story that becomes us" (171). This chapter therefore charts these texts not as maps of unexplored Vietnamese territory, but as incitements to puncture our habits of thinking about Viet Nam and "the Vietnam War." For readers unfamiliar with Vietnamese history, I offer a brief description of the circumstances surrounding the publication of these novels, and then suggest two major provocations that these novels stage for the Western reader.

Indeed, these novels' challenge to the dominant narratives was the feature that catapulted them to international fame. Dương Thu Hương and Bảo Ninh are among Viet Nam's most famous dissident writers. Bảo was denounced by the Communist Party; Dương has been the recipient of several publishing bans, was imprisoned for seven months, expelled from the Communist Party, and had her passport revoked and guards posted at her home for 12 years.[2] Dương sent her second novel out of the country to have it published, which led to her imprisonment for "smuggling 'state secrets' out of the country" (Schafer, "Land Reform" 204). In 2005, international pressure led to her passport renewal, and the following year she emigrated to France. She continues to publish novels internationally, but none of her work since 1991 has been published in Viet Nam. Bảo continues to work as an editor and essayist in Viet Nam, and released a collection of short stories in 2005, but has not published another novel.

Their censorship and state harassment are the more dramatic for having both been celebrated revolutionary veterans before their falls from grace. Dương was a member of the Youth Brigade in 1967, sent to the front to entertain and cheer the troops. Of her unit of 40, she was one of three to survive. She fought for 10 years in the central highlands, and then volunteered again to serve on the Chinese border during hostilities between China and Viet Nam in 1979. She worked as a screenwriter before shifting to fiction, and was already a popular and outspoken writer in Viet Nam when *Paradise* became the first of her works to be translated into English in 1993.[3] Bảo shares similar military credentials and similar popularity. Also a Youth Brigade soldier, he too survived the war that killed most of his comrades: of the 500-soldier brigade he joined in 1969, he was one of only 10 who survived to 1975. *The Sorrow of War* became a cultural phenomenon: a bestseller internationally and domestically, and also the subject of party denunciation.

As insiders-turned-dissidents, Bảo and Dương have been celebrated as paragons of the "disillusionment" of the generation that defeated the Americans, but that was dismayed at postwar Viet Nam.[4] As Harriet Blodgett notes, this disillusionment narrative has found ready audience in the West; and as Lan Duong writes, Dương herself embraces her identity as the "traitorous daughter of the national family" (Lan Duong 90). Even though *Novel* was clearly published as an act of rebellion, smuggled to France against government orders, neither her earlier *Paradise* nor Bảo's *Sorrow* were construed initially as acts of subversion. Both novels were at first honored within Viet Nam; their critiques originally were produced in accord with new government policy directives. The novels expressed disillusionment, but did not seek simply to condemn a failed nation state or to decry communism. While, to Dương's dismay,[5] her novels have been used by anticommunist readers to justify their cause, she first published them in a context of apparently state-sanctioned freedoms.

Context: Đổi Mới and disillusionment

In 1986, the Communist Party of Viet Nam announced a change in its policies regarding cultural productions. Previously, as John Schafer describes it, "Vietnam's communist leaders required novelists to support the national endeavor by authoring stereotyped works that featured typical characters and themes and that focused on the goals of the collective struggle" ("Collective" 13). Like its ally the Soviet Union, Viet Nam relaxed controls on cultural expression in the 1980s. The Sixth Party Congress announced a new paradigm of "Đổi Mới": literally "renovation," enacted through a series of "open door" policies. Resolution #5 in 1987 increased the "freedom of creativity" for writers, and crucially recognized that "freedom of literary creativity must be accompanied by freedom to criticize" (quoted in Healy 43). This announcement opened not only the door, but also the floodgates, and Bảo and Dương, along with many other writers, fully took up its invitation.

It was within the context of Đổi Mới that Bảo and Dương penned *Paradise* and *Sorrow*. The novels follow Party Secretary Nguyễn Văn Linh's advice to "portray bad people and bad things to arouse public indignation and censure" (1987; quoted in Schafer, "Land Reform" 203). Thus, while *Paradise* and *Sorrow* were eventually deemed treasonous (and publishing *Novel* was deliberately dissident), for Bảo in particular, exposing "bad people and bad things" was patriotic: "his last duty as a soldier" (50). *Paradise* focuses on a young woman protagonist, Hằng, who grows up caught in a tug of war between her mother Quế and her paternal aunt Tâm, instigated by her maternal uncle Chính. The present-day actions of the novel are few: adult Hằng lives in Russia as an "exported worker," travels to Moscow at the behest of her Uncle Chính, and then travels home to Viet Nam for her Aunt Tâm's death and funeral. The majority of the novel is devoted to flashbacks of Hằng's childhood and family history. It is a tragic tale of abuses passing as righteousness. Beginning with the disasters of the North Vietnamese Land Reforms of the 1950s, Dương portrays the impact of Party rules upon the family. Uncle Chính, a local functionary, destroys his sister's happy marriage because her husband is not of the peasant class but is an intellectual from a small landowning family.[6] Motivated by self-interest, Chính then pressures Hằng's mother (who has become a single mother because of his interventions, and is eking out a subsistence for herself and Hằng as a street vendor) to give up her "shameful" petty-capitalist ways and begin a career as a factory worker, employment that would benefit his own ambitions within the Party. Even this purportedly principled ambition is hollow, shown when he later tricks Hằng into coming to Moscow, ostensibly because he is ill, but really because he wants her help with the black marketeering venture he and fellow Party cadres are running. Dương's novel thus portrays decades of campaign errors, cadre hypocrisy, and bureaucratic exploitation, pushing the concept of "constructive criticism" to its limit. Although wildly popular, it proved more than the Party could stand: after selling over 40,000 copies, *Paradise* was banned in Viet Nam and Dương labeled a dissident writer (Schafer, "Land Reform" 203).[7]

Bảo Ninh's *Sorrow*, too, was a bestseller, and won Viet Nam's first prize for literature in 1991 (Healy 49). The novel's structure is postmodern, shifting narrators and time periods, and offering fragments rather than a linear trajectory.[8] As Madeleine Thien describes it, the stories in *Sorrow* seem to spontaneously generate further stories: "Here, the dead remember other dead, they call up their own ghosts, so that we are always remembering, and living, through an infinite corridor of others" (n.p.). There is, nonetheless, a unifying consciousness for most of the book: Kien, recruited in 1965 into the North Vietnamese army, fights for 10 years, is present for the "Fall" of Saigon in 1975, and tries to cope in the novel's present with postwar depression by writing a text he never hopes to publish. (He abandons it and vanishes from the novel itself near the end, when an anonymous narrator finds the manuscript the reader has until this point been reading.) Far from the Party's heroic nationalist narrative of anti-imperialist passion, disciplined principle, and collective solidarity, Bảo depicts rampant but unadmittable despair, uncontrollable violence, broken dreams, and pain. His battle scenes emphasize loss, as whole battalions are reduced to two or three survivors. Almost every woman in the novel is raped, and the assaults are committed by both enemy and allied soldiers. Postwar life is not a hard-won utopia, but more of the "vulgar and cruel life we all experienced during the war" (47). Overall, the novel itself offers "a horror song of our times" (43). Like Dương's *Paradise*, Bảo's

Sorrow took the freedom to criticize further than the Party could tolerate. While hugely popular among veterans, it was condemned by party officials and the Hanoi Writers' Union (Goldenberg n.p.). Although never imprisoned, Bảo too was subject to years of governmental surveillance.[9]

Novel, the second novel by Dương to be available in English, was censored in Viet Nam before it ever appeared. Already expelled from the Communist Party after the publication of *Paradise*, Dương submitted the manuscript of *Novel* to publishers in Hanoi (which are governmentally controlled) in 1990, but it was rejected. She surreptitiously faxed the manuscript to colleagues in Paris. When the Vietnamese authorities found out, publication in Viet Nam was banned and Dương was imprisoned under charges that in sending out her novel manuscript she was "stealing state secrets and selling them abroad to foreigners" (McPherson n.p.). International pressure, including the receipt of the international Hellman-Hammet award (given to "persecuted writers"), secured her release in late 1991 (Taí, "Disenchantment," 83). *Novel* has been published only outside Viet Nam: first in Vietnamese through a private press in California, then in French translation in Paris in 1994, and in English translation in New York in 1995. Like Bảo's *Sorrow*, Dương's *Novel* tells the story of a North Vietnamese soldier. Quan, recruited in 1965 and still fighting in the novel's present day of 1975, is sent to help Bien, his childhood friend and fellow enlistee, now confined within his military camp as a madman. As Quan travels to find Bien, the novel describes his encounters along the route and his memories of past encounters and battles. Like Bảo, Dương offers a chronicle of horror.

As in *Sorrow*, the soldiers of *Novel* are not fervent revolutionaries or patriots, but war-weary young adults who frequently ponder desertion. Fame and glory are not valuable prizes but forces of dehumanization, bribes that turn a father, lover, child, or friend into a "machine" (93). Party cadres are not honorable leaders, but "ignoramuses who never even learned the most basic morals. They study their Marxism-Leninism, and then come and pillage our vegetable gardens and rice fields with Marx's blessing. In the name of class struggle, they seduce other men's women" (133); "For so long, it's just been misery, suffering, and more suffering" (137). In addition to structural ills, *Novel* investigates the protagonist's own complicity, as when his visit home feeds the very propaganda machine he resents: "after that meeting, twenty-eight young men volunteered for service," crows the hamlet's cadre (151).

Together, Dương and Bảo attack both abuses of power within a nation-state and also the practice of building a nation-state: "Glory" is debased to being "drunk on a vision" or "an endless settling of scores" (*Novel* 285, 286), while the founding of a national legacy results only in the vainglorious erection of "triumphal arches," and the inculcation of bleak passivity: "'What happens afterward?' 'how do I know? We're all in the same herd of sheep'" (*Sorrow* 47, 288).

Even as Dương and Bảo help us to understand Vietnamese perspectives on twentieth-century Viet Nam, we need to be wary of applying a short historical lens that understands their critiques in isolation. Both Dương and Bảo are contributors to the larger phenomenon called "Renovation Literature."[10] As charted by Dana Healy, Renovation Literature offers critical rather than idealized portraits of contemporary society, focuses on individuals rather than "collective life," tracks a cultural decline in traditional morality, and reassesses national history (46–47). In a self-reflexive moment, Bảo's novel locates itself as a work of renovation literature. The main protagonist, Kien (whom Bảo acknowledges is a self-portrait[11]) is a writer, and the novel describes Kien's authorial "task" as "to expose the realities of war and to tear aside conventional images ... Kien's heroes are not the usual predictable, stiff figures but real people whose lives take diverse and unexpected directions" (50).

Renovation Literature itself builds on a prior tradition of literature as political commentary. In the 1930s, Vietnamese Critical Realist writers, influenced by the Soviet Union's literary experiments of the 1930s, "focus[ed] their critical gaze on social issues, emphasizing the oppression of ordinary peasants and workers and the inequities of contemporary (colonial) society" (Tái, "Disenchantment" 89). As Shawn McHale points out, Critical Realism offers not only a literary precursor for class critique, but also a precedent within Vietnamese Marxism for valuing individuality. Early twentieth-century Vietnamese writers such as Tran Duc Thao argued that the development of the individual and of the collective were intertwined and of equal importance (McHale 18).

In their collection of feminist Vietnamese poetry, Nguyễn Thị Minh Hà, Nguyễn Thị Thanh Bình, and Lady Borton trace the history of literature as political commentary even further back, reminding us that Nguyễn Thị Bích Châu's fourteenth-century poem, "Ten Points to Remember Before the Cock's Crow," enumerates principles of governance that are "still cited today as a course of guidance" (8). Poetry and politics have long been intertwined in Viet Nam, with major military and political figures also famous for their poetry, from Nguyễn Trãi in the fifteenth century to Hồ Chí Minh in the twentieth century. Indeed, Borton, Bình and Hà note that Viet Nam's primary national heroine, who led the first successful revolt against Chinese rule 2,000 years ago, was both a warrior and a poet: "In 40 CE, Trúng Trắc stepped onto the platform at the flag-worshiping ceremony before the battle began against the Chinese. Standing in front of her officers, she unsheathed her sword and recited her [poem] 'Oath at Hát River'" (1).

Not isolated as writers, Dương and Bảo are also not without precedent for their ideas. One immediate precursor, argues Schafer, was Trần Mạnh Hảo's *Separation* (1989). *Separation* directly foreshadows *Paradise*, offering a similar "catalogue of communist failings, beginning with [North Vietnam's] disastrous land reform program of the mid-1950s and continuing through the New Economic Zones of the post-war era" (Schafer, "Collective" 17). While Dương's portrait of postwar party abuses was radical, her critique of the mid-century Land Reform was very similar to denunciations by the architects of that campaign themselves. In 1956, Hồ Chí Minh and Võ Nguyên Giáp admitted that Land Reform "went to the point of overestimating the enemy and thinking there were enemies everywhere" (quoted in Schafer "Land Reform" 185). Hồ and Giáp denounced the simplistic and absolute class determinism that characterized that campaign, and acknowledged the error of assuming that "class standing determines everything" (Giáp, quoted in Schafer "Land Reform" 184, 185).

In addition to lengthening our historical context for these novels, we readers also want to attend to contextual specificity. *Paradise*, *Novel*, and *Sorrow* are written by North Vietnamese dissidents. While important, their perspectives are necessarily partial. As James Banerian argues, this partiality of perspective "gets the hypocrisy but misses the discipline" of the North Vietnamese military (654). *Novel* and *Sorrow*, both retrospective accounts of the war, were written out of their authors' postwar dismay. Especially for readers seeking to learn about the war, this perspective requires augmentation by other perspectives, both political and historical, addressing not only the period of the American war but also the prior war against the French, or even further back, into the periods of French and Chinese colonialism. This contextualization might begin with Lê Minh Khuê's "Distant Stars" (1997) for a story of wartime idealism (as well as her less optimistic, postwar "Tony D"); Trương Như Táng's *Viet Cong Memoir* (1986) for insight into the political, psychological, and cultural campaigns of the National Liberation Front that complemented the active combat role of the North Vietnamese Army soldiers; Bùi Diễm's *In the Jaws of History* (1987) for an ambassador's perspective on the Republic of Viet Nam; Văn Tiến Dũng's *Our Great Spring Victory* (1977) for a triumphal North Vietnamese account of the war; and Mai Elliott's *Sacred Willow* (2000) for a civilian narrative spanning four generations.

While we broaden our perspectives beyond disillusionment, we want also to attend to multiplicity among those for whom the war was cause for dismay. The disillusionment of these two veterans of the North Vietnamese regular army is not the same as the disillusionment of Vietnam Veterans Against the War dismayed with subsequent American imperialist activities; or that of antiwar protestors distressed by totalitarian policies of the reunified Vietnamese state; or that of South Vietnamese army veterans disconcerted by American rapprochement with Viet Nam's current government. The disillusionment of postcoloniality in a neoliberal context is not the same as the disillusionment of Empire checked. Indeed, Schafer suggests that the critique in *Paradise* is actually not of communism, but of corruptive consumerism, both in the Land Reform era and in the globalized market economy Viet Nam entered during the 1980s:

> Peace and the market economy produced more opportunities for corruption, more chances to wheel and deal for personal aggrandizement. After years of sacrifice during and immediately after the war many people were determined to live well, and some were not about to let moral scruples get in the way. Unscrupulous wheeler-dealers are key characters in many Vietnamese post-war novels. (205)

Further, we must keep in mind differences in the act of discursive disobedience in a capitalist democracy versus disobedience in a totalitarian Communist nation with their respective disciplinary modes. No US novelists have been jailed for their stories about the Vietnam War. Even within the Vietnamese context, the State's perspective on cultural challenge has altered over time. As Viet Nam sought to increase its involvement in global trade and tourism, it modified its own disciplinary tactics toward Dương Thu Hương, shifting from judicial prosecution to "constant persecution," and from incarceration to censorship: the government "tolerated her limited mobility ... but they disallowed the circulation of her works domestically" (Lan Duong 119).[12]

Lastly, it is also important to remember that the veteran generation, disillusioned or no, is currently in the minority in Viet Nam. The postwar population has exploded, and currently over 60% of the population is under the age of 30—thus, they have known only a Viet Nam at peace, under Communist one-party rule, and increasingly enmeshed in the globalized neoliberal economy. Prefacing their collection of contemporary women's poetry, Hà and Borton emphasize the youthful energy of postwar culture: "These young women poets are from the first generation of Vietnamese in many centuries to grow up during peacetime. They had enough to eat. They enjoy freedoms that their grandmothers, who matured during Confucianism, never imagined. These younger writers assert the rightful place of women" (29).

Overall, the prominence of Dương and Bảo in the West is deserved, and yet even as we acknowledge the disillusionment many Vietnamese feel in the wake of reunification, and the validity of their criticisms, we need also to examine our own appetite for this narrative. Lan Duong notes that *Paradise*'s reputation as "speaking truth to power" makes it highly marketable in the West: "In the United States and France, [Dương is] privileged because of [her] critiques of the state, especially since [her] work comes from inside the Party and within the country" (92). Contextualizing these novels allows us to value and assess Dương's and Bảo's contributions in relation to their cultural predecessors and peers without privileging them as representative.

This discussion cautions against facile generalizations about Bảo's and Dương's novels. But it is not meant to deny the very powerful criticisms these novels do offer. The first of these, to which we now turn, is criticism of the ideological seductions upon which state formation relies.

Provocation 1: Glory and sacrifice are sucker punches

About *First Blood* (Kotcheff, 1982), the paradigmatic American Vietnam War movie, Keith Beattie argues that "the patriot is the real hero, and the definition rests as much upon his willingness for self-sacrifice as upon the distinction [Rambo] makes between 'country' and 'government'" (94). Despite abuse and betrayal by the government bureaucracy, the patriot hero valiantly "performs his duty in the name of his country" (94). William Searle reads *Novel* and *Sorrow* as performing this same distinction, arguing that these texts vilify the Party while celebrating nationalism: "Communism is overshadowed by Vietnamese patriotism, dwarfed by it, shamed by it" (233). Beattie, however, suggests that Dương's *Paradise* and Ninh's *Sorrow* contrast with Rambo's narrative of revalorization (102–103). Extending Beattie, I align *Novel* and *Sorrow* with *Paradise* as challenging the value of duty and sacrifice altogether. Thus, more than offering a universal message that "war is hell," Dương and Bảo dispute those who would add "but worth it." Their venom is directed at those who glorify war, recruit others into war, and profit by beguiling others to their deaths.

One of the most notorious scenes of *Novel* pulls back the curtain on recruitment as hypocritical exploitation. Riding on a train to see how "the people" live, two officials parade their power-hungry manipulations before the very people they are bragging about duping: "That ideal, well, the kids need it. And it's all we need to turn them into monks, soldiers, or cops . . . Building a civilization is difficult. But guaranteeing a small number of people a civilized existence, why there's nothing easier . . . Now that's the ultimate pleasure: the gratification of power" (*Novel* 160–163). The cynical manipulation of "kids" into becoming "soldiers" for the benefit of a "small number" and their "gratification of power" is the foundation for a pyramid scheme of ambition and status. Not only do party officials and village recruiters falsely promise high rates of glory-returns, but also parents become middle men, recruiting their own kids as the next level of "investors" in order to pay the parents's profit share. In *Novel*, Quan insists that the family has paid its enlistment quota already, and his beloved little brother should stay home. But their father urges the opposite: "From the depths of his ignorance, my father's ambition had overcome him: he too had wanted to reserve his place at the victory banquet" (124). The father recruits his younger son into an investment scheme that depends on constantly expanding induction, but ultimately produces and pays back nothing. Quan's brother enlists, and dies.

The scheme is supported by a marketing machine that spins seductive visions of glory from gut-wrenching realities of despair. Quan's firsthand experience of the Tết offensive in which he "buried with my own hands countless numbers of my companions" is eviscerated by the communist party newsletter which "celebrates the glorious victories on the B3 front during the Tết offensive." Thus Quan learns "that lies are common currency" in the economics of war propaganda (83).

Sorrow critiques recruitment's pyramid scheme through Kien's step father, who urges Kien, when he considers enlistment, to value actual life over empty promises of deferred return: "a human being's duty on this earth is to live, not to kill . . . guard against all those who demand that you die just to prove something" (58). Recruitment is here redefined baldly as the demand to die. The "something" left so precisely vague by Kien's step father is contrasted with the concrete specificity of the death toll. Kien urges us to "look at who won the war . . . to know that the kindest, most worthy people have all fallen away, or even been tortured, humiliated before being killed, or buried and wiped away by the machinery of war" (193). Dương's Quan makes the same point: Hoang, the "purest soul" of the unit, the "sensitive idealist," as well as "men like him [are] snuffed out by the violence, the depravation" while those who "liked to invent new ways to kill" and find "the soldier's lot to be the perfect way of life," survive to create the postwar society (216–220). Marilyn Young notes that war is premised on the idea of necessary sacrifice. Dương and Bảo unmask "necessary sacrifice," exposing the reality of war as a perverse eugenics: those who make good peace get killed off (24).

The ideology of war's necessary sacrifice to build a better future is passionately debunked. Quan finds quaint a cadre's belief that the war is fought to do "something greater . . . to build communism on earth, to realize the dream" (76). Instead, Quan sees war as a violent "yearning for revenge": "we shot like madmen, to cleanse ourselves of the pain, the despair" (*Novel* 222). All three works present the sacrifice of lives for war as too great (too many dead), too damaging (those who could produce a good peace/nation die), and too exploitative ("the ones who loved the war were . . . the politicians, middle-aged men with fat bellies and short legs" [*Sorrow* 75]).

Paradise's critique of sacrifice extends beyond the sacrifices of war. As Young notes, *Paradise* is fundamentally "about the nature and limits of sacrifice" (25). The novel criticizes the cynical demand to sacrifice by party officials—this time in the figure of Uncle Chính, who demands that Hằng drop whatever she is doing to come help him because he's "very ill" (11, 219). He is not sick. He just knows that "come help me smuggle my crates out of Russia because I don't speak fluent Russian and you do" won't get her there. His willingness to exploit her for his own profit is both a version of the officials on Bảo's train, who manipulated "kids" to sacrifice themselves to the war for their own power, and is also an extension of that manipulation into civilian life, as the Party continues to make such demands even past the ostensible exigencies of war.

Dương's critique, however, is not simply of corruption and cynicism. In the figures of Hằng's mother and aunt, even sincere sacrifices motivated by love are revealed as abusive. Quế, Hằng's mother, and Tâm, Hằng's paternal aunt, each respond to the experience of trauma by embracing self-sacrifice. The two women, once compatible neighbors and sisters-in-law, are driven asunder when Quế's brother Chính, a party functionary, defines Quế's husband and in-laws as landlord enemies of the peasant class to which he and Quế belong. Tâm and Quế are both made miserable by Chính's actions. Tốn (Quế's husband and Tâm's brother) flees the village, returning to his wife only for a short visit (during which Hằng is conceived), and eventually commits suicide. Quế never recovers financially or emotionally from the loss of her husband. Tâm, equally embittered by the loss of her brother, devotes her life to a revenge that consists of regaining her wealth through hard work, and seeking to pass her gains and her bitterness on to Hằng.

Unfortunately, Tâm's patronage devastates Hằng's relationship with her own mother, Quế. As soon as Tâm's resources start to elevate Quế and Hằng from abject to moderate poverty, Hằng notes that Quế "stopped doting on me and calling me her 'dear child.' She had become distant and reserved" (102). Rather than competing for Hằng's affections, Quế copies Tâm's performance as patron aunt: she works ever harder to amass a modicum of financial wealth, not for herself, but to give to her own brother's children. These are the children of Chính, the brother who destroyed her marriage and Tâm's wealth, setting in motion Tâm's vengeful sponsorship of Hằng, which alienates Hằng from Quế, who compensates by sponsoring Chính's children. To Tâm, this is an unbearable circle whereby the villain profits even from her attempts at revenge, and she forbids Hằng and Quế from sharing with Chính's family any of the resources she provides. This results only in further dividing Hằng and Quế, as their relationship "degenerated" from respect to "coldness tinged with irony" to a final explosion of resentment that ends with Quế expelling Hằng from their home (188). Both Quế's and Tâm's sacrifices are caught in and reproduce a cycle of exploitation and alienation.

Through this tragic cycle, Dương offers a critique of nationalist valorization of feminine sacrifice. As analyzed by Lan Duong, Vietnamese "state feminism" celebrates a feminine heroism that ostensibly elevates women, but actually renovates and perpetuates the three traditional Confucian submissions (to father, husband, and son) and the four traditional virtues (of industry, appearance, prudent speech, and exemplary conduct). While Viet Nam has legitimate bragging rights for developing and acknowledging female leadership and professional involvement in their revolution against the French and defeat of the Americans, Lan Duong points out that subsequent canonization of this involvement actually undercuts women's empowerment, through a fetishization of revolutionary womanhood that ironically "fossilizes their agency in the past" (and suggests that they have now fallen from such prior agency) (13). This fossilization promotes not continued revolutionary leadership but docile conformity to the needs of contemporary global capitalism. State feminism, Lan Duong argues, defines the feminist modern woman as docile "industrious worker and nurturing mother" (114).

This heroic yet compliant vision of revolutionary womanhood can be seen in three quite different contemporary museum displays of self-sacrificing "state feminism." The Fine Arts Museum in Ho Chi Minh City (HCMC) and the Vietnamese Women's Museum in

Hanoi both devote rooms to portraits of "Heroic Mothers," while exhibits about women revolutionaries who had been imprisoned and tortured by French and American authorities are featured in both the Vietnamese Women's Museum (Hanoi) and the Southern Women's History Museum (HCMC). With notably similar content and rhetoric, all of these exhibits emphasize sacrifice. The prisoners are lionized for their suffering in jail, for surviving electric shock, beatings, and other forms of torture. The Heroic Mothers received their national honors because of their losses: the qualification for this status is to have had sons and husbands killed in the war. This national award celebrates them, as Helle Rydstrøm notes, "for the intercorporeal ways in which, as mothers, they are related to lost sons" (293).

In such a context of valorized feminine suffering and sacrifice for the sake of the nation, Dương's critical portraits of loving sacrifices of Tâm and Quế for family members challenge the docile state feminism Lan Duong outlines. Sacrifice is here redefined. Not a generous giving of oneself to benefit another, it becomes a self-interested form of martyrdom and revenge. The benefits of the sacrifices are dubious: Tâm's material patronage leaves Hằng trapped in an emotional debt she can never repay, and after her aunt's death, she refuses to live in the home her aunt has restored for her. Quế's patronage benefits her nephews, who get enough to eat due to her provisions, but this nurture of her brother's children comes at the cost of neglecting her own child, who nearly starves and lives in a hovel. Both loving sacrifices produce alienation and indifference. While Hằng is grateful to the aunt she loves, her aunt's actions caused a rift between Hằng and Quế that deprives her of the maternal love she once enjoyed. Even when Tâm "wins" by working herself to the bone to re-amass a small fortune (a house, a small farm, a noodle-making business, enough money to send presents to Hằng, and to leave her a cash inheritance), Hằng emphasizes loss instead: "Would she regret this war with my mother, this lifelong struggle that only I would pay for?" (242). Quế's devotion to Chính's family is never reciprocated. The relief she provides brings anxiety as well, since in Party housing, any unusual material wealth raises the suspicions of neighbors and can get the family in trouble. Although it brings Quế happiness to support Chính's family, Chính is clearly undeserving. At the close of the novel, when Quế lies in the hospital, Hằng has to lie to her mother to spare her the knowledge that Chính won't even come visit her there. Sacrifice ultimately abets selfishness and alienation rather than forging community.[13]

Provocation 2: From "'Nam vs. The World" to the worldedness of Viet Nam

The early twenty-first century is a moment of transition in Western thinking about Viet Nam, in which it has become a commonplace among scholars to insist that the Vietnam War was not just something that happened to Americans. Yet this commonplace, which seems self-evident given that the war was fought in Viet Nam and that Vietnamese casualties dwarf American ones, is still in need of reiterating in a context where the majority of American representations of the war still depict it as an American experience. More than 25 years after John Hellmann described and criticized this phenomenon in *American Myth and the Legacy of Vietnam*, American trauma still dominates American narratives about the Vietnam War.

Challenging this perspective, Bảo's and Dương's novels insistently focus on Vietnamese combatants. For American readers, they "begin or contribute to a process of dissuading the American reader from his or her exceptionalist and culturally-narcissistic assumptions that what mattered most about the war was American suffering" (74).[14] One way they achieve this revision of perspective is through the chastening contextualization of the American experience within the Vietnamese one. While the American traumas were severe and significant, focusing on them to the erasure of Vietnamese traumas becomes obscene when faced with the difference of magnitude. Christian Appy points out that although the fear of the draft affected an entire US generation, in actuality, "the 2.5 million men of that generation who went to Viet Nam represent less than 10 percent of America's male baby boomers" (18). In contrast, nearly 75 percent of eligible North Vietnamese men were drafted (Rydstrøm 283). In South Vietnam, where the ground war was fought, the distinction between combatant and civilian is not even possible: any citizen could become involved as a combatant at any moment, and for villagers living near the seventeenth parallel, 100% of the population was affected. Casualty rates for American servicemen and women in Viet Nam totaled 58,220. From 1961 to 1975, Vietnamese casualties totaled between 1.5 and 2 million (Appy 17). To borrow Appy's image, "Had the United States lost the same proportion of its population [as Viet Nam did], the Vietnam Memorial would list the names of 8 million Americans" (17).

In part, this difference was related to a different scale of time served. As Searle notes, "It is good to remember that for the North Vietnamese, there was no one year or thirteen month tour of duty; enlistment was for the duration" (227). The protagonists of *Sorrow* and *Novel* both serve from 1965 to 1975, and repeatedly emphasize the extremity of loss: "Out of my hundred-strong company, only Thai, myself, and seventeen soldiers survived" (*Novel* 237); Battle "North Star had been dazzling and our battalion ceased to exist. Of the company, twelve soldiers survived" (*Novel* 266). *Sorrow* describes "30 April, Victory Day" as the day when "Of the entire scout platoon sent into the airport, only he had survived" (*Sorrow* 100).

Beyond supplementing American trauma with Vietnamese, these novels push the Americans off-stage. *Sorrow* and *Novel* are both set in a present day after the American combat operations have ended. Both contain flashbacks to earlier years, but even then, Americans are noticeably rare within the action of the text. One of the most interesting of the rare moments when the Americans are invoked is in *Sorrow*, when [new recruits] hear the news that the United States is entering the war: "We're fighting the Americans" (175). Not the self-congratulatory David and Goliath analogy that would become a cliché of the war, *Sorrow* soberly registers the entrance of the superpower as an ominous and world-changing realization of the soldier that he is about to be going head to head against the war chest and atomic arsenal of the US military. The news transforms Kien and his girlfriend Phương into "a doomed generation, already victims of a new, long, war" (175).

In Dương's war narrative, *Novel*, Americans are almost never seen. Instead, they are replaced by their objects: "an American ballpoint pen" (*Novel* 105), the B-52s and the bombs they drop (195–196), and Vitamin B12 serum ("American, really good quality," 269). As abstractions, the Americans serve as impetus for civilian sacrifice (a poor villager insists that Quan take her family's rice so he will "find the strength to . . . fight the Americans") or a marker of deferred happiness "when those American bastards leave" (198, 200).

There is only one appearance of an American person in *Novel*: as the war ends, Quan's company captures "an American among the prisoners" (282). No POW Rambo fantasy, however, this story is instead of a wayward journalist, a "naïve . . . colossus." Rather than inciting hatred against "a foreign invader!" (284), Dương's scene deconstructs such bellicose nationalism. Quan imagines similarities with the colossus: "He too must have been drunk on a vision of himself marching till dawn with medals across his chest" (285). The encounter provokes Quan not to destroy the invader, but to realize the self-destruction of animosity: "We had wedded our dignity to that hatred, confused survival with destruction" (285).

Bảo, too, rarely depicts Americans, but in their few appearances, they are aligned with atrocity rather than with empathy. In one scene, American soldiers track Kien and Hoa as they carry their wounded. Hoa shoots their search dog "and the dog only" in order to distract her trackers from her wounded comrades (190). The American platoon catches her, and then "without losing their control or lifting their voices, they set about stripping Hoa and, the dog handler first, roughly fucking her. Some of them stayed back, but the way they had all come to a standstill, and with others waiting their turn, it appeared they would end their patrol with the rape" (191). In contrast to Dương's deconstructive empathy, Bảo offers deadpan indictment.

These few Americans in *Sorrow* and *Novel* give more presence to US forces than does *Paradise*. Although the plot of *Paradise* spans the period from the 1950s to the 1980s, almost no mention is made of the American war waged from 1965 to 1973. By sidelining the United States, these novels reassert the existence of the civil war intertwined with this Cold War occupation. The civil war between North and South Vietnam would not have existed had not the United States "enveloped in the protection and self-esteem of the United States that half of Vietnam below the 17th parallel which the 1954 Geneva Agreements had said was just a truce zone, but which American statesmen had pronounced a sovereign state and called South Vietnam" (Sheehan 375).[15] But that civil war is no less real for being manipulated in its construction. South Vietnam itself is not much depicted, but the cultural wounds of the war as an intranational rather than international event are shown in such portrayals as the "most ironic of teachings" blasted at victorious soldiers as they rode the "reunification" train home: "to ignore the spirit of reconciliation, to beware of the 'bullets coated with sugar,' to ignore the warmth and passions among the remnants of this fallen, luxurious society of the South. And especially to guard against the idea of the South having fought valiantly or been meritorious in any way" (*Sorrow* 80).

Whereas *Sorrow* reminds us of internal division, *Novel* offers similarity across both sides of that civil war, displaying the banal sameness of fundamentalism, whatever its ideological allegiances. When Quan and his platoon capture a "puppet soldier" (from South Vietnam), Quan's interrogation baffles the prisoner, as Quan reveals the use of identical rhetoric by both opposed sides: "Why did you enlist? . . . To defend the beloved motherland? . . . To fulfill the patriot's duties, to prove yourself worthy of the Lac Hong? . . . To serve the country, swearing to spill the last drop of your blood?" (242–243). Quan strips the sincerity and specificity of this patriotic duty, redefining it as an arbitrarily applied lie: "On both sides, you died believing you had attained your ideal" (247). The only truth is the devastation this lie produces, which does not discriminate between sides: "On both sides you screamed, you killed in mad, frenzied bursts, shrieking for joy when the blood gushed, the brains shattered; . . . Then the survivors limped off the battlefields to swell the reserves, to join the ranks of future combatants" (247).

In addition to diminishing the literal presence of American players on their novels' stages, Bảo and Dương stylistically rebut one of the common conventions of US veteran discourse about the Vietnam War. Such discourse frequently assigns a geographic marker to the psychological disorientation that many veterans experienced in active combat. The combat experience, time, and place become "'Nam." In part, this nomenclature reflects the literal transportation of these soldiers halfway around the globe to fight in unfamiliar terrain. But it also symbolically attempts both to ground and bind their experiences, to give a physical aspect to the surreal experience many of them describe, and to quarantine that experience away from "the World," which is home, normalcy, love, peace, civilization, reality.

It might seem to go without saying, but these Vietnamese novels make Western readers realize that this distinction is an epistemological possibility only if Viet Nam is not your home, your normality, your civilization. American veteran narratives train readers in the psychological experience of thinking of PTSD as a kind of psychic oxymoron—being mentally transported to a jarringly other time and place within the current and incommensurate time and place. *Sorrow* and *Novel* stage a different invitation: to imagine navigating postwar stress not in its uncanny disruptions of "normality" but in its inevitable embeddedness in normality. For Kien in *Sorrow*, flashbacks are not breaks in logic and locale but are entirely consistent: "riding the same tram, it was inevitable that at times the memories would return" (157).

These novels also break with another leitmotif of American literature, in which, in contrast to the surrealistically alien Americans, the Vietnamese are so integrated into the landscape as to become a literal part of it. The ubiquitous references to the "VC melting into the landscape" after an attack not only dehumanize the Vietnamese but also more specifically *topographies* them, making them simply part of the land. (At its most extreme, this becomes a Möbius strip of personification and topographication, in the trope "the jungle itself was shooting at us").

In the novels of Bảo and Dương, however, the Vietnamese population is not just some kind of armed and dangerous vegetation. Nor are they pastoral native informants whose knowledge and familiarity with the land is essentialized. The landscape in which Bảo and Dương's soldiers live and fight is often thoroughly alien and unsettling to them, as when the scout assigned to Quan's unit in *Novel* gets hopelessly lost trying to lead the platoon through jungles she does not know at all, or when Kien wanders in circles trying to get to Bui before a local member of a minority tribe finds him and helps him find his destination. Far from topographying their characters as an extension of the landscape, Bảo and Dương depict the landscape as separate and often dangerous, and whereas American narratives equate violence and landscape in images of the jungle sniping at soldiers, in *Novel*, the land has been *made* dangerous by the war: Bien dies from tetanus after stepping on a piece of buried shrapnel.

Two further differences in the way Bảo and Dương relate the humans and the landscape (vs. topographication) expose the ideological significance of topographication. First, they shift from topographication to haunting. While topographication turns people into geography, the haunted landscapes in *Novel* and *Sorrow* mark and recall the loss of human life. The Vietnamese are not ahistorically merged with the land, of which they become an appendage. Instead, the specific violence of the war and its human destruction haunts the land, as the Screaming Souls Jungle continues to howl (*Sorrow* 7, 26). Through this contrasting treatment, Bảo and Dương expose a colonizing mentality that sees land and people as interchangeable and equally available for conquest (in part because the people are not seen as people but resources, such as the land), and instead offers the personification of the land as a consequence of colonizing trauma and violence, not a precursor to it. It is the massacres that produce the ghosts in the valleys, not the spooks of the land that produce the violence.

Second, Dương and Bảo shift from tropes of topographication to those of cannibalism. In both *Novel* and *Sorrow*, the starving soldiers hunt whatever protein they can find in the mountains.[16] Of the various wild game in Viet Nam, both Dương and Bảo choose the hunting and eating of one particular species to describe in detail: the orangutan. Both Kien and Quan are horrified at the sight of orangutan stew. In *Sorrow*, the whole platoon is aghast at the proximity to cannibalism: "oh, God, when it was killed and skinned the animal looked like a fat woman with ulcerous skin, the eyes, half-white, half-grey, still rolling. The entire squad was horrified and ran away screaming" (7). In *Novel*, Kien's platoon has turned overcoming their squeamishness at eating such near-human flesh into a rite of passage for macho conformity. But Kien cannot overcome the general horror of cannibalism and the personal horror of fratricide: "the horror at . . . the taste of human flesh in my mouth" combines with his particular vision of the ladled up orangutan hand as not only "like a child's" but also nauseatingly akin to "my brother's tiny feet kicking in the air" at birth (11, 10, 15).

These scenes of orangutan eating are readily legible as allegories of the cannibalism and fratricide that constitute civil war itself—a nation killing and consuming its own members. Further, however, they provocatively rebut the topographication of American narratives. Whereas topographication de-humanizes, these scenes personify. Topographication is a trope that induces numbness and eases the erasure and taking of human life. Personification is a trope that induces empathy and calls attention to the horrors of taking and consuming life, whether human or humanlike.

Conclusion

Interviewed in 2004 by an American high school student, Bảo stated that "There is no 'winning' in war. You are forced to fight until one side gives up. That should never be considered winning" (*Special Feature*). In the humanist and philosophical sense of war being a universal tragedy, that is certainly true. But in the global political sense, it is also important to remember that there was a winner of this war: the People's Republic of Viet Nam. That victory produced two important losses: the Republic of Viet Nam was lost, a loss that reverberates palpably among its former citizens,[17] and the US military was defeated, a reminder of vulnerability that America seems determined to repress. Isabelle Pelaud notes that the United States "lost international respect and moral authority with its defeat in the Vietnam War" (58). In the past two decades or so, however, American neoimperialism has taken the end of the Cold War as an almost personal validation. Yen Le Espiritu has called this historical revalidation the "we-win-even-when-we-lose" phenomenon ("The We-Win"). Careful attention to these novels in their cultural context, and to their resignification of both Vietnamese and Western presence, provokes Western readers, particularly US readers, to see these novels' critiques of the war project and its aftermath not as further evidence that America was right all along, but as a challenge to such self-centered readings—that is, the challenge of taking these novels seriously as novels that are not about us.

Notes

1 On memorializing the Vietnamese past and contemporary transnational Vietnamese identity constructions, see: Aguilar-San Juan, Dang, L. Duong, Espiritu, Lieu, K. Nguyen, Nguyen-Vo, Pelaud, Sturken, and Tái, *Country*. On the American/Vietnam

War as an American trauma, see Franklin (*Vietnam*), Hellmann (*American Myth*), Kinney, and Liparulo, "Beyond." Note: Vietnamese nomenclature puts the surname first, so Bảo Ninh's "last" name is Bảo.
2. About Bảo, see Goldenburg; about Dương, see Allen, L. Duong, McPherson, Schafer, "Land Reform," Searle, and Tái, "Disenchantment."
3. For a description of the stories Dương published in Vietnamese prior to the publication of *Paradise*, see McPherson, and Tái, "Disenchantment."
4. For chartings of postwar disillusionment literature, see Banerian, N. Nguyen, Sachs, and Tái, "Disenchantment."
5. See Tái, "Disenchantment" 83.
6. For an overview of the North Vietnamese Land Reform Campaign and analysis of several Vietnamese novels in this context, see Schafer, "Land Reform."
7. For a more detailed account of Dương's popularity and censorship, see McPherson.
8. For a thorough reading of the novel's postmodernism, see Liparulo, "Incense."
9. In 1999, when I visited Viet Nam and requested an interview with Bảo, he declined, stating that should we meet, I would thereafter be followed and harassed by government officials.
10. Other major writers of Renovation Literature available in English include Nguyễn Huy Thiệp, Phạm Thị Hoài, Nguyễn Duy, and Lê Lựu.
11. See Bảo Ninh, *Special Feature*.
12. Interestingly, the same period has seen an increase in overtly repressive and rigid modes of censorship in the United States, such as censorship in Arizona of books deemed disobedient to a nationally prideful narrative.
13. In labeling the conflict between Tâm and Quế as a "war," Dương invites consideration of this familial story as an allegory for both the war and the postwar recovery of Viet Nam. In this spirit, Young reads *Paradise* as a "political allegory disguised as a family chronicle" (24). L. Duong sees a similar allegorical message that the "obligation" to the national family is "wrongheaded" (102).
14. Liparulo expressed this hope in regard to *Sorrow*, but it applies also to *Novel* ("Beyond").
15. See also Appy: "without American intervention (according to almost all intelligence reports at the time and historians since), Vietnamese unification under Ho Chi Minh would have occurred with little resistance" (16).

16 One of the most glaring contrasts to American vet soldier narratives is the difference between the material excess of the American war chest (chronicled most famously by Tim O'Brien) and the destitution of the Vietnamese troops, for whom one tin of meat is a cherished luxury, so rare that it can function to identify a soldier killed in combat (*Novel* 42).
17 See Aguilar-San Juan, K. Nguyen, Nguyen-Vo, and Pelaud.

3

"Ten years burning down the road": Trauma, mourning, and postmemory in Bobbie Ann Mason's *In Country*

Joanna Price

Bobbie Ann Mason's novel *In Country* (1985) tells of 17-year-old Samantha Hughes's exploration of the choices available to her as she stands on the threshold of womanhood in the small town of Hopewell, Western Kentucky in the early 1980s. Sam's adolescence is shaped by mourning for the loss of her father in the Vietnam War and concern for her uncle Emmett, a veteran still traumatized by the war. Sam's search for the "truth" of her father's experience in the War takes her to the private testimony of his letters and diary, the narrative fragments that the Hopewell veterans share with Sam and each other, and, finally, the public space of commemoration at the Vietnam Veterans Memorial (VVM) in Washington, DC. Through this narrative, Mason explores how mourning as a result of the war in Viet Nam contributes to the subjectivity of her characters, and their relation to "the nation," a relation which is shaped by cultural determinants of their identity such as their gender, age, and roots in a changing South.

This chapter offers a reading of *In Country* in the light of theories about trauma, memory, and mourning that have been produced since the end of the Vietnam War—some of these theories being produced in response to studies of the effect of the war on survivors and others who feel connected to it.[1] Referring primarily to the psychoanalytically informed work of Lauren Berlant, Marianne Hirsch, Marita Sturken, and Judith Butler, it discusses Mason's exploration of her characters' negotiation of personal and national identity in post-Vietnam War America. It argues that through its portrayal of an American adolescent's mourning for losses in and attempt to understand a war she did not experience, Mason's novel continues to resonate today, anticipating contemporary questions about what constitutes an ethical response to mourning arising from the large-scale loss of life through acts of military or other aggression.

On the road to Washington

In Country opens with Mason's depiction of Sam Hughes, her veteran uncle Emmett Smith and her paternal grandmother making a road trip to the VVM in Washington, and it closes with their responses to the Memorial. According to Lauren Berlant in *The Queen of America Goes to Washington City* (2002), Mason's evocation of the group's journey to Washington participates in "a national plot: the pilgrimage to Washington" (26). This "plot" involves the rite of passage of the protagonist, often a child, through an encounter with ideas of national identity—or what Berlant calls "the fantasy norms of the nation form" (27)—in the capital, the assumption of which identity will produce an "adult citizen" (26).

Mason's depiction of her characters as they make their way to Washington indicates the different, and particular, personal histories and subjectivities which they will bring to bear on their mourning at the memorial, and through which they will have to negotiate any ideas of national identity that the memorial might invoke. Emmett, the Vietnam War veteran, brings his "old Army jacket" on the trip, and suffers from head pains and "pimples and bad nerves," which his niece believes are symptoms of a condition caused by the defoliant Agent Orange and also of Post-Traumatic Stress Disorder (PTSD). More humorously, his pimples appear to be indicative of delayed adolescence, a notion that also implies

Emmett's development was arrested when he was a young soldier in the war. As a War veteran and would-be adolescent, Emmett's relation to "the nation" is both marginal and liminal.

Sam's grandmother, Mamaw Hughes, is present on the trip to the memorial to mourn her son Dwayne, who was killed in the Vietnam War before the birth of his daughter. In her portrayal of Mamaw, Mason draws attention to her Southernness: her sense of propriety as she worries about having to use the restroom and "sleep in the same room with a man" (10) illustrates a Southern fastidiousness about "manners and customs," as Owen Gilman points out (50). Mamaw also frets about the geraniums she is taking to the memorial, and recalls her discomfort when staying with Sam's mother at the start of their trip: "I'm still so embarrassed, spilling dirt on Irene's nice floor. I guess she thought I was just a country hick, dragging in dirt" (6). Mamaw's self-consciousness about being "country" becomes, Mason suggests, an embarrassment about being southern as she travels to Washington.

Sam's mourning for the loss of her father also involves confronting the shame she feels that her father is a "country" boy, and exploring what that means for her own identity. Her mourning takes place in a changing South, and these changes shape her understanding of and response to the loss of her father in the Vietnam War.[2] As enjoined by her mother, Irene, Sam's participation in the ritual of mourning at the VVM will include witnessing how southern identity is part of the national identity invoked by the names on the memorial: "It was country boys. When you get to that memorial, you look at the names. You'll see all those country boy names on the wall" (235).

The summer of 1984: The Vietnam War and postmemory

The second part of the novel, set mainly in Hopewell, is focalized through Sam and charts the events that bring the characters to the memorial. Mason's evocation of the summer of 1984 as "the summer of the Michael Jackson *Victory* tour and the Bruce Springsteen *Born in the USA* tour, neither of which Sam got to go to" (23) immediately establishes popular culture, here specifically music, as a significant mediator of Sam's experiences. Mason continues: "At her graduation, the commencement speaker, a Methodist minister, had preached about keeping the country strong, stressing sacrifice. He made Sam nervous. She started thinking about war, and it stayed on her mind all summer" (23). The allusions to Springsteen's album and the minister's speech provide a frame for Sam's thoughts about war, and indicate the context in which she is to explore the subject. The title track of *Born in the USA*, whose opening lines Mason quotes in her epigraph to the novel—"I'm ten years burning down the road/Nowhere to run ain't got nowhere to go"—tells of the narrator's loss of his brother in the battle at Khe Sanh and the problems the narrator, a Vietnam War veteran, encounters readjusting to American society upon his return from the war. The lyrics indicate the difficulties veterans experienced in being accepted back into a society that variously associated them with the perceived wrongfulness of America's involvement in the War, the loss of the War, and atrocities committed by Americans in the War. The minister's speech at Sam's graduation, however, indicates a change in political rhetoric about America's involvement in war by the summer of 1984. During his 1980 presidential campaign, Ronald Reagan had "told an audience of military veterans that the Vietnam War had been a 'noble cause' that 'should have been won'" and that "it was time for the nation to get over the 'Vietnam syndrome'," a phrase which referred to the American public's reluctance after the war in Viet Nam to become involved in a conflict that America might lose, and which might "be undermined by a collapse of support on the home front" (Hagopian, *The Vietnam War* 11). In the same speech, as Patrick Hagopian notes, a further and, to many, more palatable strand of Reagan's revisionism occurred in his attempt to recuperate the veterans of the War: "We dishonoured the memory of fifty thousand young Americans who died [in the War] when we gave way to feelings of guilt as if we were doing something shameful, and we have been shabby in the treatment of those who returned" (quoted in Hagopian, *The Vietnam War* 37–38). The belligerent rhetoric that accompanied Reagan's attempt to resuscitate national pride provides a reference point for Sam's sense of the nation as she travels to Washington: listening to the news about the 1984 presidential campaign, she observes that "Reagan wants to go to war" (18).

As Sam reflects on her experience of growing up in Hopewell and what she knows about the war in Viet Nam, it becomes apparent that much of that experience and knowledge has been shaped by her Uncle Emmett, and that Emmett's own post-War life has been affected by both his experience of trauma during the War and changing cultural responses to the War. From photographs, as well as Emmett's and her mother's stories, Sam learns how, after the War, Emmett adopted a countercultural lifestyle with his "hippie" friends, whose gestures included antiwar protest. Sam recalls hearing about how Emmett and his friends flew a Viet Cong flag from the clock tower of the courthouse and that, according to Emmett, "The funny part . . . was that nobody even recognized it was a Vietcong flag" (24). By the summer of 1984, Emmett and Sam occupy a somewhat marginal social and economic position, working occasional or part-time jobs and Emmett being in debt to the government's Department of Veterans Affairs (VA) after dropping out of the university course the VA paid for him to attend.

Sam recalls how, as she and Emmett pored over a stamp album of "old colonial countries" in which "Vietnam was Indochine," Emmett used to tell her "war stories" that gave her "a picture of Vietnam" as "a pleasant countryside, something like Florida." However, Sam's mother "stopped the stories. It upset her to be reminded of the war" (51). Unable or unwilling to talk about their losses in the war, Irene and Emmett seem suspended in mourning: they watch repeats of the television series M*A*S*H, set in the Korean War but commenting on the Vietnam War, and Sam recalls them crying over the final episode (107). The program enables Sam, however, to acknowledge the loss of her father, before her birth. She remembers how after watching the death of Colonel Blake on the program "she went around stunned for days. . . . Each time she saw that episode, it grew clearer that her father had been killed in a war" (25).

Sam's reflections on what she knew about the War as she grew up with Irene and Emmett reveal that its traumatic effect on their lives was constantly present, but rarely spoken about. Mason's exploration of the often unspoken transmission of the emotions associated with traumatic events to the descendants of the survivors of those events can be usefully elucidated by the concept of "postmemory." This concept was formulated by Marianne Hirsch to describe the effect of the memories of survivors of the Holocaust on their children. Hirsch postulates: "Postmemory is a powerful and very particular form of memory precisely because its connection to its object or source is mediated not through recollection but through an imaginative investment and creation" (22). One's own life will always seem insignificant and "belated" to the person who experiences postmemory. Hirsch explains: "Postmemory characterizes the experience of those who grew up dominated by narratives that preceded their birth, whose own belated stories are evacuated by the stories of the previous generation shaped by traumatic events that can neither be understood nor recreated" (22).

Sinéad McDermott, in her reading of *In Country* as a representation of Sam's postmemory of the war in Vietnam, cites as "a key passage" Mason's description of how Sam sees her father, Dwayne Hughes, in her only photograph of him (55). Sam tries to find connections with the 19-year-old in the picture—he wears "a dark uniform with a cap like the one [she] had worn when she worked at the Burger Boy"—but she concludes "she couldn't see any resemblance to him" (58). Sam's response to the photograph indicates how she will try to understand her father and his experience of the war by finding similarities between his experiences and her own in order to achieve empathy with him. This process will involve identification with him and other American soldiers in the War through "imaginative investment and creation," as Hirsch put it, in their experiences. McDermott points out that in a later formulation of postmemory by Hirsch, she describes it as "a question of adopting the traumatic experiences—and thus also memories—of others as one's own, or, more precisely, as experiences one might oneself have had, and of inscribing them into one's own life story" (quoted in McDermott 9). For McDermott, this formulation draws attention to the ethical issues that accompany postmemory, as a way of relating to the past, as inherent in the process is "the potential for . . . appropriation" of the experiences of another (9).[3] Hirsch "resolves this ethical difficulty," McDermott observes, by proposing a model of identification that, rather than "interiorizing" the other, "goes out of one's self and out of one's cultural norms in order to align oneself, through displacement, with another" (quoted in McDermott 9). Mason's depiction of Sam's postmemory, McDermott argues, will show Sam exploring these different forms of identification as a way of relating to others' experiences of the past.

"Bringing it all back home": The Hopewell veterans

Sam's attempt to understand her father's and uncle's experiences of war involves her imagining what the feelings of various others in Viet Nam might have been. Foremost among them are the group of War veterans in Hopewell. Through her depiction of the veterans, and Sam's relationships with them, Mason explores the effect of trauma on American survivors of the war: how society's treatment of the veterans compounded that effect and how memories of the war affect the "postmemory" of subsequent generations. While some of the veterans announce their adjustment into mainstream American society as a matter of pride, most have had difficulty in adjusting to societal norms on their return from the War. Emmett and Tom feel unable to have relationships with women, for instance, and many of the men prefer to seek out each other's company. They are aware that their reception in Hopewell has been less hostile than that of veterans elsewhere in America, but they also see how popular cultural representations pathologize or criminalize veterans. Earl, for example, declares: "On TV, they make us all out to be psychos and killers" (113). Sam also has grown up aware of local speculation about the veterans, including Emmett: "Now and then a rumor would surface. At one time, neighbors had the idea that Patty Hearst was hiding out with Emmett and Irene" (24). The dedication of the VVM in Washington in 1982 has only emphasized a more general lack of public recognition of veterans. Jim, the most politicized of the Hopewell veterans and organizer of the local veterans' group, comments: "We want to let everybody know vets are not losers . . . I'd like to see a big welcome-home party downtown. Lots of places had one the year they put the memorial up in Washington. But nobody did a thing here" (59).

Mason shows that the veterans' position on the margins of society has arisen from both mainstream society's treatment of them and their own responses to their experiences in the war.

Earl claims to have made his peace with what happened—and what he did—in the war: "I've got memories, but I've learned responsibility. I've come to terms with what I did. You never forget it, but you go on living. You have to. You have to think of the future" (113). However, other veterans show symptoms of having been traumatized by the War. Mason's portrayal of the effect of trauma on the Hopewell veterans reflects the clinical research of the time into Vietnam War veterans' responses to the War, and its appropriation in popular cultural representations of veterans. Jim's comment, "We never even had those rap groups a lot of vets used to have" (59), refers to the meetings between veterans and their psychiatrists in the 1970s that combined "antiwar planning and group therapy" (Luckhurst, *The Trauma* 60). The psychiatrists argued in their "politically inflected 'advocacy research,'" as the psychiatrist Robert Jay Lifton called it, that the effect of the Vietnam War on American soldiers was caused by the particular nature of America's involvement in and conduct of it, and their reception on returning home (60). A key achievement in the psychiatrist advocates' campaign to attain recognition of and treatment for the conditions of the Vietnam War veterans was bringing about the inclusion of PTSD as a classified illness in the American Psychiatric Association's third edition of the *Diagnostic and Statistical Manual* (*DSM III*) in 1980. As Judith Lewis Herman explains, informing the identification of symptoms of PTSD in *DSM III* is the theory that:

> traumatic events may sever [the] normally integrated functions [of physiological arousal, emotion, cognition and memory] from one another. The traumatized person may experience intense emotion but without clear memory of the event, or may remember everything in detail but without emotion. (34)

The symptoms of PTSD, according to *DSM III*, may "come on acutely, persist chronically, or . . . appear belatedly, months or years after the precipitating event" (Luckhurst, *The Trauma* 1). A report to Congress, commissioned in 1982 and published as *Trauma and the Vietnam War Generation* in 1990, noted both the delayed appearance and high incidence of PTSD in Vietnam War veterans (Luckhurst 59).

Writing *In Country* during the early 1980s, not long after the publication of *DSM III*, with its medical authorization of the concept of PTSD, Mason endows several of her veterans, and in particular Emmett, with its symptoms.[4] Sam's response to what she terms "the delayed stress of the Vietnam War" (89) is central to her postmemory and to her understanding of the veterans, and by extension her father and the war in Viet Nam. Emmett, obsessed with digging a trench around a wall of their house to repair a crack in the foundation, wryly offers a metaphor of his psyche: "My basement's flooded and my foundation's weak . . . And my house might fall down while I'm here" (110). Displaying the symptoms of PTSD, he becomes startled easily and has flashbacks to the war. Sam is aware that by focusing on birds, Emmett is able to remove himself from both his present situation and his traumatic memories. He searches in particular for the egret, a bird which he explains he saw in Viet Nam, and which has consequently come to represent to him his "only good memory" of the country and the War: "Once a grenade hit close to some trees and there were these birds taking off like quail, ever' which way. We thought it was snowing up instead of down" (36). Concentrating on birds becomes a way of dissociating himself from scenes of destruction.

By observing and listening to Emmett, and interpreting his behavior and speech as responses to trauma, Sam seeks both to help him recover and to learn more about "the floating signifier of 'Vietnam,'" as Kalí Tal has termed it (*Worlds* 61). Sam also turns to historical accounts to find out more about America's involvement in the war, but gets "bogged down in manifestos and State Department documents" (55). She has difficulty in picturing "the landscape of Vietnam": a "made-for-TV movie about the Vietnam War" filmed in Mexico is an unsatisfactory source of knowledge, leaving her wondering "Did corn actually grow in Vietnam?" (70). However, when Sam asks the veterans about their experiences in the War, they warn her that she would not understand. Even her mother tells her that "the war had nothing to do with" her (71). The assumption in these warnings is that Sam is excluded from knowledge of what the War was like above all because she is a woman. Emmett, for instance, tells Sam "Women weren't over there . . . So they can't really understand" (107).

This message is apparently contradicted by the "Vietnam story" of Anita Stevens, Emmett's former girlfriend (115). Anita tells Sam how in 1969 she traveled on a bus with boys in "soldier uniforms" who were "shipping out to Vietnam the next day" (115). Anita concludes: "that was *my* Vietnam experience . . . it was *real* and I was right there" (116). She uses her story to emphasize the effect of the war on her, a point underscored by Mason's account, elsewhere, of having had a similar experience to Anita's. She comments: "no personal loss or connection motivated this story [*In Country*]. The closest I came was the story Anita tells . . ." (*In Country*, 2005, "P.S." 8). While this story illustrates how women were affected by the War, it also draws attention to the exclusion of the majority of American women from the War itself.

Gender after the war in Viet Nam

Assumptions about women's relation to war are part of the many narratives about gender that circulate around the adolescent Sam. By 1984, the effects of second-wave feminism had percolated into mainstream American culture. Irene Hughes, Sam's mother, enjoins her to leave Hopewell to attend university in Lexington, and the family discusses Walter Mondale's selection of Geraldine Ferraro as his running mate in the presidential election campaign, a national representation of the increasing empowerment of women. But Sam is also aware that the local narratives about femininity in Hopewell remain largely unchanged, as is exemplified by her friend Dawn's quick acceptance of the fact that she is pregnant and will consequently marry her boyfriend and stay in Hopewell. Dawn's pregnancy and Sam's mother also recently having had a baby bear out to Sam the biological determinism of some of these narratives of femininity. Anxieties about having to embody these narratives are expressed in the nightmarish images that disturb both Sam and Dawn. Dawn tells Sam how, on buying a chicken at the grocery, "I had the sickening thought that the chicken was giving birth to a creature, but it was all in parts, so they had to be stuffed in a little bag" (176). Dawn's vision resonates with a nightmare Sam has had after discovering Dawn was pregnant:

> That night, Sam dreamed she and Tom Hudson had a baby. In the evening, the baby had to be pureed in a food processor and kept in the freezer. It was the color of candied sweet potatoes. In the morning, when it thawed out, it was a baby again . . . the dream woke her up, its horror rushing through her. (83)

Sam's imagination is haunted not only by the pregnancies of Dawn and Irene, but also by the harm the war in Viet Nam has done to babies: she is concerned about the birth defects of children of some of the men exposed to Agent Orange, and many of the images of the War that she remembers evoke Vietnamese women and children. She recalls watching a report on the television of the fall of Saigon: it "showed some people walking along a road with bundles on their backs. Some were carrying babies in their arms . . . a child in a T-shirt and no pants ran down the road, and its mother called after it . . ." (51). Later, observing that Irene's baby "was more like a vegetable than a human—with its odd sick smell and pulsation" (162) and that "Irene carried it around with her in fascination, unable to part with it," Sam recalls how "In Vietnam, mothers had carried their dead babies around with them until they began to rot" (164). Resistant as she is to the life narrative that Irene's maternity embodies, Sam's response is sensitive, nevertheless, to the plight of Vietnamese women and their children. Through her evocation of Sam's conflicted observations of maternity in her own culture and Viet Nam's, Mason charts Sam's responses to both her femininity and the Vietnamese people, positioned as "other" by her country.

In trying to negotiate her culture's narratives about gender, Sam also encounters the challenges to American masculinity brought about by the war in Viet Nam. The War is often represented as having "irretrievably damaged" American masculinity (Sturken 70). According to Susan Jeffords, "The male Vietnam veteran—primarily the white male—was used as an emblem for a fallen and emasculated American male" and through the "rehabilitation" of the veteran, American men could be "remasculinized" (Sturken 70). By excluding Sam from the possibility of understanding their experiences in the war, the Hopewell veterans reassert an embattled masculinity. But Sam also reads their bodies, in particular Emmett's and Tom's, as signifying their emasculation by the War. Pete, however, inscribes his own body while in Viet Nam, having "a map of the Jackson Purchase region of western Kentucky tattooed on his chest" (47) in an attempt to determine for himself what it signifies, and thereby both "remasculinize" and "re-Americanize" it.

Aware of how culture codifies gender through its narratives about the body, and how in turn those narratives affect one's lived experience of the body, Sam attempts to take control of her own body and what it signifies. She takes the birth control pill and jogs, and Tom tells her "I've never felt muscles on a girl like you've got" (129). She fantasizes their approaching sexual encounter through an identification with her projection of Tom's experience in the War: "She felt she was doing something immensely daring, like following the soldier on point. A pool of orange light from the mercury lamp was the color of napalm" (124). Sam is attracted partly to the way Tom's body displays the wounds of the War: "He's real sexy . . . he looks sort of like Bruce Springsteen, but he got wounded in Vietnam and his back is stiff. He moves kind of jerky" (81). Through her frequent comparisons of Tom with Bruce Springsteen, Sam also replaces the signifier of the wounded body of the veteran with her ideal of "remasculinized" American manhood. Watching Springsteen's new video of "Dancing in the Dark," a song from the *Born in the USA* album, Sam comments, "He turns me on *high*," then reflects "It made her sad. She kept thinking about what it would be like to dance with Tom . . . But he could never move with Bruce Springsteen's exuberant energy" (97). Springsteen, who gives voice to the suffering veteran in *Born in the USA*, is himself "remasculinized" through the newly muscular physique he presents in the "Dancing in the Dark" video.[5] The comparison of Tom and Springsteen, both of whom Sam associates with the Vietnam War and her own desire, reveals Sam's adolescent orientation to both the past and the future. The "energy" Springsteen evokes and stimulates in Sam becomes American energy when Mason describes Sam's feeling as she travels to Washington: "Everything in America is going on here, on the road . . . They are at a cross-roads . . . She's in limbo, stationed right in the center of this enormous amount of energy" (17).

Dwayne's texts: "Humping the boonies"

In seeking to learn more about her father and his experience in the War, Sam turns to Dwayne Hughes's "texts"—the letters and diaries he wrote in Viet Nam. She finds the letters in the bedroom Irene has vacated. This room is, as Lauren Berlant has pointed out, "a kind of shoebox museum" (32) full of the consumer paraphernalia of femininity in the late 1960s and 1970s. Sam approaches the products of these decades as a bricoleur, borrowing from them to graft them on to her own life and culture in the 1980s. For example, she buys a red ceramic cat money bank from K-Mart and, in a gesture that echoes countercultural playfulness, decorates it with sequins from her mother's "old formal" and "beads, pearls and rhinestones" from her mother's jewelry.[6] Similarly, she listens to songs of the 1960s interspersed with contemporary rock music on the radio, feeling that the music of the earlier decade will connect her to that time, her mother, and the soldiers in the War.

While popular culture affords Sam the freedom, Mason suggests, to both read and creatively adapt its signifiers, Dwayne Hughes's letters frustrate her attempt to find anything in them other than the banal expression of sentimentality, patriotism, and religiosity. Even the revelation that Dwayne chose "her" name—"Samuel . . . If it's a girl, name it Samantha"—is a disappointment, in that "he was counting on a boy" and Sam is unable to find the name where Dwayne located it in the Book of Chronicles (182–183). Unsatisfied by Dwayne's letters, Sam goes to visit his parents on their farm outside Hopewell. There, in a further effort to understand Dwayne's experience, she tries "to see [the farm] in a new way . . . to see what her father had known, the world he knew before he went to Vietnam," but she feels only disdain for Dwayne's "country" life: "Everything he knew was small and predictable: Jesus bugs, blue mold, hound dogs, fence posts" (200).

Dwayne's diaries, which her grandparents give her, are free of the self-censorship of his letters, and Sam reads his account of killing—"We got two V.C. I think one of 'em's mine"—and death in the War: "Two days ago, we come upon a dead gook rotting under some leaves, sunk into a little swamp-like place. Interesting to see the body parts broken down, like we studied in biology. It had a special stink. Dead gooks have a special stink, we know by now" (203). These accounts are interspersed with Dwayne's praise for his "team," and his questioning of why they are in Viet Nam: "it's all for her [Irene] and the baby, or else why are we here?" (202). However, the image of Irene proves elusive and "she floats away" (203). Sam's immediate response to Dwayne's words is revulsion, followed by identification: "She recalled the dead cat she dug up once in Grandma's garden, and she realized her own insensitive curiosity was just like her father's. She felt humiliated and disgusted" (205). She attempts to distance herself from Dwayne and his "ignorant and country" parents who, she imagines, must have "made up a more pleasant story" in order to forget what they had read in the diary. In her revolted imagination, the dirt and decay of her grandparents's farm and the family's "country" attitudes merge with Dwayne's attitude toward killing and the Vietnamese, and the decay of the corpse in the fetid landscape of Viet Nam:

> Sam couldn't get the sensations out of her head: the mangy dog, the ugly baby, the touch-me-nots, the blooming weeds, the rusty bucket, her dumb aunt Donna . . . And the diary disgusted her, with the rotting corpse, her father's shriveled feet, his dead buddy, those sickly-sweet banana leaves. (206)

Feeling that she needs to understand Dwayne's account of killing and death, Sam flees to the local swamp, Cawood's Pond, to reenact being "in country," "humping the boonies" by spending the night alone there. Dwayne's diaries have reinforced the deterministic gender narratives that Sam has encountered in her efforts to learn about the War: "If men went to war for women, and for unborn generations, then she was going to find out what they went through. Sam didn't think the women or the unborn babies had any say in it. If it were up to women, there wouldn't be any war" (208). In particular, Sam is disturbed by the suggestion both in the diaries and in what the Hopewell veterans have said to her that the men enjoyed aspects of the War. Tom has explained, for example, that "'Pete had the time of his life over there . . . nobody else could ever know what you went through except guys who have been there'" (78). Sam attempts to reenact her father's experience—"She was in her father's place, in the foxhole in the jungle, with a bunch of buddies" (217)—but she acknowledges that her simulation at Cawood's Pond cannot recover the experiences of the men in the Vietnam War. She also concludes that the cultural opposition between men and women is a false one: "Soldiers murdered babies. But women did too. They ripped their unborn babies out of themselves and flushed them away, squirming and bloody" (215).

When Emmett arrives to look for Sam, he reinforces the point that she cannot understand the men's experience in the War. When

Sam comments that her father "was awful, the way he talked about gooks and killing" (221), Emmett explains: "Look here, little girl. He could have been me. All of us, it was the same" (222). At the conclusion of the scene, Emmett further emphasizes Sam's exclusion from knowledge of the War: "You can't learn from the past. The main thing you learn from history is that you can't learn from history. That's what history *is*" (226). However, elements of Mason's representation of the scene at Cawood's Pond work against a logic of exclusion, and contradict the moral Emmett draws about history.

The scene effects a transformation of both Sam, bearer of postmemory of the war, and Emmett, sufferer of PTSD. In seeking to bring about Emmett's "cure," Sam works with what Hagopian, in a different context, calls a "cultural script,"[7] as illustrated by an episode of M*A*S*H she has watched [222]), whereby talking about repressed traumatic memories will enable him to confront them. Moreover, this "script" informs the text itself: Emmett does indeed tell of his primary scene of trauma in the War (hiding from the enemy under the corpses of his patrol), an articulation followed by the expression of his "sorrow" which, Sam observes, "was full-blown, as though it had grown over the years into something monstrous and fantastic" (224). However, a counter-narrative of Emmett's posttraumatic years in Hopewell for both Emmett and Sam emerges at Cawood's Pond. It is verbalized in their discussion of "care." When Sam points out "you're saying you don't care about anybody. But you cared enough about me to come out here," Emmett explains "This is what I *do*. I work on staying together, one day at a time. There's no room for anything else. It takes all my energy." Sam reasserts "You cared" (225).[8]

It is "care" that suffuses Sam's vision of Emmett as he departs from the swamp: "From the back he looked like an old peasant woman hugging a baby. Sam watched as he disappeared into the woods. He seemed to float away, above the poison ivy, like a pond skimmer, beautiful in his flight" (226). Mason draws together several of the narrative and metaphoric strands of the text in her description of Sam's perception. The description also incorporates, through its imagery, the point of view of Dwayne and Emmett, which suggests Sam's empathy with them. Emmett's resemblance, in Sam's transforming perception, to "an old peasant woman hugging a baby" resonates with the images she has recalled elsewhere in the text of Vietnamese women with their babies. It evokes a compassionate way of seeing the Vietnamese which differentiates itself from Dwayne's objectifying and dehumanizing gaze. Sam's transfiguration of Emmett into an "old peasant woman" is also attuned to Emmett's own challenges to cultural demarcations of gender and ethnicity, and the ideology they support. A photograph of Emmett after his return from the war, for instance, depicts him with his countercultural friends, "all of whom had long hair" so "it was hard to tell the males from the females" (234). Later, Emmett wears "a long, thin, Indian-print skirt with elephants and peacocks on it" to watch M*A*S*H, as "a joke because Klinger wears dresses on M*A*S*H*"(27). To Sam, observing him on that occasion, "Emmett looked stately in his skirt—tall and broad, like a middle-aged woman who had had several children" (32). Then, as now through her vision of Emmett leaving Cawood's Pond, Sam recognizes Emmett's own openness to gendered and ethnic otherness.

Sam's allusion to Emmett seeming "to float way" also responds more sympathetically to part of what Dwayne has written in his diaries—"When I get her [Irene] in my mind good she floats away" (203). Similarly, Sam's final image of Emmett as "a pond skimmer, beautiful in his flight" reworks Emmett's own desire to transform a traumatic present and, subsequently, memories of trauma, by focusing on birds. Sam, a reader and bricoleur of cultural artifacts and signs, here has a vision made more open and compassionate by her borrowings from other people's ways of seeing. It is an empathetic way of seeing that suggests imaginative care about others and that Sam *is* "learning from history."

Sam's and Emmett's responses to the scene at Cawood's Pond illustrate contemporary beliefs about the effect of expressing a memory of trauma on the survivor and on the witness to that articulation. Emmett, empowered by telling Sam his memory, takes control of their lives and initiates the trip to Washington. Sam, however, bearer of postmemory, "change[s] places" with Emmett (229) to display symptoms of PTSD: dissociated from what is happening, she lacks energy and feeling and, usually an adept reader of her culture, she is unable to find coherence in it. However, her feeling of dissociation and her identification with the estrangement from the American landscape that she imagines returning soldiers must have felt also carries the potential for critique of patriotic sentiment:

> America the beautiful. It is beautiful indeed, Sam thinks now on the road. The United States is so peaceful and well-organized. The farms are pretty, the interstates are pleasant . . . She didn't fit into that landscape. None of it pertained to her . . . The soldiers must have felt that, as though they belonged nowhere. (231)

Reading the VVM

As Sam, Mamaw, and Emmett approach the VVM, each of them becomes a reader of its ambiguous symbolism. They are struck by its color, its shape, and the fact that it is embedded in the earth. Mamaw remarks "It's black as night," and to Sam it appears as "a massive gash in a hillside," a "black wing embedded in the soil . . . It is like a giant grave, fifty-eight thousand bodies rotting here behind those names" (239). The possibility of flight, and hence transcendence, alluded to in the image of a wing (which resonates with Emmett's attempts to escape trauma by focusing on birds) is undercut by the comparison to "a giant grave," a disabling gesture repeated in Sam's observation that the "V" is "like the wings of an abstract bird, huge and headless" (239). The family's initial response to the blackness of the memorial, and Sam's impression that it is a "gash," like a "grave," echoes the controversy about Maya Lin's design of the Memorial: critics argued that the blackness, in contrast to the "ennobling" white of traditional war memorials, and that it was dug into the ground, rather than rising into the sky, connoted the "shame" associated with America's loss of the war (Buckley 66).

Mason's evocation of her characters' responses to the Memorial shows that it allows conflicting responses and negotiation over its meaning, rather than imposing a single and nationalistic significance. The location of the Memorial on the Washington Mall situates it among monuments that commemorate key moments in the founding and consolidation of the nation: Sam is interpellated as a "citizen" of the nation by the Lincoln Memorial and the Washington Monument which she sees reflected in the wall of the VVM. However, Sam has developed throughout the narrative as a critical reader of her culture's signs, as is symbolized by her bringing to the Memorial the *Born in the USA* album, whose cover depicts Springsteen "facing the flag, as though studying it, trying to figure out its meaning" (236). Sam believes that the Monument and the flag she sees reflected in the wall "seem like arrogant gestures, like the country giving the finger to the dead boys, flung in this hole in the ground." This is followed by a more ambiguous response: "Sam doesn't understand what she is feeling, but it is something so strong, it is like a tornado moving in her, something massive and overpowering. It feels like giving birth to this wall" (240). Mason's choice of simile to evoke Sam's response to the Memorial suggests a reconciliation of the opposition between men going to war and women having children that has troubled Sam throughout the narrative.

The ambiguity of the symbolism of the Memorial, which allows both patriotic and critical responses, is extended through the presence and differing practices of its visitors. Among these are veterans of the Vietnam War, some of whom find community with each other (and the dead) in the space it affords, and others use the space for political expression, either against the war or on behalf of other causes. While their bodies testify to a "multiplicity of memory stories" (Sturken 12), the visibility of wounded veterans at the Memorial also contributes to its symbolism. Sam observes "a spraddle-legged guy in camouflage walk[ing] by with a cane. Probably he has an artificial leg" (240) and "a man rolls past in a wheelchair" (242). Veterans, physically injured by the War or psychologically "wounded" by it, also symbolically embody the "wounds" the War inflicted on the nation. In the discourse of "healing" that has surrounded the Memorial since its inception, healing the wounds of the veterans, including those afflicted by their grief,[9] has also come to stand for "healing" the nation (a nation "wounded" by the loss of the war, its casualties, and the social and political divisions in America that accompanied its conduct of the war).[10]

A narrative about healing shapes Mason's account of her characters' visit to the Memorial and the images she uses to represent it, but elements of the text trouble this narrative. Sam and her grandmother search for Dwayne Hughes's name among the more than 58,000 names on the wall, and, expressing their need for embodied contact with him, climb a ladder to touch his name.

Lauren Berlant reads this scene as evoking Sam and Mamaw's assumption of national "citizenship" as they see their private loss publicly marked at a site of national commemoration, a membership of "the nation" that the Memorial also confers posthumously on Dwayne:

> The monument makes the father's life public: only the immortalizing impersonality of U.S. citizenship can bring Samantha and her family resolution, happiness and peace. Engraved in monumental time, it is as though his physical self were only now truly dead, a name and not a living story, while in contrast his national self still lives in a state of pure and enduring value. (33)

Sam and Mamaw's inclusion in "the nation" to which all the names on the wall can be read as testifying is also indicated by Mamaw's comment, "all I can see here is my reflection" (244). The reflective black granite causes visitors to see themselves in the walls, giving them the impression of being part of the history commemorated by the Memorial. This effect is paralleled by a significant moment in Sam's narrative as she finds "her own name," "SAM ALAN HUGHES," in the directory, then locates it on the wall: "She touches her own name. How odd it feels, as though all the names in America have been used to decorate this wall" (245). Her identification with the soldiers in the War seems complete, and her claim to belong among those affected by the War, although she did not experience it, seems to be validated. This inference from Sam's discovery of the name is supported by Mason's account of her own visit to the Memorial in 1983 when she was writing *In Country*, and of finding her "own" name there—"Bobby G. Mason." Mason concludes: "I knew then that Vietnam was my story too, and it was every American's story. Finally, I felt I had a right to tell a small part of that story . . . I knew we were all in it together" (*In Country*, 2005, "P.S." 6). The fact that Sam Alan Hughes's name is *not* identical to Sam's or Bobby G. Mason's to Bobbie Ann Mason's problematizes this conclusion, however. Sam's discovery of the nonidentical name on the wall points to the strand of the text that attends to a commonality that can accommodate difference, rather than Sam's fantasy narrative of identification that erases difference. This ambiguity is deepened in the novel's final image. In response

to Mamaw's expression of consolation by her Christian faith—
"that white carnation blooming out of that crack . . . gave me
hope. It made me know he's watching over us" and her question
"Did we lose Emmett?"—Sam points to Emmett looking at the
names on the wall: "He is sitting there cross-legged in front of the
wall, and slowly his face bursts into a smile like flames" (245). At
first, Emmett's smile seems to testify to the healing effect of the
Memorial. However, his "cross-legged" pose and Sam's likening of
his smile to flames also recalls images of Buddhist self-immolation,
most famously by the Buddhist monk Thich Quang Duc in protest
against the persecution of Buddhists by the then US-backed South
Vietnamese government in 1963, and later in protest against the
war in Viet Nam. Sam's perception of Emmett's smile is again
attuned to Emmett's openness to ethnic otherness, and Mason's
image could be read as referring to a South East Asian history that
includes American imperialist intervention.[11]

The novel's concluding scene at the Memorial casts in relief
some of the issues around mourning for losses in the Vietnam War
that the narrative of Emmett and Sam has raised. *In Country* has
explored what mourning may mean for those who experienced
trauma and grief during and as a result of the War, and for those
who grew up "belatedly" inhabiting the traumatized world of the
other. It also invites us to think, particularly in the concluding
scene, about how the memories and mourning of individuals are
assimilated into narratives about the nation. For Lauren Berlant,
for example, although finding Dwayne's name inscribed in the
Wall enables Sam and her grandmother to identify with national
citizenship and confers a "national self" on Dwayne, this is not the
resolution of the processes of mourning or identity that it might
seem: "the name of the father inscribed with so many others in
stone on a national monument portrays the mute historical blank
that defines a larger part of the collective and personal content
of traumatic political memory" (33). In this assertion, Berlant
suggests that "political memory" of a traumatic event works like
an individual's memory of it: as the survivor of trauma may be
unable to express or indeed remember the scene of trauma, so a
culture's traumatic past is represented as historically unknowable.
Questions of the knowableness of the past—or of *how* the past
might be known—have beset Sam Hughes's attempt to learn about
the War, undertaken within the matrix of mourning.

Marita Sturken, theorist of the practices of mourning undertaken by visitors to the VVM, takes an optimistic view of the possibilities that individual and collective remembrance afford. She states:

> We must rethink culture's valorization of memory as the equivalent of experience. If memory is redefined as a social and individual practice that integrates elements of remembrance, fantasy and invention, then it can shift from the problematic role of standing for the truth to a new role as an active, engaging practice of creating meaning. (259)

By this account, Sam Hughes's efforts at historical empathy through identification, as well as her creative reading and adaptation of the signifiers of her culture, could be read as a productive way of responding to the past that challenges dominant political narratives about history.

Conclusion

In her book *Precarious Life: The Powers of Mourning and Violence* (2006), Judith Butler reflects on the American response to the events of September 11, 2001, including President George W. Bush's "calling for 'an end to grief'" only 10 days later and his declaration "that *now* it is time for resolute action to take the place of grief" (quoted in Butler 29, 149). She observes that to "arrest cycles of violence" we must "ask what, politically, might be made of grief besides a cry for war" (xii). Butler considers how the consequences of grief are influenced by practices of representing and remembering the dead. For instance, the "narratives" used in reporting "the final moments of the lost lives in the World Trade Center" have a "humanizing effect" (38), as is the case in "public obituaries" to America's dead, which also constitute "so many acts of nation-building" (xiv). The nonrepresentation of other lives lost in the conflicts following 9/11 reveals, Butler argues, "the differential allocation of grievability that ... operates to produce and maintain certain exclusionary conceptions of what is normatively human." Hence, she asks, "what counts as a livable life and a grievable death?" (xiv–xv). Butler contends that mourning affords the opportunity for rethinking social and political relationships because it draws our attention to "relational ties" that involve "fundamental dependency and ethical responsibility" (22). She calls for recognition of the humanity of others and of the constitutive interdependence of oneself and others in our "mortality, vulnerability, agency" (26) as embodied subjects. Butler's appeal for a form of mourning that would lead to a sense of "ethical responsibility," particularly in acts conducted in the name of the American nation, is anticipated by Mason's representation of American mourning after the Vietnam War.

The final scene at the Memorial, when read as culminating in Sam's vision that "all the names in America have been used to decorate this wall," could be regarded as a celebration of the reconsolidation of American community and nationhood. As such, it is an exclusionary response that—in the commemorative tradition of war memorials—erases the loss of Vietnamese lives in the war. However, the novel's concluding image, Sam's observation of Emmett's smile, draws attention to the text's emphasis on Emmett's attunement to otherness and Sam's responsiveness to the "vulnerability" of herself and others, including the veterans, as embodied subjects. Sam's awareness of the "mortality" and "vulnerability" of the body also marks the images of suffering of the Vietnamese that haunt her. Butler points out that "in the Vietnam War, it was the pictures of the children burning and dying from napalm" that most shocked and outraged "the U.S. public" because these pictures "disrupted the visual field and the entire sense of public identity that was built upon that field" (150). It is not these particular images, but images of Vietnamese women with children—sometimes dead children—that contribute to the nightmarish phantasmagoria in which Sam's sense of the suffering and vulnerability of others fuses with her own sense of biological and cultural vulnerability as a woman. These images are transfigured in her vision of Emmett as he leaves Cawood's Pond, a scene in which Emmett and Sam have articulated a relationship based on "care." On the road to Washington and at the VVM, this relationship, now including Mamaw, persists, offering an alternative model of connectedness to the prevailing Reaganite "images of a normal, familial America that would define the utopian context for citizen aspiration," as Berlant puts it (3).

Butler observes that grief may enable us to apprehend "a mode of dispossession that is fundamental to who I am" by revealing how, as embodied beings, we are "implicated in lives that are not our own" (28). In *In Country*, Mason has explored the "dispossession" her characters feel in their mourning for losses in the war in Vietnam: Sam and Emmett are, differently, dispossessed of a life free of the traumatic shadows of the war, and both recognize that their dispossession entails being "implicated" in the lives of others. Through her exploration of her characters' experience of trauma, mourning, and postmemory resulting from America's involvement in the Vietnam War, Mason continues to invite readers to reflect on that War, and what can be learned from it today.

Notes

1. See Luckurst's account of the contribution the diagnosis and interpretation of Vietnam veterans' Post-Traumatic Stress Disorder has made to the understanding of trauma, in *The Trauma Question* 1 and 59–65 and see Kalí Tal, *Worlds of Hurt* and Judith Lewis Herman, *Trauma and Recovery*, for influential theories of trauma that draw upon the study of PTSD in Vietnam veterans.
2. The novel's representation of how the characters' mourning for losses in Vietnam incorporates reflection on Southern identity has been explored by several recent critics, including Hinrichsen (233–234) and Krasteva (78–79, 84).
3. See also Hawkins and Hinrichsen for a discussion of Mason's treatment of the ethical issues raised by "postmemory" in the novel.
4. See Herzog's discussion of how Emmett manifests the symptoms of PTSD (204).
5. See Cullen's discussion of what Springsteen's changed physique in the "Dancing in the Dark" video represents (119).
6. See doCarmo's reading of Sam's decoration of the ceramic cat (593–594) to illustrate his argument that *In Country* explores what John Fiske "calls 'excorporation . . . the "tearing" or disfigurement of a commodity in order to assert one's right and ability to remake it into one's own culture'" (589).
7. In his essay "Voices from Vietnam," Hagopian asserts, "Even when they remain true to events, veterans' stories may adjust to societal expectations—or what veterans *believe* their audiences want to hear" (595).

8 Krasteva argues that through "the relationship between mother and daughter" (85), Irene "initiates" Sam "into the code of reciprocity and affirms its ritual of caretaking," which Krasteva sees expressed between Sam and Emmett at Cawood's Pond (88).
9 Herman notes how Robert Jay Lifton and Chaim Shatan, the two leading psychiatrist advocates for the veterans in the 1970s, both claimed that grief was a significant element of the "traumatic reaction" of the veterans (69). See also Jonathan Shay's discussion of the importance of grief in the veterans' experience of trauma (*Achilles* 39–68).
10 See Hagopian's discussion of the discourse of healing and its appropriation in political rhetoric in *The Vietnam War* (15–19, 73–75).
11 Hinrichsen also reads this image as alluding to "U.S. involvement in western imperialism," thereby making us aware of "our own complicity with complex global histories" (246), and for McDermott it shows how "Emmett's openness to transformation . . . gestur[es] towards an encounter with other potential histories of Vietnam than those represented in Mason's novel" (19).

4

War, gender, and race in le thi diem thuy's *The Gangster We Are All Looking For*

Isabelle Thuy Pelaud

When the United States won the first war in Iraq in 1991, President George H. W. Bush declared that the Vietnam Syndrome was over.[1] As we near the fortieth anniversary of the end of the Vietnam War, however, the term "Vietnam War" continues to resurface in journalistic and political accounts every time the United States is involved politically or militarily overseas. The Vietnam War, according to scholar John Carlos Rowe, has been "the most chronicled, documented, reported, filmed, taped, and—in all likelihood—narrated war in history of the United States" (173). Yet, Rowe continues, despite this substantial literature that focuses on military, political, and historical events, very few accounts of the war and what followed from the perspectives of former Vietnamese allies of the United States are known to the larger American audience (173). Even less is known of Vietnamese American women.

The mass exodus of Vietnamese people starting with the end of the Second Indochina War in 1975 was a turning point for a country with a history marked by colonization, conquest, and war. For over 25 years, South Vietnam was an ally of the American government in what was the longest war in the history of the United States. Some South Vietnamese soldiers spent their entire adult lives fighting alongside the Americans against the North Vietnamese, believing that the United States, the strongest superpower in the world, could not lose and would continue to support them until they defeated the communist forces. For some South Vietnamese women, the war meant having to find ways to survive and raise their children without a husband. When the war ended, southern Vietnamese felt abandoned, if not betrayed. They feared for their lives and for the lives of their family members, and many attempted to flee. The forced migration of Vietnamese people represented the largest population movement to America since World War II.

Writings by Vietnamese in the diaspora reflect in part the wide range of human experiences that comes with being a refugee or the child of a refugee. Their experiences, perspectives, and writings are not the same as those of Asian immigrants who came to the United States by choice. While mourning the loss of their country and at times having experienced trauma, diasporic Vietnamese people struggled in the United States to rebuild lives fractured by downward mobility, language barriers, and discrimination. Gender dynamics were deeply affected and domestic violence was not uncommon.[2] It is no coincidence that memories of Viet Nam play a significant role in Vietnamese American literary productions. The past is assiduously scrutinized through fiction and creative nonfiction. It seems to haunt the lives of narrators like ghosts, at times scary and at other times comforting, driving both emotions and actions. The engagements by Vietnamese writers moving forward in a globalized world while looking back toward Viet Nam have created new identities and definitions of citizenship.[3] These identities contrast sharply with Hollywood movies about the Vietnam War, which tend to portray people of Vietnamese descent as insignificant and inferior. Vietnamese American women writers, for instance, do not create female characters as prostitutes, passive exotic victims ready to sacrifice their lives for their white man, as in the Broadway musical *Miss Saigon*, or as a Dragon Lady, as embodied by the First Lady of South Vietnam from 1955 to 1963. This chapter brings forth the notion that Vietnamese American identities and imaginaries are multilayered, complex, and diverse and that Vietnamese American women writers of the 1.5 generation in particular are exponentially burdened by being refugees, people of color, and female.[4]

The author: le thi diem thuy

What are the costs of forced immigration for Vietnamese American women writers?[5] In *The Gangster We Are All Looking For* (2003), le thi diem thuy vacillates among the need to tell the past through literary means for the purpose of healing, the strong desire to be published on her own terms, and the wish to protect her family by not exposing too many family secrets. In this short novel, le tells the story of a Vietnamese American family from the perspective of a young child who left Viet Nam with her father by boat. The mother, for reasons that are not explained, initially stays in Viet Nam. Father and daughter arrive in San Diego in 1978 with few belongings. The family struggles financially and memories of Viet Nam inform their daily life. The daughter is seen as a stranger at school while being preoccupied with the loss of comfort and familiarity that came with forced immigration. When the mother finally arrives in the United States, the situation becomes more volatile, as the parents fight often.

An interview le thi diem thuy gave to *Nha Magazine* (a magazine about Vietnamese American culture run by Vietnamese Americans in San Jose, California) suggests that even though she was writing fiction she might have engaged in self-censorship to protect the image of her family. During the interview, le recounts an exchange she had with an audience member during a public reading: "'You know, you shouldn't refer to the father as a gangster,' an older man in her audience told her. 'Why not?' she asked. 'It's not good to make people think these things,' the man answered, to which she said: 'I have to—that's who he [the character] is.'" Reflecting on this exchange, le says: "He was up to no good, that father. [laughs] I mean, how else am I going to put it? He was a young man, unemployed, up to no good." She then adds:

> In the Vietnamese community and the Southeast Asian community, [gangs are] like one of the biggest things. And I can't even talk about this gangster figure from another time? I'm

not allowed to use the word, even though it's the most obvious word around! Like, what are we supposed to do? . . . It pissed me off, because I thought this is *nothing*. (T. Tran 82; emphasis in original)

In this passage, le thi diem thuy expresses the frustration that accompanies her role as a Vietnamese American female writer. The phrase "pissed me off" and the italicization of the word "*nothing*" denotes a rise in her tone of voice that suggests she had censored certain stories to protect her family. Her frustration with the audience member's objection denotes the sense that her self-censorship came at a cost that is not only not valued, but also judged as not being enough. Not to use the word "gangster" to refer to the father character and by extension, not to speak about his excessive use of physical force toward family members, would have been, from the perspective of the older man in the audience, preferable.

The italicization of "nothing" points to Erin Ninh's argument that Asian-American daughters carry a unique weight because immigrant parents expect daughters to be "dutiful and grateful to family and nation both" (17). In the context of resettlement, Ninh argues, the "second-generation daughter is perpetually produced as the unfilial subject," caught in what she calls "a system of 'designated failure,'" as opposed to the "selfless parent" who routinely threatens to violently disown the child to discipline her (16). In addition to always being in a position of failing, Lan Duong further explains, Vietnamese women writers of the diaspora who do not "follow patriarchal rule" and fail to "reproduce the nation and its ideologies" are considered traitors to an imagined "national family" (15). Le's exclamation, "this is *nothing*," signals that the narrative in *The Gangster* may have been crafted carefully with such concerns in mind. If le's observation mirrors the censoring process by which a Vietnamese American woman's story is created, the following question needs to be asked: can a Vietnamese American woman writer *safely* craft a recognizable identity without betraying the filial duty owed to her community when faced with memories of domestic violence? Must she adhere to her memories? Why is a book marketed as a novel still treated as the representation of the real and the author critiqued for her creativity and courage? My use of the term "identity" draws here from Stuart Hall, for whom it is both an "unending process" and "the names we give to the different ways we are positioned by, and position ourselves within, the narratives of the past" (112).

Not only has le thi diem thuy been considered a treacherous daughter in her community for referring to the fictional protagonist father as a gangster, but also her positioning in mainstream society as a woman of color *and* a Vietnamese American refugee writer further restricts her ability to speak. As an Asian-American woman and as a refugee of war, she has the double expectation to tell her autobiography. Although *The Gangster* is a novel, reviewers and audience members tend to regard the book as autobiographical.[6] In the *Nha Magazine* interview le displays a clear tension with her imagined readers.

> Nha: It's interesting that [mainstream people] are interested in the autobiographical nature of the book. What do you say in response?
>
> Ltdt: What do I say? Well, I always say, "No, it's not me. It's a work of fiction because many things happen in this book that never ever happened to me or to my parents. I have siblings in life and the girl does not have living siblings in the book." I also say that it's like I'm a fellow traveler—I move through the same geographies that they move through . . . It's autobiographical in part but not in whole. (T. Tran 84)

In the interview, le insists that the names, family compositions, characters' genders, and the course of events in the novel are different from those in her life. She is indeed not interested in mirroring what happened to her in the past but wishes to follow familiar characters wherever they lead her. "There is a whole pleasure to the process for me about being with these characters and seeing what happens to them . . . to have [this book] be trumped by 'she's me or not me' is so unfair to the process," she says (T. Tran 84).

Aware of her location as a woman of color, le thi diem thuy resists portraying her female character as authentic-imagined-woman-other or in Elaine Kim's words, "a seductive female sex partner" who poses "no apparent threat" ("Asian Americans" 100). Simultaneously, le refuses to reveal the scars of war in ways that serve "America's need for its citizens to heal and forget the

Viet Nam syndrome as it consolidates and continues to expand its empire" (Pelaud 58). "The obsession with facts strips away the mysteriousness of experience," le explains. "There's a much messier way in which ... you have war, you have refugees, and then people are here. It's almost as if they haven't absorbed that they've gone through a war until they land on the other side of the world from where the war happened" (T. Tran 87). For le, memory is something that is messy and subjective, and "does not necessarily register what actually took place, but rather what we preconceive to have happened or what others inform us has happened" (Machida 124). Yet, due to America's geopolitical relationship to Viet Nam and le's race and gender, she understands there is little room for her text not to be read as authentication of the real. What is more important, she says, is to capture what she calls the mysteriousness of experience. While le resists faithfully representing the past, her comment also reflects empathy for her parents and the losses they have suffered. It also points to the limitations of language to represent trauma ethically.[7]

The culture represented in the novel is not fixed but the product of what Lisa Lowe calls "living, inventing, and reproducing cultural alternatives" (124). As the author herself explains, the book is "autobiographical in part but not in whole." The past is both a source of inspiration and a place that may facilitate closure and healing, but it does not claim to reveal the truth. Walking a tightrope between the desire to tell, create, and withhold, the author emphasizes tactics of surviving everyday violence produced by war, racism, and patriarchy; the whispers, for instance, the young child narrator exchanges with a butterfly she thinks is trapped inside a glass paperweight, or her habit of sinking her head under the bath water and pretending she "was at the ocean on the world's hottest day" to avoid hearing her parents fighting (le 66).

Despite the impulse to write non-autobiographical fiction, since the enormous success of Maxine Hong Kingston's *The Woman Warrior* (which was published when the Second Indochina War ended in 1975), autobiographies and creative nonfiction by Asian American women writers have dominated Asian American literature. It seems easier for an Asian American woman to find a publisher for a memoir about her relationship with her mother than for a novel that does not address racial and gender identities. In the same way, it is easier for a Vietnamese American woman writer to publish a book about the refugee experience and memories of the Vietnam War. In a review published in *San Francisco Chronicle*, Lara Adair writes, "Le should just learn to trust us. Or forgive us" (M3). The word "just" highlights that the reviewer does not understand the complex power relationships that a woman of color and a refugee daughter have to navigate. In le's words:

> People feel an enormous amount of permission to get intimate with women ... The culture has a huge appetite for confessional mode and a confessional way of presenting oneself ... I think this is so bogus and so about the appetite of the viewer. It's gross! (T. Tran 84)

Not accounted for in Adair's comment is the author's lack of trust toward her readers who view Asian American women through stereotypical and voyeuristic lenses. Vietnamese American women writers have the *triple weight* of protecting the family from embarrassment and shame; of conforming to national cultures that exoticize and orientalize them;[8] while having to privilege the refugee experience and personal memories of Viet Nam in ways that have more to do with America's guilty conscience than with the desire to understand the fullness and complexity of what it means in the United States to grow up in poverty with parents buried in the past and whose story is invisible in the narrative of the nation.

It is thus in part to evade such pressures that *The Gangster We Are All Looking For* is told from the perspective of a child who does not understand what is going on around her. From this perspective, the narrator is not accountable for what she sees. In le's words:

> The narrative is told largely from the perspective of a child. Children see—they absorb a lot through their visual sense—but there's a difference between seeing and understanding, or seeing and knowing. She can't help but see. It does not mean she really knows what's going on or even that she understands.

> There's a way in which the reader is responsible for seeing and understanding more than the girl can at times. (T. Tran 86)

From the child's description of her surroundings, readers cannot obtain reliable interpretations of or draw conclusions about her parents. The author can thus evade the accusation of being a traitor of family and community and become what Lan Duong calls a "treacherous subject." The child grows up in an environment that is indisputably violent. But this is all she knows. Shifting the responsibility of interpretation to the readers, le resists the woman writer's threefold burden of representation. Instead, the narrative invites readers to engage in doing further research about Vietnamese history, race relations in America, and gender dynamics in the Vietnamese American community.

The story: *The Gangster We Are All Looking For*

The author's wish to tell-without-revealing can be traced in both the form and content of the narrative. The narrator in *The Gangster We Are All Looking For* is neither heroine nor traitor. She does not denounce violence but does not hide it, either. Flight and resettlement in the United States were brutal for the family because, unlike ordinary immigrants, they did not leave Viet Nam by choice. They left because the father had been incarcerated in a reeducation camp. Although how he was able to leave the camp is not revealed, one can infer from the details—how he risked his life and his young daughter's without his wife present on an extremely dangerous journey by boat—that the decision to leave Viet Nam was a matter of life and death. The despair that comes from risking one's child's life is not to be overlooked. Once they finally arrive at a refugee camp, an elderly American couple sponsors them to come to San Diego with four young Vietnamese men they met at a refugee camp. The husband, a Navy man during the War, feels responsible for the welfare of Vietnamese allies who were left behind to face retaliation. Since the man dies shortly after sponsoring the five men and the young girl, his widow asks her son, Mel, to house the refugees. They become, the young girl suspects, Mel's unwanted inheritance. By and large, though, the girl is left to her own devices once in the United States:

> No one explained to the child what was going on. A few months after they arrived, she asked to be taken to the beach to meet her mother:
> Ba shook his head. "No. Not possible. There's no reason for us to go there."
> "But Ma's there," I said.
> "No, she's not," Ba said, leaning down to zip up my jacket.
> "You told me she was at the beach," I said.
> "Not the beach here. The beach in Vietnam," Ba said.
> What was the difference? (le 13)

This concluding question suggests that the daughter is left unattended and is expected to navigate her new uprooted life on her own. The father has not told his daughter why they escaped Viet Nam by boat, why the mother was left behind, or where the United States is geographically in relation to Viet Nam. Without explanation, the daughter waits to go back home. Instead of interpreting her experience, all she can do as a child is to describe through her senses.

In exchange for shelter, Mel asks the men to do maintenance and repair work in the condominiums he rents out. Of the refugees, the father speaks the most English and so serves as translator for the other Vietnamese men to Mel. In these exchanges, the girl notices, Mel's voice "shines bright in your face like a flashlight aimed at your eyes when you're sleeping," in contrast to her father's voice that sounds like "echoes from deep down like a frog singing at the bottom of a well" (10). As she describes it:

> His voice is water moving through a reed pipe in the middle of a sad tune. And the sad voice is always asking and answering itself. It calls out and then comes running in. It is the tide of my Ba's mind. When I listen to it, I can see boats floating around in his head. Boats full of people trying to get somewhere. (10)

Seeing the refugee life through a young girl's senses, readers can imagine the child sitting in a corner of a room, listening to the short conversations about walls that need to be painted and doors that need to be replaced. After Mel's, her father's voice lacks power, and the comparison she makes between the two voices highlights the invisible cost of resettlement and having lost one's country. The father is lost, vulnerable and, as readers learn later, at the edge of despair. He can barely hold his life together. The daughter describes his voice as sad, and sees how each of his sentences ends as a question. For the young girl to notice this, a change must have taken place. In addition to signaling a loss of paternal authority, the words "tide" and the repeated "boat" indicate that the sadness and far-away tone are intricately linked to the journey of displacement. The father is not fully present and a part of him remains elsewhere, trapped on a boat in the middle of a big ocean. What happened there is not uncovered and readers are left to guess. All they know from the daughter is that the father's voice has changed and that he is not emotionally available for his daughter. Her need for safety and comfort is not met.

The sadness in the child's father's voice hints at the possibility of trauma. Her father has nightmares and sheds tears "in the garden every night" (27). The impact of those tears is compounded by the absence of a recipient. Without someone to receive them, tears have no power. "What does crying mean in this country?" one of the other Vietnamese men, the "uncles," asks before himself answering, "nothing comes of it. Just water for Mel's lawn" (27). The father is separated from his wife, and adequate personal or institutional care is not available to him. Like the stories of Vietnamese refugees produced around that time, his tears are invisible to most Americans: those on the right did not want to be reminded of a war they had lost or of their former allies, and those on the left were not keen on reading about human rights violations committed by the regime left in power after the War ended (Pelaud 25). In the end, the exact cause of the tears is not known, suggesting that there is not one single cause for trauma or what the child calls her father's sadness. Instead, the novel as narrated by the child underlines the absence of the father she once knew and of resources available to help him address his trauma and his daughter's needs.

With a father not fully present, the young daughter takes it upon herself to handle the family's dire emotional situation. But the state of affairs ends badly when the child becomes the parent. Her intense desire to regain control for her family is manifested in a dream where she stands on the shoulders of her father and the four uncles, holding tight onto a street sign and showing them the way: "As we sailed through the streets on our sign, I held the glass disk like a telescope up to my eye and through the body of my butterfly, I saw Ma standing on a faraway beach" (le 32). If only they could reunite with her mother, everything would be fine, thinks the daughter. The butterfly that will make this possible, however, is inside the sponsor's "glass disk," or paperweight. Hoping to free the butterfly, the child throws the paperweight into the air, accidentally breaking the sponsor's precious collection of glass animals locked inside a glass cabinet. The trapped butterfly represents the father trapped in the past: events that possibly occurred on the boat, the loss of his country, and the separation from his wife. The daughter's act of trying to free the butterfly from the paperweight metaphorically mirrors her desire to help her father. The destruction that ensues, however, and the consequences of that destruction (the family and four uncles having to leave the house of the sponsor) foreshadows a future marked by a past frozen or framed "into an eternal present in which one remains forever trapped, or to which one is condemned to be perpetually returned" (Stolorow 20). The process of resettlement, this scene suggests, is intimately intertwined with the trauma that took place in Viet Nam after the war ended and during the journey of departure.

When the mother finally arrives in the United States, the family dynamic is precarious and volatile, burdened as the family is by poverty and a constant longing for Viet Nam.[9] "War," the young narrator says, "has no beginning and no end. It crosses oceans like a splintered boat filled with people singing a sad song" (le 87). In the family's minds, however, Viet Nam is not reduced only to the American war there.[10] If Viet Nam is where the father fought and was incarcerated in postwar reeducation camps, it is also where the narrator's brother accidentally drowned and where her grandparents disowned her mother for having eloped with her father. The identity of the family is transnational. What happened in Viet Nam and during their journeys to the United States shapes their decisions and actions years after resettlement.[11] A decade after they arrive, her father's crying and nightmares turn into gambling and heavy drinking. In protest, the mother shaves her head. To the girl, both parents remain distraught: "He liked to sing when he was drunk, and when she was mad, she liked to scream and throw things" (le 65–66).

Just as the child described her father's despair as sadness, she describes the presence of domestic violence without directly naming it. The daughter remembers when a photograph of her maternal grandparents in Viet Nam came in the mail and her parents started fighting. "Ba threw the fish tank out the front door and Ma broke the dishes. They said they never should've got together . . . Ba said, 'Don't cry. Your parents have forgiven you.' Ma kept crying anyway and told him not to touch her with his gangster hands. Ba clenched his hands into tight fists and punched the walls" (92). The narrator avoids the fight by fixing her gaze on the broken tank:

> When he throws the fish tank out the front door, yelling, "let me see the gangster!" I am drinking up the spilt water and swallowing whole the beautiful tropical fish, their brilliant colors gliding across my tongue, before they can hit the ground, to cover themselves in dirt until only the whites of their eyes remain, blinking at the sun.
>
> All the hands are in my throat, cutting themselves on broken dishes, and the fish swim in circles; they can't see for all the blood.
>
> Ba jumps in his truck and drives away.
>
> When I grow up I am going to be the gangster we are all looking for. (93)

Similarly when she was a little girl listening to her father translating English into Vietnamese for the uncles, the narrator is invisible and can do nothing about the circumstances. Unlike when she was a child, however, the affirmation in the last sentence, "When I grow up I am going to be the gangster we are all looking for," implies that all hope of ever fixing the situation is now lost. With the loss of hope comes the removal of protective layers of childhood fantasy. The continued loss of control results in the child's chilling awareness that she will forever carry her father's anger. Her identification with the fish that fell out of the tank and are wriggling on the ground represents death since without hope, a part of herself can no longer live. To survive the lack of air and yet still fulfill her role as protector of her father, she takes imagined and physical actions detrimental to her own well-being. She assumes the task of hiding the memories by metaphorically swallowing them. In the process, the images of the fish and hands swallowed become stuck inside her throat.

The self-destruction resulting from the girl's desire to protect her father is emphasized in the next scene, in which the narrator runs out of the apartment and faces the kids standing outside to gather information for "their gossiping mothers." She starts dancing "like a crazy lady," dancing "like a fish," wiggling her "head and whip [ping her] body around." When she stops, she stares at them:

> "What're you looking at?" I ask.
> "Lookin' at you," one boy says, half giggling.
> "Well," I say, with my hand on my hip, my head cocked to one side, "I'm looking at you too," and I give him my evil one-eyed look, focusing all my energy into my left eye. I stare at him hard as if my eye is a bullet and he can be dead. (94)

Although she has lost hope, the daughter protects her father. The contradiction between her need to survive *and* to protect her father are like the fish and fists stuck in her throat, lodged inside her body. In the process of resettlement, a vital part of the child has been sacrificed. Like the father and the butterfly of her childhood, she is stuck inside a glass prison in which anger is concealed through the impulse to escape. The image of the fish and fists stuck inside her throat gestures toward the notion that what impedes her expression and by extension representation of that anger is the guilt of having failed to rescue her father. Freedom from this prison of glass is depicted as impossible and all attempts doomed to end in destruction. The child is both the victim of the imprisonment and the perpetrator. Like her father, she will "build and break things with my hands" and "turn away from the people I loved" (116). Unlike him, however, she will "not disappear into herself when haunted," but will "leap out of windows and run" (117). The resigned tone of her voice brings to the surface a tragic and yet invisible cost of being the daughter in this refugee family.

The children waiting outside to gather gossip about what is going on inside the apartment may be compared to readers of *The Gangster We Are All Looking For*. How does one heal and create, the novel leads readers to ask, when the legacy of war, racism, and patriarchy taints all attempts at representation and by extension the processing of the harm it causes? To fully trust, forgive, remember, and tell are not options and as a result wounds are both opened and concealed. "There is not a trace of blood anywhere except here, in my throat, where I am telling you all this," the protagonist says (99). The act of trusting the reader is costly to a degree comparable to self-mutilation. The simple act of having witnessed despair results in violence. The narrator recalls:

> One night when my father was sitting on the couch looking sad and broken, he turned and realized there was someone standing where he had thought there was only a shadow. He came for me then because I had seen him. I leapt through a window and ran from the house, but before I could make it to the street, he caught me by my hair and pulled me back inside. Gripping my head with one hand, he raised the other and demanded to know what I had seen.
>
> To protect myself, I tried to forget everything.... (117)

To remember is not depicted as a voluntary act, but as something that comes in spite of herself and is mitigated by the attempt to forget for the purpose of survival. In this context, the story stands as a failure to forget and supports Viet Thanh Nguyen's notion that "the ethical challenge for the artist working with and among refugees cast out of their homeland is to suggest memory's incompleteness, especially in the presence of furious desire, the contradictory yearning to imagine one's memory as whole or to forget altogether" ("Speak" 30). The guilt that accompanies the act of remembering against one's will mixed with the desire to tell without trusting the one who reads the story creates a specific gaze. The image of the narrator does not coincide, for instance, with that of the grateful refugee nor of the exotic Asian woman. She is neither a "good daughter" who closes her eyes and patiently waits her turn to subject others to the ruthlessness she endures, nor a "bad daughter" who betrays her family.[12] While this creative representation dislodges fixed binaries, the search for *her* Gangster or father figure is one marked by much pain, one that carries the potential for self-destruction and destruction.

Conclusion: Vietnamese Americans and US literature

Since the American War in Viet Nam left a mark in American history as a national crisis both domestically and internationally and much of that history has been rewritten in ways that centered on healing the American national wounds caused by the Vietnam Syndrome, even decades after the war's conclusion it still is important to insist on the full humanity of Vietnamese Americans and in the process remind readers that Vietnamese Americans are American, too. Even today, fewer than 50 books and short story collections by and about Vietnamese Americans have been published by nationally recognized publishers. Such selective publishing practices prevents mainstream American society from understanding the experiences, history, and culture of a growing Vietnamese American community as well as the impact the community has had on the larger society. Yen Le Espiritu has pointed out that a number of books produced and written about the Vietnam War tend to offer one-dimensional portrayals of Vietnamese people, while ignoring, for the most part, their traumatic experiences due to postwar displacement (*Asian American*). Particularly in the United States, due to this history Vietnamese American artists, whose works draw from the experiences of the Vietnamese American community, continue to face the difficulty of finding recognition among American critics and audience members because the works remind them of a war America wants to forget. The images produced by mainstream Americans during the Vietnam War as well as those produced after the lost War have forged one-dimensional representations of the Vietnamese. These representations impact how Vietnamese in the diaspora are seen, understood, and perceived; by extension, these representations may also have influenced how Vietnamese Americans represent themselves. Read against such context, Vietnamese American literature provides alternative portrayals of the American War in Viet Nam and its legacy. This literature points, for instance, to the complexities and contradictions of abandonment and protection—entering the nation that has, from the refugees' perspective, abandoned them but emphasizes having defended, rescued, or enriched them. Vietnamese American literary texts such as *The Gangster* tackle the contradictions and, to various degrees, the ambivalence that takes place when one is invisible in the history of the nation in which one lives, and highlight the enormous resilience and will it takes simultaneously to heal from trauma while having to reconstitute a new life in a foreign land through a new language, a shift of gender roles, and with very few resources. The writers, it is important to note, neither portray themselves or their characters as victims deprived of agency, nor as perfect subjects who work hard and succeed without human cost. Vietnamese American women writers, as in the case of le thi diem thuy, do not romanticize family and community. Instead, their work makes clear that wounds of war and displacement cannot be healed. Such interpretation leads readers to question how wars are represented and whose histories are hidden within discourses of war.

Due to their forced departure, many Vietnamese writers in the diaspora, in contrast to other Asian immigrants, are heavily engaged with the Viet Nam of the past and thus the nostalgia can be carried from one generation to the next. Since the first generation was forced out of Viet Nam and was not always able psychologically to find closure with the past due to the chaotic circumstances of departure by plane or the secretive nature of escape by boat, the population as a group maintains a strong emotional attachment to the homeland. The generation that follows is deeply influenced by the first generation's mourning of the past and its complex relation with it, but is more emotionally detached from Viet Nam than their parents. The creative stories of the 1.5 generation who immigrated as older children are particularly rich in their complexities and attempts to articulate new concepts of home. Present in some of their works is a longing for Viet Nam and its dramatic history. The country is often referred to as a place where life was more complete and made more sense, and it is used as a frame of reference or explored with various degrees of ambivalence. Often central to these works are the explorations of the links between the past and the present through family dynamics. In *The Gangster We Are All Looking For*, le examines what it means to grow up with parents who are emotionally absent and traumatized by the war. The exploration of memory and trauma can deepen understanding of the various coping mechanisms and distinctive cultures that emerge from forced departure. This focus highlights the human cost of war for all people, not only those from Viet Nam. By analyzing how Vietnamese writers and artists represent the Vietnam War and themselves, readers see that these experiences and identities are diverse, always in flux, and vary greatly depending on one's time of arrival, class, gender, sexuality, and exposure to trauma.

Yet it is equally important, I argue, not to read and interpret Vietnamese American literature only in relation to the tropes of war and trauma. To do so would obscure the humanity of Vietnamese American people, deny their full history, and only present them as victims paralyzed by grief and deprived of agency. The longing for Viet Nam and the writers' relationships with the past is mitigated by their reception in their host country, after all. In the West, Vietnamese refugees have become "people of color," joining to various degrees those who have been either excluded, exploited, and/or mistreated because of their race. As Asian Americans, however, Vietnamese Americans have at times also been upheld as model minorities and as such have remained invisible. Discussions about race are highly significant for the United States because of its vexed history with people of color and because non-white people are likely to outnumber whites in the United States by the year 2050.[13] Gender, I have also shown in this chapter, plays a significant role in shaping how a text may be written and read. Sexism outside and inside the community often makes Vietnamese American women into subjects to be desired or sacrificed. Either too visible or too invisible, they are burdened by the expectation to reveal their inner world, which they understand is fraught with stereotypes generated by the Vietnam War, the established and less threatening framework of the Asian American mother–daughter relationship story, and by the pressure to be a good daughter responsible for protecting the image of the family and the community. To write in this context is almost a lose–lose proposition, whereby one simultaneously resists serving as an easy resolution to the Vietnam War, as a token of multiculturalism, and as a concealer of the dirty laundry of home and community. This balancing act can be painful and holds the potential to impede the act of writing itself.

By taking war, race, and gender into account when reading Vietnamese American literature, the gains and costs of identity politics surface. Vietnamese American writers have benefited from a form of cultural pluralism that has taken place as a result of the civil rights and feminist movements in the United States during the Vietnam War. This special platform has facilitated the integration and resettlement of Vietnamese Americans a great deal. Vietnamese Americans have enjoyed certain services available to minorities and have also been able to build ethnic enclaves by choice without strong pressures to assimilate, as was the case for Japanese Americans after World War II. Asian American women writers have also benefited from an established ethnic canon that privileges women's narratives. The study of race, gender, and ethnicity is taught in universities, and ethnic novels and autobiographies by Asian American women have special shelves in bookstores. Yet refugee, race, and gender politics also have been adversely experienced by writers as limiting creativity. According to literary critic David Palumbo-Liu, there is what he calls a "minority discourse," which, he says, offers too-easy resolutions to a generalized problem of racial, ethnic, and gender identities. According to him, such perceptions deeply inform the contracting, marketing, and distribution of Asian American literature, which in turn influences their production.

How do Vietnamese American women writers imagine communities when the dispersal process breaks up families and social relationships? More importantly, what kind of communities are these authors representing? Lan Duong says that the Vietnamese diasporic community's efforts to construct a monolithic discourse mandating being "with" or "against" one's community places on women a unique pressure to conform. A Vietnamese American woman writer of the 1.5 generation who wishes to tell her story in a creative way is subjected to a *triple burden* of being a refugee and a woman, but also a minority. She is pressured not to reveal family secrets as filial piety makes it difficult for her to tell her story as a fiction informed by memory. In addition, she does not trust mainstream readers because she suspects they hold a voyeuristic gaze mitigated by exotic stereotypes shaped by a long history of race inequalities and prejudice that is itself enhanced by the length and loss of the American War in Viet Nam. In this context, it is important that le's narrative be read and understood as fluid, invented, and continually negotiated in relation to a past carefully and selectively remembered, forgotten, hidden, and imagined.

Notes

1 I thank Anh Thang Dao and Brenda Boyle for their substantial comments and contributions to this chapter.
2 See Kibria.
3 See Pelaud.
4 The term "1.5 generation" is used in the United States to refer to people who are born in other countries but immigrate to the United States as school-aged children. Thus, most of their schooling is done in the American educational system but they carry with them the cultural knowledges, especially language, of their original countries.
5 Asian Americanists King-Kok Cheung, Lisa Lowe, Elaine Kim, Yen Le Espiritu, Shirley Hune, Gail Nomura, Sonia Shah, and Laura Huyn Yi Kang effectively deconstruct the two stereotypical images of Asian American women: the exotic yet docile and submissive woman, and the heartless, hypersexualized demoness. To counter the stereotypes, they have examined how these images have been used to maintain white supremacy, manage anxieties about racial diversity, or support war efforts against Asian nations. In the process of analysis and deconstruction, they provide alternative representations and create reflections "of the terms and conditions by which Asian/American women [themselves] have been rendered legible, visible, and intelligible" (Kang 17).
6 Reviewer Lara Adair treats the novel as autobiography. She writes: "We want to follow the girl when she flees—find out where she went, how she managed . . . But perhaps this book tells us all we need to know about who she turned out to be, which is a writer of great promise" (M3).
7 See Goellnicht.
8 This argument is made by Lisa Lowe in *Immigrant Acts*, 65.
9 The image of the family in *The Gangster* does not correspond to the model minority image. Parents are deeply disappointed with the reality of life in America without English or marketable skills, without support from the state of its former ally, isolated from extended family and community, and haunted by the experiences

that occurred in Viet Nam and during their journey of departure. The living situation in America is dire:

> I lived upstairs, in a one-bedroom apartment with my mother and my father. She worked as a seamstress, doing piecework at our kitchen table. He worked as a welder at a factory that made space heaters. Neither of them wanted to be doing it; Ma wanted to have a restaurant, and Ba wanted to have a garden ... The three of us slept in one room. My parents' double bed was separated from my single bed by a side table with a lamp on it. (le 43)

10 This representation of Viet Nam brings us back to an oft-cited poem by le thi diem thuy, "To my sister le thi diem trinh: Shrapnel Shard on Blue Water." See http://www.thedrunkenboat.com/thuy.htm (accessed July 23, 2012).
11 See Schiller et al., ix–xiv.
12 Asian Americanist feminists have reconstructed the notion of bad and good women for some time. In "'Bad Women': Asian American Visual Artists Hanh Thi Pham, Hung Liu, and Young Soon Min," for instance, Elaine Kim tells the story of how her mother represented her own mother, known as a "bad woman" in Korea, as a "good mother" because she left her husband and immigrated to the United States to physically save her child from a gambling and violent father (573).
13 This change may lead to collective anxieties with the potential of expressing itself in ugly ways, especially during times of national economic difficulties and wars.

5

The home front and the front lines in the war novels of Tim O'Brien

Susan Farrell

Introduction

In what has become almost a truism, critics have argued that American fiction written about the Vietnam War focuses on the individual experience of the everyday soldier rather than raises questions about the history and morality of the War. Walter Holbling, for instance, in a 1989 article surveying American-authored Vietnam War literature, writes that "there is not much in the way of explicit ideological argument in most of the novels . . ." (124). Tobey Herzog, linking Vietnam War literature to earlier war literature, especially British responses to World War I, argues that both types of fiction depict soldiers obsessed with the "surface details" and "daily routines" of ordinary life as they attempt to exert control in the face of the chaos and powerlessness they experience during war (33–34). Katherine Kinney, in *Friendly Fire*, acknowledges the focus on soldiers' individual lives, although she explains the phenomenon differently than Herzog. She argues that since scholars, politicians, and even ordinary Americans disagree about the most basic facts of the War—"when the war began, why we fought, who we fought, or when and how and why and if we lost"—it is through the "veteran's authority of experience" that we have come to define the War: "The war has become knowable primarily through the arbitrary boundaries of the soldier's 12-month tour of duty" (7–8). John Timmerman, writing specifically about the work of Tim O'Brien, argues that "war stories must evoke the dreams and lives of individual soldiers, as opposed to giving a statistical or historical accounting of data" (101). Considered by many to be America's finest chronicler of the war in Viet Nam, Tim O'Brien is best known for his trio of novels that explore the War's impact on the psyches of the individual soldiers who fought it—*Going After Cacciato* (1978), *The Things They Carried* (1990), and *In the Lake of the Woods* (1994). While it is true that O'Brien's War novels depict the ordinary lives of everyday soldiers at war—the surface details, the rituals, the banter, the dreams of escape and home—it is important to note that O'Brien is a writer who is also keenly interested in the larger moral and ethical questions surrounding war in general and the Vietnam War in particular.

O'Brien took an interest in politics, history, and philosophy from an early age. A member of his high school debate team who, as a teenager, worked part time as a reporter for the local newspaper in his hometown of Worthington, Minnesota, O'Brien went on to become a political science major at Macalester College, where he was elected president of the student body both his junior and senior years. After his stint in the Vietnam War in 1968–1969, O'Brien enrolled as a graduate student in Harvard University's School of Government. During the summers of 1971 and 1972, and while on a leave of absence from Harvard in the 1973–1974 academic year, he worked as a national affairs reporter for *The Washington Post*. When O'Brien left Harvard in 1976, he had finished all of his PhD coursework, but decided to focus on fiction writing rather than complete a dissertation. O'Brien's extensive training in political philosophy would not go to waste, however; it would work its way into his fiction. In a lecture delivered at the Bread Loaf Writer's Conference in the 1990s, O'Brien makes explicit the relationship he sees between political philosophy and fiction writing. Good literature, he insists, must entail the practice of "moral philosophy," which he defines as follows:

> I do not mean a body of received or won wisdom. I do not mean moralizing, or preaching, or proselytizing. *Moral philosophy,*

as I'll use the phrase today, refers to a process of rigorous and careful thought about values. What should human beings value? What *do* we value? ... What happens when values of equal merit come into conflict? What are the sources of our values? What are the implications?

All of O'Brien's novels, but especially his trio of Vietnam War novels, raise larger moral and ethical questions about war: Why do people go to war? How does one cope, survive, or even behave well in wartime? What does it mean to be a coward, a hero? What obligations does one owe one's country, one's self? But O'Brien is also interested in the specific historical conditions of the Vietnam War, a war he considered unjust or at least ethically murky before he was drafted to fight in it, a war in which "Certain blood was being shed for uncertain reasons" (*The Things They Carried* 40). So, in many ways, the *big* moral question underlying O'Brien's war novels asks how to behave justly in the face of an unjust war. Further, this question is often examined through the lens of traditional gender expectations, specifically that boys become men by going to war and girls become women by building a home. Yet O'Brien challenges these traditional expectations as his female characters often partake directly in war, and as his male characters repeatedly imagine domestic spaces as alternatives to experiences on the front lines. Above all, O'Brien shows that, just as it is a mistake to easily and simply equate masculinity with a warrior mentality and femininity with a domestic one, it is also wrong to think that the domestic realm of the home front is divided from the public world of global politics that brings us war.

Readers see these concerns from O'Brien's earliest works. His 1973 memoir, *If I Die in a Combat Zone, Box Me Up and Ship Me Home*, depicts the author's anguish over whether to evade the draft or allow himself to be sent to the Vietnam War. O'Brien goes so far as to research and plan an escape to Canada and eventually Sweden from the Advanced Infantry Training he was undergoing in Fort Lewis, Washington, before ultimately finding himself unable to carry out his plans. But even more, in what becomes a dominant motif in his later work, O'Brien contrasts the cozy, domestic relationship he builds with a fellow soldier, Erik Hansen, to the masculinist expectations of the war machine surrounding him. Hansen and O'Brien attempt to separate themselves from their fellow soldiers and create a comfortable space in which they can discuss philosophy, literature, and morality. But when their drill sergeant Blyton catches the young soldiers alone together, he denigrates them by characterizing them as feminine: "'A couple of college pussies . . . Out behind them barracks hiding from everyone and making some love, huh?' He looked at Erik, 'You're a pussy, huh? You afraid to be in the war, a goddamn pussy, a goddamn lezzie?'" (47). O'Brien shows how the writing life, the world of literature and ideas that his characters so often long for, is frequently characterized as feminine, is associated with women and domesticity. Bobbi Haymore in *The Nuclear Age*, for instance, is a poet and flight attendant who represents for William Cowling a life that soars above the War. Martha, Jimmy Cross's not-quite-girlfriend back home in *The Things They Carried*, is an English major who writes movingly of Chaucer and Virginia Woolf in her letters to Jimmy. Linda, the 10-year-old girl with a brain tumor in the same collection, is associated with storytelling when she explains to Timmy that being dead is like being a book on a shelf that no one is reading.

This pull between a domestic life associated with literature and ideas and characterized largely as feminine, and a more traditionally masculine experience of war, is the main tension driving O'Brien's first published novel as well. In *Northern Lights* (1975), Paul Perry is torn between the warmth, domesticity, and security offered by his wife Grace, and the stern teachings and cold hardships advocated by his male forebears and symbolized by his more daring and adventurous younger brother Harvey, who goes to fight in the Vietnam War while Paul stays home. O'Brien's next two novels, *Going After Cacciato* (1978) and *The Nuclear Age* (1985) explore the very different reactions of two men drafted to serve in the War. Paul Berlin in *Cacciato* goes to the war, then tries to imagine his way out of it, while William Cowling in *Nuclear Age* evades the draft, eventually joining an underground political group that resists the war, albeit by using some of the same violent tactics that seem part of war itself. While the war themes in O'Brien's later novels, *Tomcat in Love* (1998) and *July, July* (2002) retreat at least partially to the background, readers still see some of the same concerns that appear in the earlier works. In *Tomcat* linguistics professor Thomas H. Chippering cannot leave his War experiences in Viet Nam—they follow him home in the form of six former Green Berets who stalk him across Minnesota, seeking revenge for Chippering's behavior during the War. While *July, July* depicts a wide range of characters, the Vietnam War affects many of them, particularly David Todd, who goes to the War and very nearly dies in a Viet Cong ambush along the Song Tra Bong, and Billy McMann, who flees to Canada and feels the separation from his friends and family for the next 30 years of his life. But this chapter focuses mostly on O'Brien's middle works—his trio of Vietnam War novels. It shows how the ethical values of the front lines versus the home front pull at his characters in these novels, from *Cacciato*'s Paul Berlin, who is a divided self, trying to imagine domestic peace in the midst of chaotic war, to *The Things They Carried*, which begins and ends with love stories to show how war and peace are intertwined, to *In the Lake of the Woods*, which shows how choices made on the front lines infect the domestic arena.

Going After Cacciato

Going After Cacciato is a complex book that explores a soldier's longing for peace, order, and domestic happiness in the midst of the chaos and violence of war. The novel's present time takes place on a night in late November 1968, as a young, frightened soldier named Paul Berlin sits watch in an observation post overlooking the South China Sea. During the long night, Berlin suppresses his frightening war memories of the previous 5 months as he imagines a detailed story in which his squad pursues a deserting soldier, Cacciato, all the way from the jungles and rice paddies of Viet Nam to the streets of Paris. Like Paul Perry in O'Brien's previous novel, *Northern Lights*, who is torn between domesticity and a more traditionally masculine life, Paul Berlin is a divided character. His very name, with its allusions to the German city divided following World War II into a communist East and a democratic West, suggests the divisions in Berlin's psyche, whose imagined story of chasing Cacciato allows him to explore the pull between building a domestic life away from war and the traditional obligations that tie him to war.

Like many of O'Brien's characters, Paul Berlin is a young soldier drafted into the War who wants desperately to behave honorably, but who struggles to live up to traditional standards of masculine bravery. As his night on the observation tower unfolds, readers realize that Berlin has been unable to control his fear during his 5 months at war. His most recent war memory, the late October desertion of Cacciato, concludes with Berlin losing control of himself during an attempted ambush of the AWOL soldier. Berlin panics during the operation, wildly shooting off his rifle, urinating on himself, and shaking with fear. The story that Berlin spins out in his mind during the late November night on the observation post is an attempt to rewrite this incident—Berlin imagines that the pursuit of Cacciato did not end with the failed ambush, but that Third Squad actually followed Cacciato all the way across Viet Nam, into Laos, Burma, India, Afghanistan, Turkey, Iran, Greece, and finally into Paris. But try as he might, Paul Berlin cannot banish his frightening war experiences from his made-up story. His real war memories, especially the most shameful and repressed of these memories, continually work their way into and shape Berlin's imagined pursuit story.

Most disturbing to Berlin are two memories that completely undermine traditional notions of male heroics in wartime. The first, described by Berlin's platoon mates as the "ultimate war story" (*Going After Cacciato* 203), involves the death of a young soldier named Billy Boy Watkins, who, during Paul Berlin's first taste of combat, experienced a heart attack after being shot in the foot. Said to have "died of fright on the field of battle" (208), Billy Boy brings home to Paul Berlin what could happen to him if he cannot control his fear. Berlin's most deeply hidden war memory, though, is his implication in the fragging death of the platoon's commanding officer, Lieutenant Sidney Martin, an event so horrendous and so contrary to Berlin's received notions of cowardice and bravery that portions of the incident remain repressed in his memory. Readers see the small group of soldiers plotting the murder, platoon sergeant Oscar Johnson claiming that it is an act of self-preservation. Lieutenant Martin, a stickler for standard operating procedure, had insisted the men search Viet Cong tunnels before blowing them up, a dangerous endeavor that has already killed two of Berlin's fellow soldiers. Readers find out as well that a new commanding officer, Lieutenant Corson, is sent to replace Martin after a "sad thing" happens to Martin in Lake Country. But readers never see Martin's actual death. The fragging, described in chapter 34, "Lake Country," ends with Sidney Martin's hands showing at the lip of the tunnel and the officer pulling himself up and out, even though all indications elsewhere in the book suggest that the men threw a grenade down the tunnel, murdering Martin. The actual fragging runs so counter to romanticized, sanitized depictions of war, especially prevalent in World War II films, that Berlin cannot face it; his imagination intrudes, masking the reality of what happened to Martin.

Berlin is haunted by the ghosts of World War II—the so-called good war—in which there seemed to be a moral imperative to fight and in which the military enjoyed widespread support at home. Tim O'Brien's own parents were World War II veterans, his father a member of the Naval Reserve who saw duty in the Pacific and his mother a WAVE (Women Accepted for Volunteer Emergency Service). In his memoir, O'Brien remembers playing World War II games as a child, he and his friends pretending to be their fathers, "taking on the Japs and Krauts along the shores of Lake Okabena" (*If I Die* 12). In *Cacciato*, Berlin's father is a World War II veteran as well. While he does not appear much in the novel, he is nevertheless a key figure, often serving in Berlin's imagination as both listener and judge to his son's Vietnam War experiences. Just as Berlin's father steered Paul through the Iowa woods of his childhood, Berlin views his father as a guide through the wilderness of Viet Nam. Paul frequently remembers his father's advice to keep his head down, to learn from experience, and to notice the good things that will happen in the midst of the devastation of war. But Berlin also imagines himself justifying his actions to his father—explaining how he almost won the Silver Star and arguing that he never truly "joined" the other men in his platoon (210), a special pleading that suggests his guilt about the fragging death of Lieutenant Sydney Martin. Berlin's father also plays an important role since he bridges the gap between traditional expectations of male bravery in war and the domesticity most often associated with women. The elder Berlin has both successfully fought in a war and returned home to build houses in Fort Dodge, Iowa. Also, building a home is something that Paul longs to do. As the older man tells his son, the houses he builds will be "strong and lasting" since they are made from "good materials and good craftsmanship and care" (48), values that directly oppose the waste, destruction, and carelessness associated with war.

Berlin's longing to live out a domestic alternative to war, to build homes rather than destroy them, is most fully expressed through his imaginative creation of Sarkin Aung Wan, a young, half-Chinese, half-Vietnamese war refugee, who meets up with Third Squad while fleeing the destruction of her family and home. Despite Berlin's inability to enter the mind of an actual young Vietnamese girl whom Doc Peret treats for facial sores—"did she feel, as he did, goodness and warmth and poignancy . . . did the girl *like* him? . . . what *did* she want?" (262)—in his imagination, Berlin can shape the girl into his ally, in the invented form of Sarkin Aung Wan. While critics such as Renny Christopher and Kalí Tal have critiqued O'Brien's portrait of Sarkin as reflecting stereotypes of Asian women, it is important to remember that Sarkin is an invention of Paul Berlin's imagination, and Berlin, after all, is a 22-year-old young man raised in a small town in America in the 1950s, with all the attendant gender expectations accompanying that era. In Sarkin, Berlin can explore his own desires to escape war and build a home by projecting them onto an imagined female and racial other. He imagines Sarkin as an Ariadne figure, leading the members of Third Squad from war to peace after they have fallen into a labyrinthine underground tunnel system along the road to Paris. Sarkin tells the men that in order to escape the maze, they need to "fall out"— military lingo for breaking formation. The soldiers follow her through the myriad, confusing pathways that represent the entanglements of war, up through piles of "sewage, through deepening sludge" (111)—language that anticipates the "shit field" of war where Kiowah dies in *The Things They Carried*—out of a manhole cover, and onto the streets of Mandalay, in Burma: "Civilization" (112) in Berlin's imagination. In what is clearly a rebirth scene, Sarkin acts as midwife, suggesting Berlin's own longing to leave the War behind and also his anxieties about behaving in a way that would be perceived by others as nonmasculine, as cowardly.

In his imagined story, Berlin seems to both long for and fear physical intimacy with Sarkin. Rather than inventing a full-fledged sexual relationship, he imagines the girl performing small, intimate services for him such as scrubbing the "caked filth from beneath [his] nails," which he describes as "chipping away at the war" (115). There is a sense that Berlin wants to keep Sarkin innocent, untouched, untainted. In this way, Sarkin can represent a female world separate from the War—a more innocent, uncorrupted world—at the same time that her family's tragedy and displacement, both caused by the War, give her the experiences that allow her to understand Berlin's own wartime suffering. The novel will later question Berlin's simplistic notions of an uncorrupted civilian world when the men of Third Squad witness the beheading of a young soldier in Tehran. Doc Peret pointedly tells Berlin to "*watch this shit*," since it is part of Berlin's "fine expedition to Paris," his imagined "Civilization" (186). The notion of two separate worlds—an untainted home front set apart from the ugly world of war—is hopelessly naïve, as Doc angrily points out.

Nevertheless, Berlin's invention of the young refugee allows him to play out his fantasy of domestic tranquility, of building a home like his father does back in Iowa. When, in Berlin's make-believe story, the squad finally makes it to Paris, he and Sarkin go house-hunting. Paris, the City of Lights, looms in the Western imagination as the civilized antithesis to the jungles and rice paddies of Viet Nam. Not only is Paris a symbol of the worldly, decadent pleasures that contrast the deprivations of war, but also, historically, Paris suggests the possibility for peace in several ways. The city, triumphantly liberated from Nazi control by the Allies during World War II, also points to the French disentanglement from their own costly and disastrous war in Viet Nam, as well as serving as the location of secret peace talks between the Americans and North Vietnamese beginning in the summer of 1968. Paris, with its connotations of peace and civilization, functions as the ideal city for Berlin to conclude his fantasy of escaping war and entering into domestic harmony: "In Paris, where it ended, it was right to fall in love, and so he did" (294). He imagines that he and Sarkin rent a World War II era apartment in the heart of the city and shop together for rugs and furnishings, Sarkin at one point pointing out to Paul that it is "better to hunt apartments than people" (301).

Yet Paul cannot simply and completely leave the war behind, even in his imagination. Soon after renting the apartment, he learns from a platoon mate of the death of former World War II general and US President, Dwight D. Eisenhower. When Sarkin asks him who Eisenhower was, Berlin replies, "Nobody . . . a hero" (303). Berlin's divided self is evident here. He understands that playing house with Sarkin shuts the door to his dreams of traditional, masculine wartime heroism, and he is not fully willing to make this concession. The contradictions evident in Berlin's imagined version of Sarkin Aung Wan finally prove too much for him to sustain. In a climactic scene near the end of the novel that mimics the Paris Peace Accords of the early 1970s, Berlin imagines himself and Sarkin trading arguments about whether Berlin should flee the War or remain. Sarkin urges Paul Berlin to step into his dreams, to make concrete his longing for peace, and to leave the War in reality, not just in his imagination. But Berlin, echoing Socrates in *The Crito*, responds that he has obligations to his family and country and fellow soldiers to stay at the War. This scene clearly partakes in the type of moral philosophy that O'Brien believes marks good literature—what happens when moral values of seemingly equal merit come into conflict? Berlin, the novel suggests, makes his choice and returns to the War. The novel ends back in Viet Nam, after the failed ambush of Cacciato. That night, the narrator tells us, "Paul Berlin slept. There were no dreams" (336).

It might be easy, on the one hand, to suggest that Berlin makes the courageous choice in ending his imagined story and returning to the War. He is finally able to sleep deeply, perhaps comfortable with his decision. Yet O'Brien complicates the ending by having Berlin confess that, despite all his fine talk of honor and obligation, what he truly fears is exile—"the dread of abandoning all that I hold dear" (320)—as well as the shame of being thought a coward. Does the fact that "no dreams" interrupt Berlin's sleep suggest that he has given up on his imagination, on his attempt to dream a way out of war, to defy traditional gender expectations that associate masculinity with warrior prowess? As he will do in all of his works, O'Brien asks readers to question traditional assumptions about courage and war. He leaves us with a question: is it more courageous to stifle one's fear in order to fight in a war that one's family, friends, and country have committed themselves to? Or is it more courageous to use one's imagination to break away from traditions that have bound us into a culture of violence, to dream about a way out of war and into domestic harmony, and to work to make those dreams real?

The Things They Carried

Like O'Brien's earlier works, his 1990 collection, *The Things They Carried*, explores the quandary of how to behave morally in the face of an immoral war. Like those earlier works as well, *Things* frames the problem of ethical behavior in terms of domesticity versus a traditionally masculine warrior mentality. While a critic such as Lorrie Smith highlights her own discomfort as a female reader of the collection and argues that it resides comfortably "within a larger cultural project to rewrite the Vietnam War from a masculinist and strictly American perspective" (17), I contend that the book undermines traditional dichotomies by challenging the view that war is a closed world understood only by men. When the narrator of "How to Tell a True War Story" chastises an elderly woman for not properly listening to his story of Curt Lemon, Rat Kiley, and the baby water buffalo, he thinks to himself, "It *wasn't* a war story. It was a *love* story" (85). The narrator is referring specifically to the love that Rat had for his buddy Curt, but at the same time he is nodding to a larger entanglement of love and war that we see throughout the collection. *The Things They Carried* begins and ends with stories that are, at least on one level, love stories. It suggests that those back home, including women, can indeed begin to understand the "things men do" in wartime because the home front is not nearly as separate from the front lines as we might first imagine.

Daydreaming one's way out of war plays a pivotal role in *The Things They Carried*, just as it did in *Cacciato*. The book's title story, which opens the collection, begins with a description of Lieutenant Jimmy Cross lying in his foxhole in the early evening, pretending that a girl he knows back home, Martha, loves him more than she really does. For Jimmy, Martha represents the home front, another world untainted by war. In her letters, Martha writes about her favorite authors; she quotes lines of poetry, but she never mentions the War, as if speaking about it will actually summon it into being. Jimmy, in his daydreams, muses obsessively over whether or not Martha is a virgin, wanting her to both be and not be one at the same time. Cross's strange, forceful, yet tender fantasy, in which he carries Martha upstairs to her room, ties her to the bed, but then only touches her left knee all night long, illustrates his conflicting impulses. Like Paul Berlin in his Sarkin Aung Wan fantasies, Jimmy works hard to control his sexual desires, as if keeping Martha virginal in his imagination will also keep her untainted by the War, untouched by men and the "things men do" (21).

It is when the danger of the Vietnam War is at its worst that Jimmy Cross thinks most intensely about Martha. As Cross looks into the darkness of a Vietnamese tunnel, waiting for fellow soldier Lee Strunk to emerge, he worries about a cave-in. His intense longing to be elsewhere is manifested when he suddenly, "without willing it" (11), begins to think of Martha, who represents for Jimmy the purity of his prewar self. Desiring even "to sleep inside her lungs and breathe her blood and be smothered" (11), Cross wants to *become* Martha, to lose his wartime self completely. He imagines the two of them "buried under the white sand at the Jersey shore," pressed together so tightly that the "pebble in his mouth was her tongue" (12). The pebble is a gift sent by Martha to Jimmy in Viet Nam. When Cross carries the pebble in his mouth, he is able to feel as if he has overcome the home self/war self division he feels. Carrying Martha's token inside his physical body allows him to imaginatively return to New Jersey, where he feels light and carries nothing. Yet, as was the case with Paul Berlin and Sarkin Aung Wan, Jimmy's imagined version of Martha tells us more about Jimmy Cross's own wartime fears and anxieties than it does about Martha herself, a fact O'Brien underlines in the following story, "Love," in which readers discover that Martha becomes a trained nurse, completing service missions to Guatemala, Ethiopia, and Mexico.

For Jimmy, in any case, the panacea of Martha can only be temporary. When one of his platoon members, Ted Lavender, is shot by sniper fire while urinating, Cross blames himself: "He felt shame. He hated himself. He had loved Martha more than his men, and as a consequence Lavender was now dead, and this was something he would have to carry like a stone in his stomach for the rest of the war" (16). Martha's pebble has transformed into a stone of guilt, and Cross's reaction is to try to banish the home front, with its dreams of domestic tranquility, completely from the experience of war. In fact, as a direct response to Lavender's death, the men of Alpha Company burn and destroy Vietnamese homes: "After the chopper took Lavender away, Lieutenant Jimmy Cross led his men into the village of Than Khe. They burned everything. They shot chickens and dogs, they trashed the village well, they called in artillery and watched the wreckage..." (16). In O'Brien's works, the worst excesses of war and violence come about not when characters imagine home and family—Jimmy Cross is not really responsible for Lavender's death, which is a random event that could not have been prevented—but when they banish these thoughts from their minds. The men burn the village and Jimmy burns Martha's pictures as he resolves to become a no-nonsense officer in the future, to impose "strict field discipline" on the men in his charge, all the while "distancing himself" from them emotionally (25). Cross here embraces a traditionally patriarchal view of masculinity, in which things associated with women or with femininity are deemed weaknesses to overcome. An ominous future looms for this group of American soldiers and the Vietnamese civilians they encounter as the soldiers pack up and head west, where "they would do what they had always done" (24). Like Berlin in *Going After Cacciato*, Jimmy Cross suppresses his imagination and the result is a return to the violence of war.

Perhaps the story in the collection that most clearly explores the home front/front line divide is "Sweetheart of the Song Tra Bong," in which a young American medic arranges to bring his high school girlfriend to Viet Nam. When Mary Anne Bell first arrives in country, she easily fits the stereotype of the all-American girl-next-door, who is separate from and unaffected by the violence of war. Described as a "doll" and as a "cheerleader" (96), Mary Anne looks the part as well. With "long white legs and blue eyes and a complexion like strawberry ice cream" (93), the 17-year-old girl arrives in Viet Nam wearing a pink sweater and white culottes. But very quickly, Mary Anne begins to transgress boundaries of all kinds. She spends time with the ARVN soldiers whose camp lies along the perimeter of the American base; she insists on visiting the Viet Cong-controlled village at the foot of the hill; and, unafraid to get her hands dirty, she learns to assist at surgery and to shoot and care for an M-16 rifle. As she becomes more accustomed to life at Tra Bong, Mary Anne begins to question the earlier dream of domestic bliss she had shared with her boyfriend, Mark Fossie: the "fine gingerbread house near Lake Erie," the "three healthy, yellow-haired children" (94). While O'Brien's male characters frequently disrupt traditional masculine gender expectations by dreaming of domestic tranquility in the midst of war, Mary Anne does the opposite. She embraces the masculine world of war, eventually rejecting her former dreams of domesticity. But banishing the domestic world does not have happy consequences for Mary Anne any more than it does for O'Brien's male characters.

Although Mary Anne and Mark originally "set up house" (94) in one of the bunkers along the perimeter of the camp, Mary Anne deserts this play home one night, leaving Mark behind. Mary Anne's body has changed, grown "stiff in places . . . firm where the softness used to be," and her voice has "reorganized itself at a lower pitch" (99). Meanwhile, Mark, bewildered and devastated by Mary Anne's absence, is described in terms similar to those initially used for Mary Anne—"tall and blond," "a nice kid," "good-hearted" (100). The sweethearts have swapped gender roles at this point. Mary Anne's transformation from the domestic realm to the world of war seems complete when she is found in the tent of six Green Beret soldiers, shadowy figures who live at the border of the medical detachment. When Mark, along with Eddie Diamond and Rat Kiley, burst into the Greenies' bunker, they discover Mary Anne amid a horrific scene—piles of bones and animal skins, candles, incense, an appalling, animal stench—but most disturbing of all is Mary Anne herself, singing in an incomprehensible, high voice in "a language beyond translation" (112), and wearing a grotesque necklace of human tongues. When Mary Anne tells Mark Fossie and Rat Kiley that they are in a place "where [they] don't belong" (111), she is perhaps more right than she knows. Her statement raises questions about the very presence of Americans in Viet Nam. Mary Anne's necklace of tongues—which presumably come from dead Vietnamese bodies—suggests the imperialist project of silencing the Vietnamese completely. This chilling scene demonstrates that war violence is not simply a masculine prerogative, that the boundaries between home front and front lines are more permeable than the men had imagined.

While Jimmy Cross, in the opening story, attempts to banish Martha completely from his mind, since "imagination was a killer" (11), O'Brien offers a different thesis about the imagination in the final story of the collection. "The Lives of the Dead" mingles memories of narrator O'Brien's worst experiences at the War—American soldiers shaking the hand of an aged, dead Vietnamese farmer propped up in a pigpen; gathering enemy KIAs and loading their mangled bodies into the back of a truck—with the tale of 9-year-old Linda, the narrator's fourth-grade girlfriend, who died of a brain tumor. The story opens with a line that sounds as if the narrator is in the midst of a debate with someone: "But this too is true: stories can save us" (225). With its focus on the redemptive power of the imagination, this opening line can be read as a counterargument to the claim in the initial story that imagination is a killer. Stories, the narrator points out, can be a way of fighting death, of bringing the dead back to life: "in a story, which is a kind of dreaming, the dead sometimes smile and sit up and return to the world" (225). The powerful status of fiction, of the imagination, is perhaps nowhere so well illustrated as in the plot of the movie that 9-year-old Timmy attends on his date with Linda: *The Man Who Never Was*. In the film, the Allies plant false documents on the body of a dead British soldier to mislead the Germans about the site of the upcoming landings in Europe. "The Germans find the documents," O'Brien writes, and "the deception wins the war" (232). The dead soldier's fictional identity is more influential than his actual, biographical identity, which is never revealed.

The power of story, the "illusion of aliveness" (230) that a story can create, is something that O'Brien elaborated on in an interview given right before the book was published:

> What I discovered in the course of writing this book is the reason I love story; not just for its titillation, its instant gratification of what next, what next, but for the livingness that's there as you read and that lingers afterward. Jake Barnes is alive for me. Though he is a fictional character in the taxicab at the end of *The Sun Also Rises*, he is alive in that cab with Brett. That's what I love about writing them and reading them—that quality of immortality that a story is—doesn't contain—just is. (Coffey 60–61)

O'Brien's belief in the power of stories becomes an admonishment to readers who fail to see connections between war experience and larger, more general life experiences. In "The Lives of the Dead," O'Brien deliberately juxtaposes traumatic war deaths with the traumatic death of Linda in order to undermine the old cliché of Vietnam War fiction: "if you weren't there, you can't possibly understand." As he argues in his moving 1994 essay, "The Vietnam in Me," anyone can experience what it is like to be on "wartime," which "is the time we're all on at one point or another: when fathers die, when husbands ask for divorce, when women you love are fast asleep beside men you wish were you . . . You don't have to be in Nam to be in Nam" (55).

The opening and closing stories that frame the collection, both love stories mingled with war stories, serve as the beginning and ending points of an argument that develops throughout the book. We begin with Jimmy Cross's view that the world of women and memories of domestic harmony can have no place in war, that women will never be able to understand "the things men do" in wartime, that the home front and the front lines must remain separate and distinct. But as the book progresses, this initial hypothesis is questioned. The narrator in "On the Rainy River" cannot refuse to go to war because his hometown ties and obligations weigh so heavily on him. In "How to Tell a True War Story," the narrator concludes that, "in the end, of course, a true war story is never about war. It's about sunlight . . . It's about love and memory. It's about sorrow. It's about sisters who never write back and people who never listen" (85). In "Sweetheart of the Song Tra Bong," the boundary lines separating the domestic realm from the War can be more easily transgressed than the soldiers would like to think. Finally, O'Brien chooses to conclude his collection with the story about Linda—a tale that takes place long before his War experiences—to show the connection between war experience and human experience in general. While Kiowa is dumbfounded that the dead old Vietnamese man in the pigpen, whom the soldiers in Alpha Company shake hands with, reminds the narrator of a girl he used to know, his first date in fact, readers see that the experience of death and trauma is not exclusive to war. All human beings will have to face sorrow and loss during their lives. It is a mistake to think that war can be compartmentalized as an experience completely apart from "the world," as many American soldiers referred to the home front during their stints in the Vietnam War, unknowable and incomprehensible to those back home. It is a mistake as well to think that soldiers can have separate selves, a war self and a domestic self.

In the Lake of the Woods

John Wade, in O'Brien's 1994 novel, *In the Lake of the Woods*, is a veteran who mistakenly believes that he can leave his war self behind when he returns to Minnesota after serving two tours of duty in Viet Nam. An ambitious politician who has held the office of Lieutenant Governor for 6 years, Wade has also worked diligently to conceal his involvement in the My Lai massacre of 1968. But both Wade's professional and personal lives come crashing down around him when his war past is exposed during his US Senate campaign. After suffering a humiliating election defeat, Wade and his wife, Kathy, retreat to a cabin in the remote woods of northern Minnesota to recover. When Kathy mysteriously disappears a few days later, suspicion immediately falls on Wade, but the novel offers several other possibilities for what might have happened to Kathy, stubbornly refusing to supply readers with a definite solution to the mystery of her disappearance. Did she, horrified and dismayed by the revelations of John's involvement in My Lai, leave of her own accord, taking the cabin's old Evinrude motorboat out into the lake where she either became hopelessly lost or else took her own life? Did John, fearful that Kathy might leave him and unable to bear her disappointment in him after the My Lai revelations, knowingly murder his wife and hide his act? Or perhaps John killed Kathy in a psychologically incoherent state of rage and did not even remember the atrocity he committed, accustomed as he was to denying and hiding, even to himself, the uglier parts of his life? Or is the disappearance of Kathy, and later of John himself, part of a magic trick, a "double consummation" (192) that John performed on both his "lovely assistant" and himself? In other words, did John and Kathy plan their disappearance together as a way to leave their old identities behind and start anew? Whichever solution readers find the most convincing, this novel clearly shows how the home front and the front lines are inextricably mingled together; how one's home life affects one's experiences in war; and how war experiences, in turn, infect the domestic realm.

A novel that is, in many ways, about the human inability to get at truth, *Lake* is narrated by an unnamed reporter/investigator who is himself a Vietnam War veteran. This narrator has spent 4 years investigating Kathy's disappearance, assembling evidence, and formulating hypotheses about what happened at the remote cabin in the woods and what made John Wade the man he turned out to be. Was it his childhood and family life before the War that made John Wade capable of wartime atrocities? Or was it the War that shaped him and destroyed his later domestic life with Kathy? This turns out to be a chicken and egg question. The novel provides good evidence that John Wade's domestic experiences affected his wartime self and that, in turn, his wartime experiences affected his domestic self. As the narrator in "The Lives of the Dead" observes, "the human life is all one thing" (*The Things They Carried* 236). Or, as John's mother observes in a quote from the second evidence chapter, "It wasn't just the war that made him what he was. That's too easy. It was everything—his whole *nature*" (*Lake* 27). The alcoholism and death by suicide of John's father when John was only 14 surely shaped his life in irreversible ways. It is after his father's death that John's earlier fascination with magic begins to be more than a hobby. John does "tricks in his mind" (31), using the mirrors inside his head to pretend that his father is still with him. Losing his father at such a young age seems to lend to the insecurity John feels at college when he begins to date Kathy. The "trick" John desperately wants to perform at this point is to "make her love him and never stop," an urgency that is born from fear: "he didn't want to lose her" (32). John even begins to spy on Kathy, following her surreptitiously around campus, desperate to gain access to her private life, her true self, in much the same way that the narrator is desperate to gain access to Wade's hidden psyche.

These childhood and early adulthood experiences in Minnesota contribute to the soldier John Wade becomes in Viet Nam. Pleased to be part of a group for the first in his life, John adopts the identity of "Sorcerer" at the War, exploiting his new mystique by demonstrating certain tricks that could be done "with his jackknife and a corpse" (38). After a sergeant named Reinhart is shot dead by sniper fire, John, filled with a rage reminiscent of what he felt at his father's funeral, a "force so violent it seemed to pick him up by the shoulders" (40), seems to almost leave his own body as he glides through the brush, behind the enemy position, and shoots the sniper in the face; "Later, the men in Charlie Company couldn't stop talking about Sorcerer's new trick" (40). That night, the American soldiers summon an audience of villagers at gunpoint to witness yet another trick performed by Sorcerer and his assistants: "an act of levitation" (41), as the dead man's body is hoisted into the trees to serve as a warning to the watching villagers. The death of John's father, his spying on Kathy in college, and his behavior in Viet Nam are intertwined experiences. All are connected with a fear of loss, with feelings of helplessness and rage in response to that fear, and with a performing of "tricks" in an attempt to overcome the helplessness.

Readers see the mingling of the front lines and home front as well in the letters that John writes home to Kathy from the War. The novel's narrator emphasizes the intertwining of the two realms when he writes that, before John and Kathy could get married, "there was Vietnam, where John Wade killed people, and where he composed long letters full of observations about the nature of their love" (61). The two activities—killing people and writing about love—are expressed as part of the same clause of a single sentence, suggesting a disturbing relationship between war and domesticity. In addition, John interprets what he sees in the War in domestic terms, imagining a pair of snakes he had seen along a trail near Pinkville, each eating the other's tail, not as a metaphor for the destructive appetites of imperialism, nor for the futility of war, but as a symbol of how his love for Kathy feels to him: "like we're swallowing each other up ... one plus one equals zero" (61). While in the midst of war Paul Berlin imagines building a home, a domestic space, John Wade imagines the terror of war into the domestic realm.

Even more, when John returns home, he brings the war along with him. Just as John's childhood shapes his war self, his experiences in Viet Nam shape his later, domestic life. As Sorcerer, during the War, John is surrounded by secrets. For him, as for many American soldiers, Viet Nam seems a mysterious, unknowable land: "a place with secret trapdoors and tunnels and underground chambers populated by various spooks and goblins" (72). An ethnocentric view that reflects the lack of knowledge among American soldiers (and among many American politicians) about the country's geography and history, this sense of mystery about the land and people of Viet Nam was only abetted by the secretive and dishonest way the War was prosecuted by the American government. As the narrator/reporter figure of *Lake* writes, "The war itself was a mystery. Nobody knew what it was about, or why they were there, or who started it, or who was winning, or how it might end ... History was a secret. The land was a secret" (73). Of course, "Sorcerer had his own secrets," the most serious of which was his participation in the My Lai massacre, an event "so secret that he sometimes kept it secret from himself" (73). Two months before the end of his second tour of duty, John procures a desk job in the battalion adjutant's office, where he carefully rewrites the historical record to erase himself from Charlie Company, the unit responsible for the tragedy, and reassign himself to Alpha Company. The rewritten paperwork, he expects, will, over time, erase "memory itself" (269). The novel's later recounting of previous American wartime atrocities, from the Revolution to the Indian Wars, suggests a secret history connecting the My Lai massacre to events from America's past and countering the view that My Lai was simply an anomaly, a dark, and grisly aberration in the story of America. Domestic and international politics merge as the atrocities of the Vietnam War are presented not simply as historical aberrations occurring in a country on the other side of the world but as growing directly out of the hidden sins of America's past.

Nor does John leave his penchant for secrecy or his identity as Sorcerer behind when he leaves the War. In fact, he reverts to Sorcerer while still on the airplane over North Dakota on his way home to the Twin Cities, winking at his reflection in the lavatory mirror: "'Hey Sorcerer,' he murmured. 'How's tricks?'" (41). Also it is Sorcerer, not John, who follows Kathy for two nights at the University of Minnesota before making his presence known to her. Ominously, it is Sorcerer as well who responds to Kathy's assertion that she knows she and John will be happy in their new, married life: "Sorcerer laughed and carried her inside. The trick then was to be vigilant . . . The secrets would remain secret—the things he'd seen, the things he'd done" (46). Most disturbing of all is the possibility that John may have been reliving his worst memories of the War the night Kathy died. Whether John actually murdered Kathy or not, it seems incontrovertible that on the night of her disappearance he was living on war time. The narrator imagines John boiling the plants, the jungles of Viet Nam evoked as the room acquires a "damp exotic stink" (50). He imagines as well John taking on the identity of Sorcerer, as he "glides" around the room, muttering the phrase, "Kill Jesus." While much about what happened that night remains pure speculation, Sheriff Lux does find the telephone wrapped in a dishtowel and stowed under the sink, the houseplants steamed to death, and the teakettle on the stove. Also Kathy's sister, Patricia Hood, confirms in interviews that Kathy had confided to her John's trouble sleeping—that "he'd wake up screaming sometimes. Foul language . . ." (29). Critic Bruce Franklin, in fact, argues that the novel is not as unresolved as it might initially seem, that the midnight boil scenario is clearly the most plausible of the hypotheses the narrator presents, partly because it is the only theory presented in non-hypothesis chapters. Just as America tried its best to cover up and forget about My Lai, Franklin argues, readers, uncomfortable with the horror of Wade's murder of his wife, choose other, less terrible scenarios to explain Kathy's disappearance ("Kicking the Denial").

Yet perhaps what Bruce Franklin overlooks in his otherwise persuasive argument that the novel is about denial is the narrator/investigator's early footnote cautioning that even much of what looks like fact in the book is actually "a diligent but still imaginative reconstruction of events" (*Lake* 30). In all of Tim O'Brien's work, historical truth is elusive. While the hypothesis chapters are clearly marked as such, it is important to remember that the entire novel, just like *The Things They Carried*, is controlled by a specific narrative voice, by a writer who is interpreting and shaping the history that he presents to readers. Also this narrator must finally admit that John Wade is "beyond knowing. He's an other" (101). As much as he would like to "force entry into another heart ... to perform miracles of knowing," we are left with "the implacable otherness of others" (101). The best the narrator can do, then, is to tell a story, or in this case, multiple stories, about what might have happened to John and Kathy Wade and let readers draw their own conclusions. But this concession is not meant to be seen as a failure. As the narrator writes in *The Things They Carried*, "story-truth is truer sometimes than happening-truth" (179).

While *In the Lake of the Woods* is a novel about secrets, about war, about love, about the intertwining of the home front and the front lines, it is also a novel that, like *Things* and *Cacciato*, is a metafictional meditation on the nature of storytelling. O'Brien's wartime novels are all books about the creative powers of the human imagination, about our ability to access truth, and, especially, to communicate trauma. In each novel, he uses metafictive techniques to explore the power of narrative to shape reality. In a recent interview with the *Austin American-Statesman*, O'Brien explains that what's driven him as a writer for so many years "isn't the desire to describe war. It's the opposite. It's peace" (Buchholz D1). If we are going to find new ways of thinking about the world and its problems, O'Brien suggests, we need to find new stories to tell. That is not to say that this is an easy thing to do. Each novel in the trio explored here is at least somewhat ambiguous about the efficacy of narrative. Paul Berlin suffers from a failure of the imagination at the end of *Cacciato*, and while the final story of *The Things They Carried* seems to celebrate imaginative powers as it offers the conclusion "stories can save us" (225), readers had been warned earlier that they should not feel "rectitude" or moral uplift at the end of a true war story (68). Finally, the mystery of Kathy Wade's disappearance in *Lake* is deliberately unsolvable. The recurring image of mirrors in the novel suggests that the reader's choice of solution to the mystery reflects back on ourselves, ultimately telling us more about who we are than about what really happened to John and Kathy Wade. But this outward turn reflects as well O'Brien's larger purpose of storytelling as moral philosophy—as readers we must ask ourselves about the sources and implications of the moral values that both we ourselves and our society hold dear. Is it possible to imagine ourselves out of war and into peace through the stories we tell? O'Brien's War novels challenge traditional masculine stereotypes associated with war and warrior culture as well as traditional feminine stereotypes that completely remove women from the world of war and war literature. But perhaps even more important, over and over again his works show that imagination and storytelling, often associated with the feminine and perceived to have no place in the masculine realm of war, must work alongside history if we are to get at the truth of past experiences and imagine a future that leads us away from war.

6

The ghost that won't be exorcised: Larry Heinemann's *Paco's Story*

Stacey Peebles

The announcement of the winner of the 1987 National Book Award was, for some, provocative. The nominees included heavy hitters such as Philip Roth and Alice McDermott, and many expected that Toni Morrison's lyric memorial to slavery's horrors, *Beloved*, would walk away the winner. Instead, however, Larry Heinemann won for *Paco's Story*, a raw, jittery novel about a man trying to get out from under the Vietnam War experience that is written on his psyche and on his skin. "What happened?" asked Michiko Kakutani in the *New York Times*, wondering if the jury "went out of its way" to give a less popular nominee a break. Although Kakutani calls *Paco's Story* a "well-crafted" and "often admirable" novel, she also argues that it "avoid[s] dealing with many of the troubling political and moral ambiguities raised by the war," and falls far short of *Beloved*, which is a "work of mature imagination—a magisterial and deeply moving meditation not only on the cruelties of a single institution, but on family, history, and love" (n.p.). Jack Miles, among others, took Kakutani to task for attributing her own bias to others and for the condescension apparent in her piece, noting too that Kakutani could just have easily wondered about the other excellent nominated books.

If Kakutani's article was wrong-headed, it is true that *Beloved* has only grown in reputation since its publication, and also that Morrison's novel and *Paco's Story* make an intriguing pair. Although the two novels differ in their focus on female and male characters, respectively, they each feature a protagonist who is quite literally scarred and haunted by an American institution—slavery, for Sethe, and the Vietnam War, for Paco. These two novels, closely associated by the Book Award controversy and their focus on the physical and psychological legacy of violent experience, differ in what they suggest about the possibilities for healing and for exorcising the ghosts. *Paco's Story* emerges as the bleaker portrait, one in which any kind of community proves to be a fragmenting rather than a sustaining force. It is a portrait of Vietnam as irrecuperable trauma, a ghost that cannot be exorcised—and one that has, in turn, haunted Americans' more recent wars.

Trauma is, of course, endemic to experiences like war and slavery, and part of the project of trauma studies as a field has been to draw attention to the ways that trauma and recovery have been portrayed in works of art. Although much of trauma studies has focused on soldiers' and civilians' responses to war, a significant branch of the field grew out of feminist theory and the women's liberation movement, and originally sought to bring to light women's narratives of rape, sexual assault, and general oppression. (More recent studies in this vein include those by Suzette Henke, Deborah Horvitz, and Laurie Vickroy, in which they explore issues of voicing trauma in the work of authors like Leslie Marmon Silko, Charlotte Perkins Gilman, Colette, and, appropriately, Toni Morrison.) The 1970s saw women's issues taken up more prominently by politicians, artists, and scholars alike as well as an increasing awareness of how trauma could be medically delineated as post-traumatic stress disorder, or PTSD. Trauma became more widely acknowledged as an effect of experiences like rape, oppression, and combat. In this same period, the immediate aftermath of the Vietnam War, the condition previously called shell shock, soldier's heart, or battle fatigue became known as PTSD.

Jonathan Shay shows how art can reflect the realities of combat trauma in his study *Achilles in Vietnam: Combat Trauma and the Undoing of Character* (1994), which identifies strong connections between the oral narratives of Vietnam veterans and Achilles' story as told in the *Iliad*. For Shay, the profound and debilitating emotional reactions that soldiers can experience when betrayed by a leader, for instance, or when they lose a close comrade are evident in war stories from antiquity and modernity alike.[1] But trauma studies' most influential text is Judith Herman's *Trauma and Recovery* (1992), which draws together considerations of trauma across gender lines, addressing rape, combat, and political terror. Herman explains traumatic response as a series of dialectics: the desire to deny the event competes with the need to tell the story, and the feeling of being numb contrasts with the feeling of reliving the event in question. Like Shay, Herman emphasizes the construction of a personal narrative as the crucial element in the healing process; thus the "work of reconstruction actually transforms the traumatic memory, so that it can be integrated into the survivor's life story" (175). Also like Shay, Herman recognizes the utmost importance of community in aiding that personal reconstruction: "Those who have survived learn that their sense of self, of worth, of humanity, depends upon a feeling of connection to others ... Trauma isolates; the group re-creates a sense of belonging ... Trauma dehumanizes the victim; the group restores her humanity" (214).

Both *Paco's Story* and *Beloved* depict the aftermath of severe trauma that has created complicated questions about responsibility and poses particular challenges—of differing surmountability—to the possibility of finding a sustaining community in which to reconstruct and continue one's personal narrative. Heinemann and Morrison portray past traumas as physically present for the protagonists in the form of scars and ghosts, though ultimately the female community of *Beloved* is able to alleviate those old wounds while the male community of *Paco's Story* only exacerbates the problem, suggesting quite different conclusions from these two authors about the potential for redemption. In its bleak portrait of unhealed trauma and of unsustainable, unsustaining community in the wake of the Vietnam War, *Paco's Story* is a significant touchstone in literature of war and trauma, one with continued relevance in light of more recent representations of war. Particularly in the images from Abu Ghraib, the ghost of the Vietnam War is still evident, leaving its trace digitally as well as on minds and bodies.

Paco's trauma

Paco's Story opens with a denial: "Let's begin with the first clean fact, James: This ain't no war story" (3). War stories are "out," the reader is told, because people believe them boring, "a geek-monster species of evil-ugly rumor." According to some, folks "do not want to hear about Alpha Company—us grunts—busting jungle and busting cherries from Landing Zone Skator-Gator to Scat Man Do (wherever *that* is), humping and *hauling ass* all the way" (5). The story is narrated by these grunts, the men of Alpha Company who were all killed—except for Paco—by an airstrike on Fire Base Harriette. Some people think that folks do not want to hear about all this, they repeatedly insist. Some people think that the boring tedium of guard duty, the subtleties of USO entertainment, and most of all, the air attack that vaporized everyone but Paco make for dull storytelling, but these ghosts keep on talking nonetheless, telling the tale with verbose energy and urgency. In the world of the novel, regardless of those "other folks" who would ignore what they have to say, the ghosts command the stage and the listener's ear. You are special, they imply—you are listening. You get it. You can hear what is really out there, like their screams. Those screams that "burst through the ozone" at the moment of attack are not fading but rather are "rattling all over God's ever-loving Creation like a BB in a boxcar, only louder" (17).

These ghosts' voice persists, screaming up from death and narrating the book in a jazzlike, slangy patter that does not shy away from the ugly details of violence, injury, or tedious labor. Paco, in contrast, is quiet. His story is told by the ghosts, who, in a chapter titled "God's Marvelous Plan," describe Paco's searing day-and-a-half wait for help after the attack. "Our man Paco," as they call him, is "not dead but sure as shit should be," lying in the muck and the hot sun, feeling pain that "tick[s] like a living thing, until he comes to understand it as a living thing, as if some small animal with bristling, matted fur had crawled up to him for warmth" (18–19). He grows delirious in the sun, unable even to raise his arm to shade his eyes, and the ghosts describe the insects drawn by his stench: "big black deerflies and tiny translucent maggots, small gnats with bites like hard mean pinches, which immediately become stinging welts, raw and infected, drawing pus at the least touch" (19). Paco is such a horrible sight when help finally does come that it utterly undoes the battle-hardened medic. That man is "revolted, defeated," and has a heart attack later that night. The next morning, he quits, but like the ghosts, he cannot leave Paco behind. Years later, over and over in a bar the medic tells the story of finding Paco, lingering over the terrible epiphany Paco represented; as the ghosts put it, "it was as if he saw the sheer, manifest ugliness—the blunt and pervasive, raw and stupefying ugliness—of that place for the first time. And he was suddenly, finally, ready to admit that no matter what he did or how much, it was never enough" (27–28).

Paco's story is told by many others, but it is also told by his own body—his aches and pains, the medications he has to take, and the scars that envelop him and mark the sites of shrapnel and stitches, scabs and sores, the places where "filthy debris" had penetrated him, festering in his wounds until medics picked out the pieces of cloth, wood, and burnt skin (45). If the ghosts' story is oral but disembodied, Paco himself is wholly embodied, a text without much of a voice at all. His body "tingles and thrums with a glowing, suffocating uncomfortability that is more or less the permanent condition of his waking life" (36–37). He drags that heavy text through a town called Boone, which is as far as his bus fare will take him, looking for work. The book never specifies where Boone is located, and the town remains as vaguely unspecific as Paco himself, whose last name, Sullivan, is revealed late in the story and without commentary about what this combination of names might suggest about his background or ethnicity.

Paco says little, his body and mind haunted by his war experiences, and others react to him as if he is already a ghost himself. When he walks into Mr. Elliot's small store, the elderly man "looks at Paco silhouetted like an apparition" and falls headlong into his own memory of the Russian revolution in 1917. "There is something about the expansive timbre of Paco's voice, something about his physical presence—the old man feels Paco loom in the doorway light. And suddenly the old man is overcome by an upwelling of feeling that unleashes a deluge of memories going back fifty years and more" (73). Paco finally finds work as a dishwasher at the Texas Lunch, owned by Ernest Monroe, who is also moved to tell Paco about his service as a World War II Marine on Guadalcanal and Iwo Jima, an experience he categorizes as a "sloppy, bloody butt-fuck" (128). Even Jesse, a drifter and fellow Vietnam War vet who stops in for a meal, tells his own long story. It is a moment when Paco, unusually, breaks his silence to reveal that "Doctors told me I was the only one of ninety-three guys" (162–163). He might even have said more, but Jesse's openness comes at the cost of constant motion, it seems, and so he has to leave. Although the ghosts go into excruciating detail about Paco's "slashing lacerations, big watery burn blisters, and broken, splintered, *ruined* legs," this comment about the number of others who died is the most Paco ever says about the traumatic event (18).

Paco's quiet, maimed, ghostly presence elicits war stories from those around him, but his own memories must be drawn out by the ghosts of his comrades. Paco seems largely unreflective, concentrating on his work as a dishwasher and on revealing as little about himself as possible, but the memories are still there. According to the ghosts, it is their job to bring them forth. "No, James, Paco has never asked, *Why me?*" they say. "It is we—the ghosts, the dead—who ask, Why him? So Paco is made to dream and remember" (137). In one of the book's most remarkable sequences, the ghosts describe Paco lying down after a long day of work, and their own stealthy approach:

> It is at that moment that we would slither and sneak, shouldering our way up behind the headboard, emerging like a newborn—head turned and chin tucked, covered head to toe with a slick gray ointment, powdery and moist, like the yolk of a hard-boiled egg, and smelling of petroleum. We come to stand behind him against the wall—we ghosts—as flat and pale as a night-light, easy on the eyes . . . And when Paco is most beguiled, most rested and trusting, at that moment of most luxurious rest, when Paco is all but asleep, *that* is the moment we whisper in his ear, and give him something to think about—a dream or a reverie. (138)

Paco's dreams are various, but they are all bad. He dreams of being chased into warehouses by truckloads of men; he dreams of being executed by lethal injection, the stone-faced medics stabbing their needles into never-ending lines of soldiers; and he dreams of waiting endlessly to be finally released from service, to go home.

All are painful reflections of the war experience that rendered him disabled and isolated. It is not until late in the novel, however, that the ghosts bring forth Paco's devastating memory of the brutal rape and murder of a young Vietnamese woman. The girl was VC, the ghosts insist, and ambushed the soldiers' listening post, shooting two of them dead. A soldier named Gallagher dragged the girl into camp by her hair after she had been captured, and as Paco lies in his bed after a day of work, he suddenly "cannot choose but remember" how he and many other soldiers tied her wrists behind her back and raped her repeatedly, "watching one another while they ground the girl into the rubble" of a bombed out room (174, 180). Afterward, Gallagher shot her point blank in the forehead, spraying everyone with her blood. One detail out of many that Paco remembers is how the blood was "thick as freckles, and how it sparkled," how the "quick, tingling itch of the spray [was] like a mist of rain blown through a porch screen" (183).

It is unclear what Paco's particular thoughts are about the atrocity, other than his desire to avoid the memory. But the story surfaces when Paco is listening to his neighbor Cathy have sex with a friend, and wishing he could take the man's place. The ghosts explain how Paco wants the soothing redemption of sexual contact, of physical welcome and relief:

> And he's just a man like the rest of us, James, who wants to fuck away all that pain and redeem his body. By fucking he wants to ameliorate the stinging ache of those dozens and dozens of swirled-up and curled-round, purple scars, looking like so many sleeping snakes and piles of ruined coins. He wants to discover a livable peace—as if he's come up a path in a vast evergreen woods, come upon a comfortable cabin as solid as a castle keep, and approached, calling, "Hello the house," been welcomed in, given a hot and filling dinner, then shown a bed in the attic (a pallet of sweet dry grass and slim cedar shavings) and fallen asleep. (174)

The rape, and Paco's memory of it, seems to make that redemption impossible. The ghosts force it upon him and he relives the experience, remembering everything "as clear as day," including the feeling of the girl's bowels squeezing tight, the sight of the blood on the table where the soldiers pinned her, and the sound of the men crushing the rubble of the room under their boots (181). He will not interrupt Cathy and her lover after all; his own mental interruption gets in the way. Eventually, the idle flirtation and potential for sexual union between him and Cathy grows cold. At the end of the novel, Paco sneaks into Cathy's room while she's away and reads her diary; here, Cathy is the one telling Paco's story. Her initial impressions of him as "good-looking" and "cute," despite his visible scars, give way to descriptions of him drinking and taking pills, talking to himself, "a dingy, dreary, smelly, shabby, *shabby* little man" (205). Cathy writes about a dream she had in which she and Paco begin to have sex, but he peels off his scars and lays them on her flesh. She fights it, but he continues, the scars burning and screaming when they touch her, "as if each scar is a scream" (208). It is too much. Reading it, Paco feels "as if he's met his wraith" (209). He closes the diary, writes a short note to Ernest, and leaves town on the next westbound bus. As the book ends, he disappears.

The role of community

Although the subject of *Paco's Story* is quite different from Morrison's *Beloved*, the common motifs are striking. Sethe, *Beloved*'s protagonist, is haunted by a similarly devastating memory—of her daughter, Beloved, whom she killed to prevent her from being taken back into slavery. The ghost appears first in the guise of a disembodied child who leaves tiny hand prints in a cake and shatters a mirror, and later as an embodied young woman who walks out of a nearby stream and devotes herself to Sethe (3, 60). Like Paco, Sethe is haunted by someone close to her. Just as Paco's former friends show up like a newborn, a ghostly, repeated birth of memory and violation, Beloved is another child who appears as a disturbing reminder of past violence. Also like Paco, Sethe is scarred, her old injuries from beatings creating what she calls "a tree on her back," a wide spread of old, twisted skin (18). The novel's styles are similar as well: both Morrison's and Heinemann's novels shift back and forth in time, flashing back to significant episodes, and emphasize the rhythms of oral storytelling, as *Beloved* includes stream-of-consciousness sections narrated by Sethe, her daughter

Denver, and Beloved. Despite the obvious differences in race, gender, and historical context, the stories of Paco and Sethe are remarkably similar, revealing the impact of trauma by emphasizing the legacy of physical injury and the ways that past experiences can come back like insistent children who are anything but innocent.

Near the end of Morrison's novel, a white man arrives to take Denver to her new job, and Sethe relives her primal scene, confusing him for the schoolteacher who came to take her and her children back into slavery. Crazed, she moves to attack him but is prevented from doing so by the local women, who have gathered around her house in hopes of exorcising the ghost. "For Sethe it was as though the Clearing had come to her with all its heat and simmering leaves, where the voices of the women searched for the right combination, the key, the code, the sound that broke the back of words" (308). It works: the ghost disappears, Sethe's partner Paul D returns to her, and Denver moves on in the world with ambition and potential. The community reforms, although the final pages indicate that it will always be haunted by this ghostly presence, the legacy of slavery. "They forget her like a bad dream," though occasionally she drifts in close again with the rustle of a skirt or the caress of a cheek (323). "They can touch it if they like, but don't, because they know things will never be the same if they do," the novel's last page reveals. "This is not a story to pass on," the book insists (324).

Sethe and Paco are complicated characters who have been both perpetrators and victims, scarred and haunted by their pasts, and yet their stories end differently. Paco moves on alone, but Sethe is enveloped in her community: by the women who help exorcise the ghost of Beloved; by Paul D, who knows her past but will not let her go, and insists that Sethe is her own "best thing" (322); and by Denver, who also survives the ordeal and finds the strength to move forward. Some scholars have even understood Sethe's scars as more than just the evidence of her brutal mistreatment, and argued that they also stand for the female capacity to heal, for the communal history that Sethe is a part of, or for a "family tree" of connectedness.[2] Sethe, flawed as she may be, has kin. The book itself is dedicated to the "*Sixty Million and More*" affected by slavery, and encourages the reader to identify with this traumatized woman who may have committed an unspeakable act, but did so in response to—and revolt against—the culmination of horrors that slavery visited on her and her family. Morrison writes that this is "not a story to pass on," but this could mean either that it is not a story to tell again (to pass *on*) or that it is not a story to forget (to *pass* on.)[3] In some ways, it is both—the characters may not revisit it, but Morrison has, and it is not an easily forgettable tale.[4] In this way Morrison further extends the community marked by slavery, and makes the book a monument to that history—like a commemorative "bench by the road"—of the kind she has said she was never able to find. "I can see now what I was doing on the last page," she said in 1989. "I was finishing the story, transfiguring and disseminating the haunting with which the book begins. Yes, I was doing that; but I was also doing something more. I think I was pleading for that wall or bench or that tower or that tree when I wrote the final words" ("Bench").

Slavery is an isolating, dehumanizing experience, but the community that Morrison creates both within and beyond the novel works to recognize and recuperate those profound losses. Heinemann, however, appears less optimistic. While it is true that alliances forged in war have historically been strong and sustaining, *Paco's Story* denies its title character that sustenance, as well as any recuperation or avenue to reconstitution into postwar America.

Paco is, however, a soldier, and that community—that brotherhood, as it has long been called—is considered one of significant sustaining power. As far back as the *Iliad*, it is possible to see the strength of the bonds forged by people (usually men) fighting together in war; the potential horror of the war experience is often ameliorated by this closeness, which some have said is the most intense and intimate relationship of one's life. Rather than devotion to nation or cause, many soldiers overcome their fear or their reluctance to engage the enemy by thinking of the person standing beside them, fighting both for and with them. "Whether called 'mateship,' 'the buddy system,' or 'homo-erotic relationships,' the power of love and friendship in enticing men to kill has been widely commented upon," notes Joanna Bourke. "The importance of comradeship in enabling men to 'carry on' is at the heart of most histories of 'life at the front': so much so that it has become a cliché of military, cultural history" (129–130). When soldiers return home, they often find that their comrades are the only ones who "really understand" what they went through, and those friendships can be deeply significant as veterans make the adjustment to civilian life.

Paco's Story draws our attention to this wartime community in its style of narration. His comrades-in-arms know Paco almost better than he knows himself, and certainly express no reservation or doubt about explaining all the details of his life, his thoughts, and his emotions. They were all in it together, for better or for worse—though in this case, things were more often worse than better. As an author, Heinemann has indicated his interest in male comradeship in war but also the challenges those men face when trying to understand the war and integrate that understanding with their postwar lives. A former soldier who was drafted into the Vietnam War, he said in a 1992 interview that "[t]here's still a lot of misunderstanding and ill feeling and hard feeling among a lot of Americans—men of my generation—men of our generation—who went and just can't get past that. As far as I'm concerned, for people of our generation, there's still a lot of questions to be answered about just what the war was. I mean, it was the defining event . . . The men of our generation have a lot to talk about. That isn't to say that the women don't—but this is really a man thing" (Silesky 186–187).

Perhaps, then, the male storytelling that is central to *Paco's Story* is key, a necessary task of this male community to ameliorate the trauma of war. Louis Greiff has argued that Heinemann's naming practices in the novel reflect this belief in the brotherhood of all veterans; he directs readers' attention to Heinemann's Foreword to the novel, where he talks about why the novel's narrative is addressed to someone called "James." It is a slang term, Heinemann points out, that comes from the "custom of street folks engaging total strangers by calling them 'Jim' or 'Jack' or sometimes 'Jake' in a jivy sort of way." But because "Paco's story requires language more formal than street-corner patois," Heinemann finds "James" to be more apropos (n.p.). The author notes that the name also alludes to the intellectual brothers Henry and William James; the outlaw brothers Frank and Jesse James; the brother or cousin of Jesus, Saint James the Less; and finally, it is the name of Heinemann's oldest brother, "a man I have not seen or heard of since 1970 or thereabouts" (n.p.). "James," then, functions as a synonym for "brother," argues Greiff, and the novel itself may be an "artistic effort—through a collective American male speaker and listener—to get the needed discussion under way" (386).

Conversation is a good thing, and certainly can help "achieve the clarity that potentially follows deep tragedy," as Greiff puts it (387). Jonathan Shay and Judith Herman would certainly agree. The problem with this particular case, and the reason why this solution is made to seem untenable by the narrative, lies in the particulars of this community and this storytelling. The "deep tragedy" that draws these men together is self-inflicted; the attack on Fire Base Harriette is, in fact, friendly fire.[5] As the soldiers engage with the NVA in a fierce firefight, their lieutenant "crouched over his radio hoarsely screaming map coordinates to every piece of artillery, every air strike and gunship within radio range, like it was going out of style, when all of a sudden—zoom—the air came alive and crawled and yammered and whizzed and hummed with the roar and buzz of a thousand incoming rounds" (14). The communication of coordinates works, apparently, but not in the right way. Alpha Company knew then that "this one's going to blow everybody down," and it does: "everything was transformed into Crispy Critters for half a dozen clicks in any direction you would have cared to point" (15). Then, of course, there is the rape, an unquestionably brutal act that most of them, including Paco, participate in, as well as the subsequent murder of the girl, which none of them move to prevent or condemn. They simply look down at her body afterward with "resentful and curious fascination," knowing that this is a transformative "moment of evil" but going on with their day as usual (184). Paco lies in bed "thinking about" the girl and the rape, but other than the fact that he "winces and squirms" when the memory surfaces, there is no indication of how he judges the act, or even if he does so (174, 184).

Can a community be sustaining if it has produced the horror that it endures? At the very least, this complicates the discussion that Heinemann suggests is needed. Grant Scott has argued that this horror, particularly the rape, must be considered by scholars who wish to give the book full consideration. "Critics have effectively written the rape out of the novel," he notes, "and this has allowed them to praise other parts of the book—most notably its innovative style and narrative technique—with impunity." (Scott mentions pieces by Richard Sullivan, Veronica Geng, and Reginald Gibbons as particularly egregious examples of this elision.) "But the rape scene as well as the novel itself raise serious questions about selective seeing," he continues, "about our looking away from events and actions we may deem inappropriate or distasteful" (69). Scott also notes that this male community alienates Paco as much as it includes him, and not just because Paco is the only one still alive. Although his scars are a reminder of the war's devastating impact on a generation of young men, he is also subtly associated with the Vietnamese girl: they are both combat-hardened, have healthy appetites, are good laborers, and she is ground into the debris and beaten into a state "startlingly like Paco's own state after the holocaust" (75). Both by their experience and temperament as well as the abject state of their bodies after the bombing and the rape, Paco and the girl are characters resonant more with each other than with Alpha Company.

Perhaps, then, recovery might lie in a recognition across gender lines, in relationships with women rather than identification with brothers-in-arms. But the narrative denies this too—as it turns out, sisterhood is not the answer, either. The first time Paco walks into the Texas Lunch, for instance, he sees Betsy Sherburne, a local woman who took refuge there from a sudden storm, wet clothes clinging to her body. She is, quite literally, a vision of loveliness. Betsy sits in "that strong, clean, spring-showery yellow light" and "has never been more beautiful than she is right now, and will never be again" (99). Betsy is associated with the light and with cleansing rain, a refuge from the darkness, pain, and filth that Paco has experienced. But the narrators quickly undermine this association, denying Betsy—and thus Paco—any transcendence. Betsy is "nobody's angel," they assure us. The young men in town brag about having slept with her, the ghosts tell us, and she has a reputation as the "town punchboard" (100). For her part, Betsy eyes Paco and imagines sleeping with him, but when he explains his cane to Ernest by saying that he was wounded in the war, "Betsy jerks her head around as if pinched" and looks away (103). Paco arranges his job with Ernest and walks across the street to the hotel, Betsy's beauty and her apparent prejudice quickly forgotten. Once it becomes clear that she is not really the vision she might appear to be, and further, that she will not sleep with Paco, she disappears from the story. In this "double vision" that the narrators provide, Betsy's sexuality is her defining characteristic—it both creates her beauty and negates it. But when it becomes clear that she will not be sharing that sexuality with Paco, she has no other part to play in his life.

Just about all the women in the novel, in fact, are defined by their sexuality: Betsy, who imagines how she and Paco would "fuck on that sofa bed in the side den"; the Filipino singer for a USO band who "dry hump[s] the air with sure and steady rhythmic thrusts of her nifty little snatch" and inspires a circle-jerk among the grunts in the audience; and the night nurse who gives him oral sex during his recovery, even "dust[ing] his crotch with talc" when she finishes (13, 100, 56). The Vietnamese girl and Cathy are no different—they are women reduced in the narrative to sexual conduits. But if Paco really wants to find a "livable peace," as the narrators say, he may need to try for more than just sex—not only because sex will always bring him back to the war, but also because any real communion or community will have to go beyond a mere bodily encounter. Betsy's brief cameo in the story reveals this lost and perhaps impossible potential—she enters as a goddess and ends up as just a "mighty fine . . . pussy," and a refusing one at that (100).

Cathy is probably Paco's best hope for a companion, but their teasing mutual voyeurism turns bitter for each of them, suggesting that sex, to say nothing of love, is a comfort that is impossible for him to attain. Cathy happily objectifies herself by "parading around" in her underwear for Paco to observe while on a break from work, but also watches him with great interest, "speculating about the bulge in his pants and his cute little ass" (146, 148). It is a "nice little game" that is soon supplanted by a new one, in which Paco tries to get up the apartment stairs in time to slip into her apartment before she closes the door (149, 168). When Cathy's lover visits her, Paco listens to them have sex and imagines interrupting them and taking over, "that he slides into her as easily as a warm, clean hand slips into a greased glove; that she whimpers grotesquely, encircling him at once with her arms and legs, holding him to her like warm covers" (173). He wants the pleasure of a physical action that promises ease and release, even if it is with someone whom he finds somehow "grotesque." Like Betsy, whose sexuality makes her both desirable and undesirable at the same time, Cathy's enthusiastic attitude toward sex makes Paco want her even as he finds some aspect of her desire lurid or excessive.

Paco never penetrates Cathy's body—he cannot overcome the literal and figurative distance between them, and can only communicate the story of his past trauma through his scars, his limp, and the moans that escape from him while he is sleeping. He does feel a different kind of pleasure, however, an "alien ease," when he resurrects his old booby-trap-setting skills and penetrates her empty apartment, substituting her living space for her body (197). This is the only way, it seems, that he can get inside her or make any effort to know her. He goes through her things and finds her diary, communicating with her in this intruding, nonconsensual, one-sided way because he cannot communicate in person. The "conversation," such as it is, goes badly. Paco reads about her first impressions of him, "good-looking, with nice tight buns," but then reads about her later reactions to his scars, his drinking, his hobbling around, and how he cries out when he is sleeping (202). It "gives me the creeps," she writes, and then describes her dream of Paco forcing his scars onto her (206). This horrific vision of Paco, which echoes the rape of the Vietnamese girl, makes her skin crawl; her initial desire for his body has turned into repulsion.

Susan Jeffords has argued that it is Cathy, not Paco, who is most like the Vietnamese girl, that the women are figured in the novel as literal and metaphorical ambushers and thus deserving of their punishment. Male masculinity here is "enforceable only through and upon lived bodies—specifically the bodies of women" ("Tattoos" 222, 210). Jeffords sees the book's end as a reconstitution of masculinity, because Paco's story has been "told, heard, and recorded" on both a Vietnamese and an American woman's body, his visible scars transferred to Cathy, where they may be invisible on her body but legible in her diary. In Jeffords's reading, Paco's departure "is not so much one of fear and self-repulsion as of completion"—his scars have been passed to Cathy, and in this way "the war and the masculinity it inscribes have truly come 'home'" (223).

I would argue, however, that though the book clearly highlights the objectification and abuse of women on many levels, the result is not a masculine sense of satisfaction or closure. When Paco reads the diary, he suddenly feels as if he has "met his wraith," his own ghost, and he immediately prepares to leave town. It is a recognition, I think, of his own incompletion and the impossibility of achieving any kind of community. The repulsion he feels may erupt because, despite everything, Cathy not only *does* understand something of Paco's need and isolation, but also understands that real communion with him would be paradoxically enacted as a violent struggle. The only way to share the pain of the Vietnam War, the novel suggests, is to be already dead or to be assaulted; it is not enough just to see the scars, to acknowledge them. What Paco sees, perhaps, is the ghost of his possibility for healing. In the end, Paco can only exorcise himself by getting on the next bus out of town.

Paco's status as victim and perpetrator is a tangled one. If Paco was a rapist and an abetting witness to murder, to what extent does he pay for that with his horrific injuries, which are also caused by American soldiers? Like Cathy, readers may be both drawn in and repulsed, punished for their curiosity even though, as Scott writes, "we do not have the option of looking away. Even if we did . . . the novel's ethical code would condemn us for it, as it does the Lieutenant [who ignores the scene of the rape although he knows exactly what's going on]" (77). *Beloved*'s Sethe is a character whose guilt is similarly complicated, and the abuses she endures and enacts cannot be separated from the context of slavery. To what extent should the reader condemn Sethe for loving "too thick," as Paul D puts it, for wanting to, as she says, "put her babies where they'd be safe"? (193) The experience of slavery and the Vietnam War mark Sethe and Paco in both physical and psychological fashion. The result of this tension between guilt and victimhood, suffering from violence and causing it, is a haunting—the disembodied presence of a figure who somehow stands for these bodies, hurt and hurting, attacking and being attacked. Sethe may be able to send her ghost back into the ether when she relives her primal scene, but Paco cannot—he literally cannot "fuck the pain away." The Vietnam War haunts Paco, and Paco haunts those around him, heading off to who-knows-where at book's end—your town, maybe.

Heinemann's portrait of this Vietnam War veteran is a discouraging one that does not allow for physical or social reintegration. This trauma leaves a palpable, embodied trace, and in that way it is similar to the trauma of slavery in *Beloved*. In the late 1980s, these two writers grappling with America's difficult history gave that history voices and bodies, both of real, breathing people and their ghostly Others, their troubled history walking beside them. By the twenty-first century, however, when America entered into new wars in Afghanistan and Iraq, the trauma of war would trace differently, though the ghost of the war in Viet Nam is still very much a part of the ongoing story.

The ghost of the Vietnam War

No one wanted "another Vietnam," after all—like Sethe's and Paco's stories, the Vietnam War has been invoked as a tangled memory of guilt and innocence, victory and loss, something not to be passed on, not to be repeated. In her study *Worlds of Hurt: Reading the Literatures of Trauma*, Kalí Tal begins a chapter on Vietnam War literature by quoting President George Bush speaking in 1991 about the recently concluded Persian Gulf War. "We promised this would not be another Vietnam," he says. "And we kept that promise. The specter of Vietnam has been buried forever in the desert sands of the Arabian Peninsula" (quoted in Tal 60). But the Vietnam War— the quagmire, the nightmare, the specter—did not stay buried. The threat of another war like that one prompted more comparisons when the United States sent troops to Afghanistan in 2001 and back to Iraq in 2003. As the wars continued, similarities seemed to grow, including the difficulty of finding and identifying the enemy, the harsh terrain, and the protracted nature of the conflicts. In Chapter 7 in this volume, Brenda M. Boyle notes a number of books published from 2006 to 2008 arguing that the United States had failed to learn the political "lessons" of the Vietnam War, and was thus embroiled in two wars that would ultimately be as damaging as the earlier conflict, if not more so. Even as the wars in Iraq and Afghanistan also demonstrated strong contrasts with the war in Viet Nam—the all-volunteer forces, advanced technologies, and the administration's unwillingness to commit massive numbers of troops, for instance—the potential for trauma at the political, cultural, and individual level was what haunted the discourse about contemporary war.[6]

The Vietnam War haunts the one in Iraq even more literally, however, in what is perhaps the most iconic image from that latest war. A hooded man stands on a box, wires attached to his hands and his arms outstretched—it was one of the photographs at the center of the Abu Ghraib scandal, the revelation of the torture and other abusive activities that took place in that prison facility in 2003 and 2004. The man, called "Gilligan" by the soldiers, was told that he would be electrocuted if he stepped off the box, although the wires were not electrified. The photo was circulated worldwide, appearing in news stories about the scandal and on the cover of the *Economist* in May of 2004, under a headline urging Donald Rumsfeld, the Secretary of Defense, to resign ("Resign"). As Jasbir Puar has noted, it has also been widely used in billboards, murals, and antiwar protest materials, in performance art, and in paintings by artists such as Richard Serra and Guy Colwell (102).

Why did this particular photo become an icon of the Iraq War? First, there are pragmatic reasons: "it is the only released photo to date that exposes almost no skin," Puar notes, making it reproducible in mainstream media outlets and also less confronting for the viewer. "[O]nly the legs and shins of the victim can be seen, preserving an anonymity of body that simultaneously incriminates the viewer less than some of the more pornographic images" (102). But the photo also radiates what Puar calls a "distressing mystique." It calls up associations with the Ku Klux Klan and with the burqa, but those associations are vague, unsettling. Like Paco's scars, the image may be as ambiguous as it is revelatory. What, exactly, is going on? "[T]he power of an image does not necessarily reside in what it depicts but in its seeming truth, however inscrutable that truth may be," write Philip Gourevitch and Errol Morris. The image of the man in the hood is one of "carnival weirdness: this upright body shrouded from head to foot; those wires; that pose that recalls, of course, the crucifixion; and the peaked hood that carries so many vague and ghoulish associations . . . So we seize on the figure of Gilligan," they write, "as a symbol that stands for all that we know was wrong at Abu Ghraib and all that we cannot—or do not want to—understand about how it came to this" (182–184).

The image was indeed a strange and shocking one for many, though forced standing, as this man was made to do, is not a new coercive technique. As Darius Rejali has reported, it shows up as practice in a number of historical contexts. In the early twentieth century, the British Army, the French Legionnaires, and the Gestapo all used the method. The technique is valued, says Rejali, "because it leaves few marks, and so no evidence" (n.p.). The CIA documented its effects in the 1950s—extreme swelling, blisters, increased heart rate, and eventually kidney failure. In the 1970s, Brazilian police added electricity to jolt the victims and prevent collapse, thus extending the torture. The Brazilians called this "the Vietnam," because it "combined tortures used by the North Vietnamese (forced standing) with tortures used commonly by American and South Vietnamese interrogators (electrical torture from field phone batteries)" (n.p.). "And now," says Rejali, "the ghost of 'the Vietnam' appears in Iraq" (n.p.).

In 2004, the Vietnam War's ghostly presence was still with us, although the nature of the haunting has changed since Heinemann told Paco's story. Instead of disembodied voices with a distinct identity, this photo shows a voiceless, faceless person—a ghost in black—his body the subject of coercion but one that will bear no trace, no physical record of that treatment. Soldiers have to be taught how to do this, Rejali argues, noting that practices like this do not spring up without precedent. These are "stealth tortures that leave no marks," he says, an obvious advantage for the torturer—or those ordering the torture. His comment points to the tangled question of guilt in evidence here, one that Errol Morris tries to draw out in his documentary about the scandal, *Standard Operating Procedure* (2008). In the film Lynndie England, who appeared in another widely circulated photo leading a naked prisoner on a leash, says that the goings-on in Abu Ghraib initially struck her as "weird" and "wrong," but that "the example was already set . . . It was okay." Sabrina Harmon, who took the picture of the man she calls Gilligan, notes in the film that because the wires attached to him were not electrified, the treatment was "just words." In fact, her view is corroborated by Army Criminal Investigator Brent Pack, who reviewed all the photographs for criminal wrongdoing. Since Harmon's photo shows a man put into a stress position but not electrocuted, he deems it "standard operating procedure." Megan Ambuhl voices Morris's primary fascination with the photographs when she comments on one of a blood-smeared floor: "Your imagination can run wild when you just see blood," she explains. "The pictures only show you a fraction of a second. You don't see forward, you don't see backward. You don't see outside the frame." Indeed, Ambuhl herself was cropped out of the picture showing Lynndie England with the man on the leash, perhaps because the man who took the photo, Charles Graner, was dating England but was secretly involved with Ambuhl as well. "In the pictures that came out in the media, all you seen was me," England says. "You didn't see Megan. 'Cause that was the cropped picture. Graner told me he just wanted her out of the shot . . . Maybe it was to secretly protect her."

The layers of guilt and implication are convoluted. Ultimately Graner was sentenced to 10 years, England to 3 years, Harmon to

6 months, and Ambuhl to reduction in rank and loss of half-a-month pay for their involvement in the scandal. Many soldiers insisted that the torture was protocol. Brigadier General Janis Karpinski, commanding officer of the prison, was demoted, but claimed that she was a scapegoat for higher-level commanders who were never charged. The photographs so central to the scandal were also the focus of the investigation and the ensuing convictions—they are the digital trace of coercive acts that might leave no physical scars. Puar suggests that the subsequent ubiquity of the photographs in the media indicates our need to see the effects of violence in order to grapple with and understand it: "The only evidence of the Vietnam comes in the form of the photograph. Its mass multiplication and mutations may speak to the need to document and inscribe into history and our optic memories that which otherwise leaves no visual proof" (102).

Not every prisoner came away from Abu Ghraib with scars like Paco or Sethe, but the trace is there nonetheless. The story of Abu Ghraib is one of layers of information, the war that lingers in data and pixels as much as it does on skin and soul. "One could argue," says Puar, "that what is exceptional is not the actual violence itself, but the interplay of technologies, circuits, and networks that enable the digital capture and circulation of these acts" (107). Like Paco's Alpha Company, the soldiers at Abu Ghraib formed a community that inflicted violence on others and also hurt themselves—their own photographs, in most cases casually taken, became the evidence of their wrongdoing.

What, then, is the legacy of *Paco's Story* in light of these subsequent wars? Heinemann's novel pushes readers away with its raw, dreadful revelations at the same time that the narrative voice reels them in, the musical cynicism revealing awful secrets of bodies violated and turned inside out by war. It is a difficult book to read, but an important one for that difficulty. It may not be a "war story" in the entertaining, heroics-filled sense that the narrators mean by that designation, but it is also not a story to pass on in either sense. It needs a witness who will not *pass* on it, and its ugliness shouldn't be passed *on*—it should not happen again.

Of course, Abu Ghraib is a reminder, if of nothing else, that war always contains atrocities within it, shameful, violent secrets that always leave a trace—on skin, in the psyche, in the data that make the whole world a witness. By creating Paco as the bearer of these scars and ghosts, Heinemann suggests that every war story is something like Paco's story if you dig deep enough. The horror and pain are always there, and can be profoundly isolating for those who survive. *Paco's Story*, as I've noted, seems much less optimistic about our ability to rally around such revelations and form a healing community than does *Beloved*. Heinemann himself, however, does rally his readers as witnesses. Within the world of the novel, witnesses may not matter very much—the fact that there are those who know his story does not seem to make Paco feel much better, or help him foster connections with the (living) people around him. But the novel itself is a reminder to us as readers that the trace of war is often indelible. Seeing institutions like slavery and war for what they are and what kind of atrocities they produce at least keeps us honest, however stunned and shaken by the experience we may be. Paco's story is an ugly story and an upsetting one, but perhaps all the more necessary because of those qualities.

Notes

1. Lawrence Tritle takes a similar tack with his book *From Melos to My Lai: War and Survival* (2000).
2. Anita Durkin catalogs the many interpretations of Sethe's scars, and among others, mentions Wendy Faris's claim that the scars link Sethe to Amy Denver and her curative female powers; Caroline Rody's understanding of the scars as a bond between the different generations of women; and Michele Bonnet's reading of Sethe's "tree" as a genealogical one that links her to her family as well as to other African Americans.
3. Durkin adds a third possibility—that it's "'not a story to *pass on*' (not a story to die, to be forgotten)" (554).
4. Morrison herself is drawing from another compelling story, that of Margaret Garner, the escaped slave who was arrested in 1856 for killing one child and attempting to kill the others rather than have them returned to slavery. In Morrison's Foreword, she notes Garner's fame in the fight against the Fugitive Slave laws, and calls Garner as a historical figure "fascinating, but to a novelist, confining" (xvii).
5. Katherine Kinney's book *Friendly Fire: American Images of the Vietnam War* (2000) contains a lengthy discussion of *Paco's Story* as one of many examples of representations of Americans killing

Americans in the Vietnam War, a trope that suggests the "idea that we fought ourselves" politically, culturally, and psychologically (4).
6 Roger Luckhurst has argued that comparisons can be seen in artistic representation as well, and that cultural narratives about contemporary war "are often displaced or filtered through the iconography of prior wars" ("In War" 722). He reads Denis Johnson's Vietnam War novel *Tree of Smoke* (2007), Guillermo del Toro's film *Pan's Labyrinth*, set at the close of the Spanish Civil War (2006), and Kathleen Ann Goonan's science fiction novel *In War Times* (2007) as works in which the war in Iraq "erupts" into narratives ostensibly about other conflicts (724).

7

American totem society in the twenty-first century: Denis Johnson's *Tree of Smoke*, Karl Marlantes's *Matterhorn*, and Tatjana Solis's *The Lotus Eaters*

Brenda M. Boyle

Revived interest in the Vietnam War

American interest in popular representations of the War peaked in the 1980s and persisted, less avidly, in the mid-1990s after the normalization of diplomatic and trade relations between the two countries. Scholars, of course, had continued to study the War, the country, and the diaspora, often from angles other than the American one, and fiction by and about Vietnamese people in the United States and in Viet Nam was published to wide acclaim. Perhaps for geopolitical reasons, however, at the end of the millennium dominant American groups tended to view the War as part of a distant past unrelated to a United States by then focused on Middle Eastern Islam, not Southeast Asian Communism.[1] In an era of what Andrew Bacevich terms "the new American militarism," because the American military purportedly had since the war in Viet Nam rectified the errors leading to its loss there, the War could be regarded as anomalous and the military celebrated. The "myths" of this new militarism endeavor to "create an apparently seamless historical narrative of American soldiers as liberators, with Operation Iraqi Freedom in March 2003 becoming a sequel to Operation Overlord in June 1944" (*The New American Militarism* 98). Conveniently, the Vietnam War had been omitted from or minimized in this militarist storyline.

Even leading up to the March 2003 invasion of Iraq, however, many critics drew parallels between it and the conflict in Viet Nam, producing a resurgent interest in the Vietnam War of four decades earlier. For instance, President George W. Bush's 2002 State of the Union address claiming that the threat of Iraqi Weapons of Mass Destruction (WMDs) demanded an invasion by a "coalition of the willing" echoed President Lyndon Baines Johnson's 1964 claim that the Gulf of Tonkin incidents warranted escalating American military presence in South Vietnam. Reports of both WMDs and the Gulf incident later were found to be erroneous if not outright misleading, but both facilitated the American Commander-in-Chief's waging war. Turn-of-the-millennium experts in American foreign policy, international relations, history, and culture, with the support of publishers willing to gamble on the experts' publications, called attention to other eerie parallels between the wars. For instance, in 2006 international relations scholar Robert K. Brigham published *Iraq, Vietnam, and the Limits of American Power*, asserting in the book's Preface, "the war in Iraq is not another Vietnam. It is far worse" (ix). In 2007, historians Lloyd C. Gardner and Marilyn B. Young produced a collection of essays by many scholars entitled *Iraq and the Lessons of Vietnam: Or, How Not to Learn from the Past*, contending that "the United States finds itself bogged down once again in a war against an enemy whose low-grade weapons defy the technological superiority of the world's greatest military power" (2) and "the real lessons of Vietnam have been ignored" (3). Rufus Phillips, a 1950s and 1960s CIA member and State Department official in Viet Nam, published in 2008 *Why Vietnam Matters: An Eyewitness Account of Lessons Not Learned*, concluding that "Overarching in Vietnam and Iraq was hubris at the top, combined with an unwillingness to listen to alternative views or to understand the enemy, the local people on our side, or our own limitations and capabilities" (309).[2] Furthermore, Ty Hawkins published in 2012 *Reading Vietnam Amid the War on Terror*, claiming that both wars threatened the foundational American myth, the story of a nation commissioned by God to liberate all of mankind (7–8). Historian David Elliott comments, "When soldiers and officials realized they were in it [the Iraq war] for the long term, the Vietnam tropes of quagmire, light at the end of the tunnel, and exit strategies became more prevalent" (21). Approximately a year after the Iraq invasion, says Elliott, General Anthony Zinni, commander of American forces of the Middle East until 2000, was using a familiar Vietnam War trope about Iraq: "I have seen this movie. It was called Vietnam" (22).[3]

Representations of the War also reappeared in American popular cultural, through pre-Iraq war films such as the Mel Gibson vehicle, *We Were Soldiers* (2002), Werner Herzog's during-Iraq film, *Rescue Dawn* (2006), and Ben Stiller's during-Iraq satire of Vietnam War films, *Tropic Thunder* (2008).[4] This post-9/11 context proved fertile ground for the publication of three novels written by European Americans, set in Viet Nam, and about the American war: Denis Johnson's 2007 *Tree of Smoke*, Karl Marlantes's 2010 *Matterhorn*, and Tatjana Solis's 2010 *The Lotus Eaters*. All three have been received warmly: *Tree of Smoke* was awarded the National Book Award in 2007 and was a finalist for the Pulitzer; after three decades of seeking a publisher, Karl Marlantes found his opus, *Matterhorn*, not only published but also lauded;[5] and *The Lotus Eaters* won various prestigious national and international awards. The three novels replicate themes in previous works of fiction about the War; after all, American readers and writers are tutored—both by novels and films—to expect certain events and characterizations in representations of the Vietnam War era. These elements of War fiction, outlined more fully in this volume's Introduction, focus on the victimization of, trauma to, and redemption of the individual (usually male) American. While these three recent novels do not disappoint reader expectations, they reveal influences not evident in earlier narratives. Although concerned with events occurring decades earlier, the current novels are influenced by American events and cultural sensibilities of the early twenty-first century.

Among others, these sensibilities include a hyper-attentiveness to national security, a focus on Middle Eastern Islam, an ongoing question about the US obligation to secure the rest of the world, and concerns about gender roles. For the purposes of this study, the most applicable current sensibility is what can be called the Support the Troops Syndrome.[6] Emblematized by the yellow ribbon, this term refers to the exhortation of Americans during the post-9/11 Iraq and Afghanistan wars to resist holding individual "troops"—US Army, Air Force, Marines, and Navy personnel—responsible for war. Allegedly, military personnel returning from Viet Nam were poorly treated and often blamed for the war itself.[7] The Support the Troops Syndrome inhibits that treatment by suppressing citizen displeasure with individual military members or executive decision makers. According to the logic of the Syndrome military people only can be sanctified, not condemned, and mourned as victims of war, not as complicit. They must not in any way be criticized.[8] In popular discourse, their having been in the military is seen as self-sacrificing and heroic behavior, judgment ensuring young Americans will continue to volunteer for the military.[9] Andrew Bacevich says this about "America's civic religion" in *Breach of Trust* (2013):

> In recent decades, an injunction to "support the troops" has emerged as its central tenet. Since 9/11 this imperative has become, if anything, more binding. Indeed, as citizens, Americans today acknowledge no higher obligation. Fulfilling that obligation has posed a challenge, however. Rather than doing so concretely, Americans . . . have settled for symbolism. With a pronounced aversion to collective service and sacrifice . . . Americans resist any definition of civic duty that threatens to crimp lifestyles . . . Cheering for the troops, in effect, provides a convenient mechanism for voiding obligation and perhaps easing guilty consciences. (4–5)

The Syndrome thus produces quietude about war and the military generally, an if-you-can't-say-something-nice-don't-say-anything-at-all mantra. In this national environment it is deemed unpatriotic, nay, treacherous, to criticize the armed forces or the US use of military might; all military actions, conducted by noble actors, are themselves noble. The result of such prevalent logic is that Vietnam War stories published after 9/11 end redemptively, concluding that though the war might have been conducted disastrously and ignobly, the uplifting outcomes of the war for individual Americans and the country made it worthwhile. Using a familiar cliché, the novels suggest that war may break us but we will heal more strongly in the broken places.[10] The Vietnam War broke Americans and they healed; the wars in Afghanistan and Iraq are breaking them, but Americans will be better for the wars. Ergo, the logic might conclude, Americans need war to be strong.

Like many of their predecessors, two of the three novels analyzed in this chapter demonstrate that "war novels" do not necessarily deal explicitly or exclusively with combat and combatants. That is, because war includes more than killing, many war novels explore elements that may not involve ending the lives of others, at least not in the conventional battlefield sense.[11] Thus, *Tree of Smoke* is concerned with CIA activities in Southeast Asia before and after the American war and *The Lotus Eaters* features war photojournalists in Viet Nam. Although the Vietnam War is known as a non-conventional war, *Matterhorn* is a conventional combat novel, comparable to Norman Mailer's WWII novel, *The Naked and the Dead* (1948), and two Vietnam War novels, James Webb's *Fields of Fire* (1978) and John Del Vecchio's *The 13th Valley* (1982). With greater historical perspective than those published shortly after the war's end, however, all three new novels address the responsibility each institution—the CIA, photojournalism, and the armed forces—has for war's enduring. Consequently, they speak as much to the US wars in the last decade as they do to that of decades ago.

Masculinities

Since war traditionally in the United States is regarded as a (if not THE) male purview, gender theory is useful to analyzing all three narratives. Gender, especially masculinity, theory is applicable given that masculinity traditionally is regarded as male behavior and the Vietnam War was the last major American conflict using an all-male force. A crucial factor in considering gender, however, is that it is distinct from biological sex. That is, one's social behavior (gender) is not a function of one's anatomy (sex). A female body does not mandate or naturally produce feminine behavior; a male body does not mandate or naturally produce masculine behavior.[12] Instead, these gender practices are taught, learned, and repeatedly practiced, or are what Judith Butler terms "performative" (*Gender Trouble*). Their repetition is what makes the practices appear natural. Furthermore, as behavior, gender is socially constructed and therefore varies by and within culture. Not only do American and Vietnamese versions of masculinities differ, but also subcultures within "American" and "Vietnamese" produce differing renditions of gender behavior. For instance, American businessperson masculine behaviors differ from American high school athlete masculine behaviors, as each constitutes discrete cultural values and practices, and within each of those subcultures—American business, American high school athletics—values and practices vary. Within any culture, therefore, masculinities abound.

R. W. Connell's conception of masculine gender systems can help to understand masculinities in modern Western patriarchal cultures. Connell asserts that masculinities within these cultures are hierarchical, and within each hierarchy there are four masculine ranks: hegemonic/dominant; subordinate; marginalized; and complicit.[13] Imagine each masculine system as a pyramid, narrow at the top and broad at the base. Males (in the current systems) vie for the limited "hegemonic" rank at the top, the impossible-to-achieve but currently "culturally exalted" position that confers on them the perquisite of determining who is subordinate and who marginal ("Social Organization" 38). In twenty-first century Western patriarchy, hegemonic masculinity usually is performed by wealthy, educated, white, heterosexual males; "subordinate," just below "hegemonic" in the pyramid, is conferred by the current hegemonic rank typically on males who do not identify as heterosexual or are identified as feminine; "marginalized" occurs most often to males who do not match the dominant group in terms of race, class, ability, religion, or ethnicity, and to females who practice masculinity; and at the broad, "complicit" foundation of the pyramid are all males (and some females) because in enjoying its benefits they bolster and sustain patriarchy (*Masculinities* 78–79). Unbeknownst to most of its practitioners, however, this masculine gender system is characterized by change and flux, so that one's status is never fixed because one shifts among pyramids. As one moves from one culture/pyramid to another, one's status easily can change. For instance, males who excel at combat may be part of the hegemonic masculinity group while in war, but when they leave war and return to civilian culture, with the shift in cultural values comes a new, reformulated hierarchy. Gendered practices valued in combat are unlikely to be similarly valued in civilian culture. What was deemed hegemonic in one culture probably is not in the subsequent one; behavior valued as dominant in one culture may be subordinate or marginal in another culture. Therefore, if a person believes there is only one form of masculine behavior that supersedes culture and history, this alteration in status will befuddle, at least. It is the unpredictable changeability of gender status that Connell terms the "crisis" of patriarchy; patriarchy is by design impermanent and therefore always in crisis, yet few of its participants are aware of that characteristic.

What these three novels have in common is they confront practices of masculinities in contemporary American war culture. They do this especially in light of some of the changes to American military culture since US armed forces withdrew from Viet Nam in 1973: institution of an all-volunteer military; integration of females into the Regular military, the military academies, and some combat roles; increased use of remote weapons/drones to fight battles; limitations on war photography and reporting; and use of counterinsurgency as a strategy. In addition to reflecting post-9/11 sensibilities, the novels also reflect a brotherhood-in-arms ethos heightened by turn-of-the-millennium commemorations of World War II, like *Saving Private Ryan* (1998), *Band of Brothers* (2001), and *Flags of Our Fathers* (2006). By insisting that males fight not for country or heroism but for love of one another, this ethos contradicts the "generation gap" of the Vietnam War era.[14] The novels reflect the generational tension as they confront the role of fathers or father-figures in sending their sons or son-figures into combat. As Michael Herr points out in *Dispatches* (1977), many young military men were (badly) influenced by the World War II glory stories of their fathers: "I keep thinking about all the kids who got wiped out by seventeen years of war movies before coming to Vietnam to get wiped out for good . . . They were insane, but the war hadn't done that to them . . . We'd all seen too many movies, stayed too long in Television City, years of media glut had made certain connections difficult" (209). Similarly, in *Born on the Fourth of July* (1976), after having accidentally killed a fellow Marine and been paralyzed by his wounds in the War, Ron Kovic inspects and is disillusioned by the patriotic rhetoric of his parents's generation: "[E]verything would not be all right, he thought, nothing would be all right at all. It was starting to be very different now, very different from what he had ever thought possible" (189).

With numerous male–male pairings in a noncombat environment, *Tree of Smoke* sometimes literally illustrates this father–son conflict, and so is discussed first in this chapter. As a combat novel with an all-male cast, *Matterhorn* spotlights this issue largely in terms of military rank and thereby more figuratively; it is examined second. *The Lotus Eaters*, whose central character is a female war photographer, is discussed last, following Judith Halberstam's advice in *Female Masculinity* that masculinity is most "legible as masculinity where and when it leaves the white male middle-class body" (2).

Tree of Smoke, masculinities, and blood sacrifice

Tree of Smoke underscores this generational issue most explicitly in the many character pairings that complicate father–son relationships. The novel features the CIA in Southeast Asia from 1963 to 1970, and concludes in 1983. It includes a large cast of (mostly) male characters, but Skip Sands is the focal character, a young, patriotic idealist who begins his CIA career in the Philippines and concludes it in Viet Nam. Disillusioned by the corrupt machinations of agency members, after many years Skip abandons the "soul-dissolving acid" of the CIA in Viet Nam to become a gun-runner in Asia; the novel winds down in 1983 with his imprisonment in Kuala Lumpur and his execution (546). He explains while he awaits his hanging, "After I left Vietnam I quit working for the giant-size criminals . . . I served . . . and started working for the medium size. Lousy hours and no fringe benefits, but the ethics are clearer. And the stakes are plain" (604). Other major characters include Skip's uncle, Colonel Francis Sands, a former World War II POW, and current rogue CIA operative in the Vietnam War who groomed his nephew for the Agency; Sgt. Jimmy Storms, Colonel Sand's enlisted accomplice and protégé;

Kathy Jones, wife to a dead missionary, occasional lover to Skip, and nurse to many caught in the crossfire of war; and Bill and James Houston, ne'er-do-well half-brothers who unsuccessfully try to escape through the US military the spiritual and financial poverty of their Phoenix home life. Secondary characters include several men allied to the Colonel's cause: Eddie Aguinaldo in the Philippines, Hao and Minh Nguyen and Than Trung in South Vietnam, and Dietrich Fest, German assassin-at-large.

The character pairings rarely are based on biological father–son relationships but are father–son figures. Skip Sands's father died at Pearl Harbor when Skip was young and his father's brother, Colonel Sands, subsequently became Skip's surrogate father and primed him for the CIA. Bill and James Houston have different (felonious) fathers but cannot remember which is whose. Hao Nguyen is uncle to Minh Nguyen but, childless himself, fathers Minh and his brother when their parents die. To some extent, Hao also fathers (and betrays) his childhood friend, Than Trung, the double agent, as Hao advises and then double-crosses naïve Trung in his dealings with the Americans. Jimmy Storm plays a sort of son to Colonel Sands, faithfully accompanying the Colonel, disbelieving the Colonel's death when everyone else accepts it, and, in needing to "get out of this machine," sacrificing himself to the "father–mother" (590–596). Dietrich Fest, the German assassin employed by the CIA, spends much of his time worrying about his father's impending death as he prepares to assassinate Trung. In the Philippines, where most white men have been Catholic missionaries and are called "father," Skip is referred to as "Pa-dair" (78) while the actual Catholic priest, unassuming Father Carrigan, is murdered by Fest (114). Fathers, it appears, are to be neither trusted nor tolerated nor actual.

This relationship between males in a war environment is troubling, the novel urges. Biological or not, fathers are everywhere but rarely are effective guides to their sons. Instead, they misguide, mislead, and often use the sons to their own advantage. Bill and James Houston are fathered by men who leave their mother, who end up in prison, and who ensure their sons will land in prison, too. Dietrich Fest's brother had been a NAZI and his father "a patriotic German, an acquaintance of Heinrich Himmler" (422); Hao, too cowardly to do it himself, delegates Minh to demand rent from another family member; and Colonel Sands uses Skip to organize and narrate his illicit, double-agent operation, the "Tree of Smoke."

In all cases, the novel leads readers to a correlation: the father is bad and so the son will be bad. Although in performative masculinity fathers and older males expressly are responsible for teaching young males how to perform as men, to impart their lessons fathers and father figures in the *Tree of Smoke* often conceal something essential from their male progeny. Before Skip arrives in Southeast Asia, Colonel Sands conceals from naive Skip his duplicitous aims in his "Tree of Smoke" operation and the CIA's "poison," and Hao conceals from Trung his double-crossing.

A radical but persuasive way to understand this conundrum of fathers, sons, and war is through what Carolyn Marvin and David W. Ingle term "blood sacrifice" in *Blood Sacrifice and the Nation: Totem Rituals and the American Flag*. Using sociologist Emile Durkheim's theory of totem to organize social groups, Marvin and Ingle assert that, although the notion of totem typically is applied only to "primitive" societies, modern American society is based on the same principle: that regular sacrifice of some of its members is needed to ensure societal coherence. This sacrifice, initiated by the totem class, or authorities of the society, both defines the boundaries of the society and relieves the tension of intersociety conflict. The boundaries also create evil outsiders, enemies, Others who can be used to conduct the sacrificial killing so that the totem class does not have to do it. Marvin and Ingle explain the challenge of maintaining a societal entity:

> The guilt we feel about the [sacrificial] killing we cannot admit to reconsolidates the group. The surrogate victim, the savior, is the son we expel into death. The ritual victim, the scapegoat [enemy], makes our anger and killing acceptable and disguises its real target. Our rage at the scapegoat [the enemy] provides a pretext to kill the savior [our sons]. With the death of enough sons, the group finds relief from internecine tensions. (79)

Using the evil outsider to conduct and justify the killing assuages citizens' guilt at sending society's sons to define (and redefine) the societal boundary. The guilt also mandates quietude about the mission, echoing the Support the Troops Syndrome.

Most importantly to social cohesion is that the need for sacrifice must be concealed, and so sacrificial designates—the "sons"—are kept ignorant of their role through various totemic rituals, such as pledging allegiance to the flag and singing the national anthem. To fill the role of warrior, the sons are induced with exhortations of patriotism, honor, heroism, courage, and manhood, so they go as willing sacrifices in the belief that they are reluctant killers (79).[15] Those who have experienced war—the "fathers"—are horrified to learn in war what their sacrificial role is but are required by the ruling totem class to withhold their knowledge from those who have not yet been (the sons) or will not go (the mothers and sisters) to war. "These insiders turned outsiders must cast off the knowledge of who sent them to die. They forswear revenge and refuse to tell what they know. If they agree, they are reincorporated [into American society]" (73). The fathers deliberately must not and do not tell the sons (or mothers and sisters) what sacrificial role they are sent to play in war. Marvin and Ingle point out this silence specifically in relation to the Vietnam War: when Bill Clinton's draft-dodging of the War became an issue during his first campaign for President, the role of fathers in sending young males to war was taboo. "The discussion did not address whether the fathers were good fathers to send the sons to a bad war," observe Marvin and Ingle. "Only the willingness of the sons to die could be publicly examined. The taboo discussion was the fathers' willingness to sacrifice them" (74).

In effect, *Tree of Smoke* is an application of Marvin and Ingle's theory, although their investigation of American totem society is limited to its domestic rituals, halting at the border of war and peace. Johnson's novel examines the masculine gender systems across the border, studying how fathers negotiate with sons as the sons learn about the previously withheld secrets; the novel does this especially in regard to the relationship between Skip and his uncle-cum-father, Colonel Sands. Although the Colonel has groomed Skip for service in the CIA, when Skip arrives in Southeast Asia—first in the Philippines and then in Viet Nam—he is untutored in war's impurities. The Colonel instructs Skip, revealing to him the totem secret. "War," says the Colonel, "is ninety percent myth anyway, isn't it? In order to prosecute our own wars we raise them to the level of human sacrifice, don't we, and we constantly invoke our God. It's got to be about something bigger than dying," concludes the Colonel, "or we'd all turn deserter" (54). The Colonel reveals here to Skip what going to war requires: mythmaking and religiosity.[16] The novel more strongly implies that going to war requires of males a complete separation from females. Men in the novel generally but Skip and the Colonel specifically have trouble with women, meaning that war's venue is an exciting alternative to peace's tranquil domesticity. Skip "was afraid of women," avoids contact with Kathy, and more or less rejects his mother for her desire to protect him (64, 609). Rick Voss does not return home often because "[w]omen and children frighten me" (159). The Colonel is disgusted with his antiwar daughter, who is dating someone repulsive for being both a "beatnik" and a "mulatto" (186), and is being divorced by his wife who, Sands says, thinks he is "in this war to run from my failures in life." The Colonel continues, conflating politics, gender, and normalcy: "I'm here because I won't go back to my homeland. Go back to what? A bewildering place full of left-leaning feminine weirdos" (427). To participate in the masculine arena necessitates a separation from the feminine. Although admission to the masculine war arena requires maleness, being male does not ensure masculinity, however. Skip doubts himself on this count: "Somehow he'd entered their world without becoming a man" (155) and feels "a girlish despair" in his uncle's presence (47). Learning from his uncle/father these secrets of blood sacrifice does not inspire Skip, though. The lesson he learns instead is dispiriting; he refuses the silence demanded in exchange for return to the homeland. As he languishes in an Indonesian prison awaiting execution, he cynically writes to Kathy: "in a war you mustn't think, you mustn't ever think. War is action or death. War is action or cowardice. War is action or treachery. War is action or desertion. Do you get the idea here? War is action. Thought leads to treason" (608). War requires masculinity and war requires action: masculinity = action = not thinking.

Matterhorn, masculinities, and blood sacrifice

As a conventional combat novel with an all-male cast, though the "fathers" always are figurative Karl Marlantes's *Matterhorn* is the most explicit among the three recently published novels about the tenets of blood sacrifice and the precariousness of the masculine gender systems. Like the other two novels, this one features a young adult, Second Lieutenant (2LT) Waino Mellas, whose life is transformed by the experience of war. Unlike the other two novels, whose narratives extend through decades and geographies, *Matterhorn* is set in a small geographic area near the Demilitarized Zone (DMZ) between North and South Vietnam and spans only a few months in late 1968 and early 1969. Consequently, its storyline occurs entirely in a combat zone, where females appear only in males' memories and literal fathers are invisible. Thus, simultaneously per the tenets of blood sacrifice males are required to engage in war against Others, and per the tenets of masculine hierarchies must jockey with one another for position in the gendered military system. Sometimes this jockeying is based on racial hierarchies and sometimes on socioeconomic ones, but military rank is the most obvious point of contention among the men, especially the officers.[17] The novel's prominent trope is the careerism of the officer ranks, from second lieutenant to general.[18] Despite a totem rhetoric of all for one and one for all, of brotherhood in arms, of collective sacrifice, each of the officers instead is motivated primarily to improve his own professional lot, almost always at the cost of others'. The consequences of such egoism are dire for all of the men in the battalion.

This careerism is patent in Major Blakely, the Battalion S-3, the officer responsible for orchestrating all of the battalion's military operations.[19] His job is to enable the orders of the battalion commander, Lieutenant Colonel Simpson, but he also uses his access, Iago-like, to influence the commander's decision making. Simpson is easily influenced, insecure as he is of his education and social class, of his drinking habits, of his ability to inspire men to great deeds, but Blakely fantasizes using his current job to become the chief of staff at Division headquarters, "advising the general on the political complications and how they interacted with the strategic complications" (128). Such fantasies lead Blakely consistently to inflate body counts wildly because they will reflect well on his reputation, but also to terrible blunders, as when he forgets to resupply a company whose supplies of food, water, and ammunition already are depleted. Blakely's image as a military professional is everything to him: "Blakely knew the value of image. It wouldn't hurt if they [battalion headquarters] got shelled every so often. He had to have real combat on his record, the kind with Purple Hearts [awarded for combat-acquired wounds] and medals. It was the best route, maybe the only route, to the top"

(201). Simpson also is a careerist, having been passed over once (281) but still hoping for promotion to Colonel and the command of a regiment: "He cared about immersion foot. He cared about security and cutting his casualty rate. But how do those things get you the notice of the commanding general?" (203). Colonel Mulvaney, the regimental commander, is more circumspect about career opportunities, perhaps because having already reached a professional peak he understands that "hypocrisy's always been part of the profession" (262). His awareness doesn't stop Mulvaney from longing to be promoted to general "[i]n this new Marine Corps of careful staff work and covering your ass with paper" (185). Major General Neitzel, the division commander, had made enough of the right career moves not only to be promoted to general but also to have "figured out that he had the raw power to make the crooked places straight and would put his Marines where he wanted, not where nature would have allowed" (247).

Lower-ranking officers are newer at the profession but are no less opportunistic about careerist positioning. Mellas's company commander, First Lieutenant (1LT) Fitch, is concerned that his company's inability to meet Simpson's orders, as outrageous as the orders are, will doom his personal fitness record and his career: "Fitch knew the Marine Corps well enough to realize that the word would get around. And in an organization as small as the Marines, he'd never be able to outrun it. No amount of explaining would help" (206). Both most-junior officers 2LTs Hawke and Goodwin recognize the careerist moves of other officers, but neither seems similarly motivated. Hawke, who cares about the Marines' welfare (98–99) but is only a Reserve officer, agrees to become part of the Regular Marine Corps because there seems nothing better for him to do (558) and ends up being mistakenly fragged; Goodwin is a "natural hunter" who simply enjoys the challenge of warring, career or not (13).

Since Mellas is the central character of *Matterhorn*, his opportunistic careerism is revealed the most. Mellas joined the Marines expressly to advance his post-military career, and he "realized that part of him would wish anything, and maybe do anything, if it meant getting ahead or saving his own skin" (6–7). Like Blakely, Mellas's actions are motivated more by the glory of having a combat record and the reputation of being a caring leader than of being a caring leader (56–57). In what to him is a zero-sum game, Mellas envies the successes of other lieutenants, especially Goodwin (103), but he also resents the careerism of his seniors when it involves using him (212). Even after a torturous and inglorious patrol and 8 days without food, Mellas "daydream[s] of glory and recognition" (248) and gathers intelligence because "bringing in solid information would make him look good" (253). When Mellas is appointed the new company executive officer (XO), he laments leaving his platoon to a brand-new 2LT, but is happy for his own advancement: "Mellas felt like a turd. But this was his chance to move up. To be the executive officer this early in his tour gave him ample time to get a company" (268).

Mellas's abrupt transformation from careerist to leader occurs more than halfway into the novel, when in an epiphany, Mellas comprehends the meaning of the Marine Corps' collectivist motto, *semper fi*: "Now, seeing the Marines run across the landing zone, Mellas knew he could never join that cynical laughter [with Princeton friends about the notion of honor] again. Something had changed. People he loved were going to die to give meaning and life to what he'd always thought of as meaningless words in a dead language" (324). His new belief staunches any further talk about his career, and the remainder of the novel illustrates Mellas's commitment to protecting the "kids," the enlisted men in the company. Mellas is not motivated by any of the exhortations ordinarily used. Instead, he is persuaded by the brothers-in-arms dictum that men fight for one another and no one or nothing else, an idea central to current totem rhetoric.

That Mellas calls the men who are subordinate to him "kids" is significant, especially because none of the senior officers in the novel uses this nomenclature and it rarely appears elsewhere in Vietnam War fiction. Its constant use by Mellas[20] reminds readers of the patriarchal organization of the military and of the father–son relationships invoked in blood sacrifice. Although usually only a few years older than the Marines he calls "kids," following his transformation Mellas assumes a fatherly role toward them. Rather than ensuring they not go into combat, or his mutinying against or killing Simpson, Mellas/father reinforces the totem's blood sacrifice by justifying the violence he and his "sons" have committed. Mellas's conclusion that killing is human nature (500)—and thereby fated, inexorable—allows his confession that he enjoys killing people, having met the "mad monkey" he says exists in all Americans (559–560). The novel concludes in a ritual that secures the totem and the dictates of blood sacrifice when the Marines "cast off the knowledge of who sent them to die" (Marvin and Ingle 73). The "kids" chant a roll-call of their dead: "Then soft voices, chanting in a weird atonal harmony, rose like spirits from the earth below . . . The chanting went on, the musicians giving in to the rhythm of their own being, finding healing in touching that rhythm, and healing in chanting about death, the only real god they knew" (565–566). Mellas's deduction that to be human is to be violent is ritualized by his "children," their innocence and forgetting a confirmation of his equation. In light of this "human nature," the careerism of Blakely and Simpson—and Mellas—is to be forgotten and forgiven.

The Lotus Eaters, masculinities, and blood sacrifice

The Lotus Eaters dwells on the relationship of fathers and sons also, though because the focal character is female and is not expected to perform masculinity, the parent-and-child roles are likely to be overlooked. In *Female Masculinity*, Judith Halberstam reminds readers, however, that the outlines of masculinity may be most visible when practiced in female bodies. Her argument can be extended, then, to the father–son relationships of blood sacrifice: that in war stories neither fathers nor sons must be male to define and defend the societal boundaries. *The Lotus Eaters* deals with war photography: its role in war, its power to influence storytelling and mythmaking, its morality, and its addictiveness. Nearly all of the photographers featured in the novel suffer from this addiction.[21] Journalism often is blamed for the war's outcome, too, because the war in Viet Nam was the United States's first televised war, and correspondents and photographers were relatively uncontrolled. "Our worst enemy seems to be the press," President Richard Nixon complained (Hammond ix). In *Dispatches* Michael Herr exemplifies the news media's free-wheeling status, free to go whenever he chooses to wherever he can find transportation.[22]

Like the focal characters in *Tree of Smoke* and *Matterhorn*, the focal character of *The Lotus Eaters* comes to Viet Nam as a young adult and the character's worldview is turned upside down by the experience. Having dropped out of college to ensure she did not miss a short-lived war (87), Helen Adams arrives in Saigon in 1965, soon after the United States escalated its intervention to full-blown combat.[23] Except for several months stateside, Helen stays until after the United States withdraws in 1973 and the North Vietnamese invade Saigon in April 1975. Although Helen arrives intending to work as a photographer, at the outset of her decade there she is neither trained nor experienced in photography, nor does she even own the "weapon" of a combat journalist, a real camera (90). She thinks of this war as an opportunity to vindicate her lifelong role as a "tomboy, refusing dolls and dresses, always hanging out with the boys."[24] She resents having been sidelined as a child because she is female: "Her father and Michael [her brother] shared the idea of soldiering and she had been left out. She cried when she had to stay in the kitchen with her mother, told to bake cookies . . . as they went out shooting" (87). Her father was killed in 1950 during the American war in Korea and her brother was killed in Viet Nam 14 years later (77). Although her brother's 1964 death as a member of the Special Forces had been reported as heroic, the description did not ring true to what Helen knew of him, and so one of her aims is to investigate his death (81). In blood sacrifice terms, Helen's suspicion about her brother's alleged heroism initiates her desire to know what exists on the other side of the border, what actually happens to the sacrificial victims the United States sends to war, taboo knowledge for females in American totem society. In terms of Connell's gender system, in coming to war Helen enters the traditional male domain and, thereby, hierarchies of masculinities where as a female she is unwelcome and marginalized.

Helen arrives, then, already with complicated relationships to her two male relatives, echoing for a reader the blood sacrifice invoked in *Tree of Smoke*. Although Helen never expresses desiring a father-figure, her father's death when she was a young girl and her brother's when she was a young woman might lead a reader to conclude that she longs for one. This conclusion could make sense, given that soon after her arrival in Saigon, Helen begins an affair with Sam Darrow, "Mr. Vietnam" (75), a much older, married

Pulitzer Prize-winning veteran war photographer who could be read as a father figure: he teaches her what he knows about war photography and provides entrance to the masculine hierarchy.[25] But Helen realizes late in the novel, 7 years after Darrow's death and while a captive of the Khmer Rouge in Cambodia that the price of entrance was to be under Darrow's "spell," that he was "poisoned" by violence and had poisoned her, too (379). The "father" had bequeathed to his protégée violence, both the totem secret and the constituent element of the Western masculine hierarchy in war. Realizing this, Helen rejects Darrow's lessons in masculine individualism in favor of those of Vietnamese Linh, "the least" poisoned and an advocate for taking one's identity from a collective, of being a "brick in the wall" (151).

Marvin and Ingle's theory is most pertinent in terms of Helen's being a female at war. Readers see that the American males in the novel already compete for dominance, journalists and combatants alike. Many of these males are dismayed by Helen's presence, as though her ability to do what they do diminishes their masculinizing war-making prowess. This idea—of competing for dominant masculinity—also coincides with Connell's social organization of masculinity as hierarchical and in constant crisis. An able competitor, Helen is threatening because she can practice masculinity but is not even supposed to be in masculinity's arena.[26] At Helen's first meeting with Darrow he is unhappy to see "another shiny, young, innocent face landing in the war, especially a female one," and another journalist complains, "So now the girls are coming. Can't be much of a war after all" (75). Gary, the man who hires Helen, comments "Headquarters is busting me about hiring women" (55); Robert, a journalist and onetime-suitor to Helen, declares after her first trek into the field, "It's not a place for a woman" (96), and later remarks snidely, "That's what's so delicious about you. You think like a man" (244). American military men are equally displeased: Frank MacCrae, a former Special Forces officer who had made Viet Nam his home for 7 years, laments that with the advent of "girl reporters" the "good ol' days are gone" (113); and as Helen prepares to photograph a dying US soldier, he moans he does not "want a woman to see me this way" (130). "Vietnam" muses Annick, the French shop owner who befriends Helen, "is a man's world. We have to make our own rules, but always the obstacle here is men" (105).

"In totem myth," explain Marvin and Ingle, "men defend culture while women maintain and consolidate it. The male principle is differentiation and exclusion, the female principle is connection and reintegration."[27] Further, totem myth "rehearses a traditional division of sexual labor in which men's bodies are sacrificed for fighting, and women's bodies are sacrificed to the nurture of children" (113). This distinction requires keeping males and females divergent; males can be designated as men only by separating from females, the "regenerative center" (115). Maintaining totem society requires that "killing authority" be retained among the (male) totem elders, so that they alone have the authority to kill, to send sons as sacrifice, and to confer that killing authority on the males sent to war. The problem of women in the military, the elders of American society suggest, is less about females being killed than about females having the authority to kill others. "Objections to women as battlefield killers taps the same issue that makes abortion controversial in the larger society," remark Marvin and Ingle. "In both cases women claim the killing power that is reserved for and must be ritually dedicated by the [male] totem" (116).

Helen's presence in Viet Nam therefore not only strains an already stressed masculine gender system of males jockeying for position, but she also claims "killing power" in arriving there in the first place, when she refuses to be "sidelined" by "human interest stories" (111), and when she aggressively seeks opportunities to be in combat situations. In effect, her shooting work as a photographer is hegemonic "killing power": "cold, clear, and mechanical" (136). After Helen witnesses a Marine kill himself rather than follow orders that were suicidal but would have won him a medal posthumously, Helen knows the totem secret: "Before, there had been this small, shiny thing inside her that kept her immune from what was happening, and now she knew it had only been her ignorance, and she felt herself falling into a deep, dark place" (218). With this understanding, in Vietnam War parlance Helen no longer is a cherry. After the Marine's suicide, she comprehends what is required of totem society's sacrificial victims; she concludes later, too, that her brother "died like an animal," not a valiant hero (363). Her knowledge endangers the totem society: women/mothers are not supposed to know about the required sacrifice or they may elect not to regenerate, to provide the sons for such a sacrifice.

As a female who has chosen to go to war, Helen figuratively is outside of the "regenerative center" of totem society. Presumably, she has the option to return to its folds without the conditions imposed on males at war: to remain silent about the totem secret, the lessons learned at war. When she returns to the States after Darrow's late 1967 death, Helen imagines "Home will fix things" (271); domestic life will obliterate the lessons she learned in Viet Nam, and "she cooked for the first time in her life" (275). The lessons prevail, though, when she urges a young man to dodge the draft by going to Canada. "If you go [into the military]," she insists, despite his parents's support of military service, "they will use you up like a piece of meat" (275). Helen's knowledge of war, without the prohibition of silence imposed on "sons," is dangerous to the totem myth. "[Y]ou're not that kind of girl" says her rebuffed suitor when she stops their sex and declares she wants to be "the kind of girl you think of when you go off to war" (281). Clearly, rejoining the regenerative center as a female is not so simple for Helen, and though she may practice war's "cold, clear, and mechanical" masculine behaviors in Viet Nam, she also is not supposed to be a member of the sacrificial class at war. Although she may opt to return to the regenerative center, Helen is more in-between, "not that kind of girl," and has no choice but to recross the boundary of American society, to return to the Vietnam War.

Ultimately, though, Helen is also banished from the regenerative center of totem society. Shortly after she returns to Viet Nam and is involved in perhaps the most hegemonic of war masculinities, an ambush, she is wounded in the abdomen. The military doctors who attend to Helen's wound, accustomed only to male anatomies, botch her surgical repair and she ends up having to have an emergency hysterectomy (300–301). As a female in totem society, Helen is refused killing power because her role is to regenerate, to produce sons for sacrifice, and to reintegrate them on their return from war. Her choice to operate across the border in the world of war, therefore, is a punishable violation; with her punishment, the removal of her reproductive organs, Helen no longer has the option to return to the regenerative center. Thus, she is neither in the sacrificial class of males sent to war nor is she in the reproductive class of females whose job it is to produce more members of the sacrificial class. Helen has no place in American totem society.

Conclusion

This conclusion—a strong, independent young woman banished from her society—would be an unpalatable story to readers longing for redemptive national unity in light of 9/11 and the wars in Afghanistan and Iraq.[28] Likewise, *Tree of Smoke*'s ending with Skip's equation of war, masculinity, and not thinking, and *Matterhorn*'s Mellas concluding that war is human nature, are equally dismal. The early twenty-first century Support the Troops Syndrome mandates uplift from these Vietnam War novels, and none of these dismal endings do. All three novels reverse course, however, in their last few, heavy-handed, surprising sentences, satisfying the mandate. Thus, rather than Helen's being raped and murdered by the Khmer Rouge boys, she is released and thereby reborn: "Helen come back from the dead" (386). Similarly, the chanted penance ritualistically performed by Mellas's "kids" absolves them of their sins, freeing them to be agents of their own destinies, not fated to violence: "He [Mellas] knew that all of them were shadows: the chanters, the dead, the living. All shadows, moving across this landscape of mountains and valleys, changing the pattern of things as they moved but leaving nothing changed when they left. Only the shadows themselves could change" (566). Finally and literally, in *Tree of Smoke* redemption is assured. Although Kathy has every reason to resent bitterly war's production of orphans, and is repulsed by the American audience from whom she has to beg funds and by the questionable results of the money's use, she decides "All will be saved. All will be saved" (614).

These brief and prosaic endings are literary feints, distracting readers' attention away from the existential woman-banished/ men-condemned/war-as-mindless conclusions and leading early twenty-first century readers back to supporting the troops. In effect, just as the veteran was rehabilitated to an honorable position during the Reagan era of the 1980s, the reader is rehabilitated by these totemic fictions of the twenty-first century. "Cheering for the troops," says Andrew Bacevich, "provides a convenient mechanism for voiding obligation and perhaps easing guilty consciences." These novels are a part of that mechanism as they assuage guilt, assuring the reader that the best way to support the troops . . . is to send them into war.

Notes

1. See Miller and Vu for a history of the scholarship published by 2009.
2. At a September 2013 conference held at the National Archives and hosted by the Texas Tech University Vietnam Center and Archive, Phillips said that it was not until he added the last chapter of his book, one linking the Vietnam and Iraq wars, that publishers were willing to consider his manuscript.
3. Ordinary Americans also noted the similarity between the wars. In a March 2003 posting to *AsianWeek*, Vietnamese American Sonny Le notes that his experience as a child of nightly rocket "lullabies" in Viet Nam is probably being experienced in Iraq. "I love this country and have faith in its core moral values," says Le, "[b]ut what I have seen . . . shows the ugly warmongering side of America that I cannot reconcile in my conscience . . . We cannot hide behind the illusion and lies that our weapons of mass destruction [e.g. 'smart bombs'] will only kill the bad guys. War kills, period." See also Dumbrell and Ryan.
4. For a discussion of *We Were Soldiers*, see Boyle, "Rescuing Masculinity," and for one of *Tropic Thunder*, see Combe and Boyle.
5. Marlantes reports that publishers frequently advised him they would be more interested in his novel were it set in Afghanistan (James).
6. See Combe and Boyle, "Coda."
7. See Lembcke; and Beamish, Molotch, and Flacks.
8. See Bacevich, "I Lost My Son to a War I Oppose." See V. Nguyen, who names this pressure to support troops "compulsory empathy" ("Remembering War" 147). See Huebner, Part III, "The Vietnam Era."
9. See Boyle, "Rescuing Masculinity."
10. See Cleland, and Hemingway.
11. See "Costs of War."
12. See Halberstam.
13. See Connell, and Connell and Messerschmidt.
14. See Steigerwald 247; Bates, chapter 5.
15. Geoffrey Galt Harpham quotes an Air Force Academy instructor participating in Harpham's seminar on Joseph Conrad's *Heart of Darkness*: "My understanding of history teaches me that violence is always going to be a part of human existence, and my moral sense says that managed violence, in the service of the right principles, is better than the alternatives. What we try to do here . . . is train. . . *reluctant killers*. We teach them how to do things that will haunt them for the rest of their lives. That's what we do. We stand there in front of our cadets, and we train them to do things they would never do if the nation didn't ask it of them. And even though the

nation asks it, and no matter how disciplined they are, they will still be haunted by what they've done. And they have to be. If they aren't, then we've only trained Kilgores [a character in *Apocalypse Now*], murderers without a conscience" (200).
16 See Hedges, 19–42.
17 Officers are more likely to have chosen to be in the military and less likely than enlisted men to have been drafted. This could partly explain officers' careerism, their drive to improve their professional lot in the military. Additionally, in the Vietnam War era it was still expected that male leaders would have served in the military, usually as officers. Until President Bill Clinton, every modern-day president had been in the US military.
18 Racial conflict dominates company-level concerns in the novel, and critics comment on this conflict most frequently. As Marlantes reports, however, he added this element to the novel late in his decades-long writing process, suggesting that it was only in hindsight and with perspective on his experience that Marlantes envisioned racial conflict as part of the story he wanted to tell (James).
19 See both the novel's glossary for all military terms as well as the Chain of Command diagram at the front of the book.
20 Marlantes also uses this word to describe young adults during the Vietnam War era. See James.
21 On this issue of addiction to war, see Hedges, and Boal.
22 This unfettered role of war correspondents during the Vietnam War can help to explain the current highly controlled standard of war reporting: embedded reporters. See Paul and Kim; and Franklin, *Vietnam*, chapter 1.
23 From 1954 until March 1965, the United States supported the South Vietnamese with at most 23,000 advisers to South Vietnamese military units. In early 1965, the United States introduced Marine combat units in Danang; by the end of the year, nearly 200,000 combat troops were in the country. 1965 is also the year that Dickey Chapelle, reputed war photographer during World War II and in Hungary and Cuba, returned to Viet Nam and met her death in November while on patrol with American Marines (Faas and Page 136).
24 Helen is depicted as conventionally beautiful by American standards: blond, blue-eyed, tall, and slim. She looks like the "girl next door," symbolizing "the way of life the United States had committed itself to defending against communism and a host of associated fears, including homosexuality, racial strife, the collapse of the nuclear family, and the disintegration of capitalist prosperity. Faced with these anxieties, American women who ventured to Vietnam were expected

to fulfill the conventional women's roles of caregivers, mothers, and virginal girlfriends" (Stur 3).

25 Darrow is an absent father to his biological son, having rarely seen the boy in his 6 years of life. He resembles the actual war photographer and Pulitzer Prize winner, Larry Burrows, who was, as is Darrow, killed (in 1971) when his helicopter was shot down over Laos.

26 In *Tree of Smoke*, Kathy plays a similarly threatening part for Skip. In *Matterhorn*, Mellas thinks "He really hated women at some level, maybe because they stayed home and couldn't get drafted. Maybe it was the power they held over him because of his yearning to be with one, just to talk with one" (210).

27 To be consistent in terms of gender, the line should refer to "masculine" and "feminine" principles, not "male" and "female."

28 See Faludi for an investigation of the gendered national narratives following 9/11.

FURTHER READING

Since wars are peculiar to their time and place, reading their fictions requires historical and cultural contextualizing. The contextualizing of Vietnam War fiction is ongoing, especially as national archives—in the United States, France, states in the former Soviet Union, Viet Nam, and other countries in Southeast Asia—are opened to scholars and as more cultural and diplomatic exchanges happen between Viet Nam and the west. The American wars in Iraq and Afghanistan have also renewed interest in war generally and the Vietnam War specifically, resulting in more fictional, critical, and historical works. With the sources cited in each of this volume's chapters, the following sources can be used further to contextualize the American war in Viet Nam.

Primary works: fiction, film, memoir

Prose fictions

A Good Scent From a Strange Mountain (Robert Olen Butler, 1992)
American Pastoral (Philip Roth, 1997)
American Woman (Susan Choi, 2003)
Better Times Than These (Winston Groom, 1987)
Birds of Paradise Lost (Andrew Lam, 2013)
Buffalo Afternoon (Susan Fromberg Schaeffer, 1989)
Fake House (Linh Dinh, 2000)
For Rouenna (Sigrid Nunez, 2001)
Grass Roof, Tin Roof (Dao Strom, 2003)
Indian Country (Philip Caputo, 1987)
Machine Dreams (Jayne Anne Phillips, 1984)
Meditations in Green (Stephen Wright, 1983)
Monkey Bridge (Lan Cao, 1997)

The Armies of the Night: History as a Novel, The Novel as History
   (Norman Mailer, 1968)
The Book of Salt (Monique Truong, 2003)
The Ha–Ha (Dave King, 2005)
The Short-Timers (Gustav Hasford, 1979)
The Waiting Room (Mary Morris, 1989)
Vietnam Perkasie (W.D. Ehrhart, 1983)

Films

84C MoPic (1989)
Apocalypse Now (1979)
Casualties of War (1989)
Coming Home (1978)
Forrest Gump (1994)
Full Metal Jacket (1987)
Good Morning, Vietnam (1987)
Go Tell the Spartans (1978)
Hamburger Hill (1987)
Hearts and Minds (1974; documentary)
Heaven and Earth (1993)
In Country (1989)
Platoon (1986)
The Fog of War (2003; documentary)
The Quiet American (1958, 2002)
Rambo: First Blood (1982)
Return With Honor (1998; documentary)
Taxi Driver (1976)

Memoirs

*An American Requiem: God, My Father, and the War That Came Between
   Us* (James Carroll, 1996)
A Rumor of War (Philip Caputo, 1977)
Black Prisoner of War: A Conscientious Objector's Vietnam Memoir
   (James A. Daly and Lee Bergman, 1975)
*Catfish and Mandala: A Two-Wheeled Voyage Through the Landscape
   and Memory of Vietnam* (Andrew Pham, 1999)
Chickenhawk (Robert Mason, 1983)

Faith of My Fathers (John McCain, 2000)
Fortunate Son: The Autobiography of Lewis B. Puller, Jr. (Lewis B. Puller, 1991)
Home Before Morning: The Story of An American Nurse in Vietnam (Lynda Van Devanter, 1983)
In Pharoah's Army: Memories of the Lost War (Tobias Wolff, 1994)
G.I. Diary (David Parks, 1968)
Late Thoughts On An Old War: The Legacy of Vietnam (Philip Beidler, 2004)
Nationalist in the Viet Nam Wars: Memoirs of a Victim Turned Soldier (Nguyen Cong Luan, 2012)
Our War (David Harris, 1996)
Perfume Dreams (Andrew Lam, 2005)
The Eaves of Heaven (Andrew X. Pham, 2008)
The Passing of the Night: My Seven Years as a Prisoner of the North Vietnamese (Robinson Risner, 1973)
The Twenty-Five Year Century: A South Vietnamese General Remembers the Indochina War to the Fall of Saigon (Lam Quang Thi, 2001)
Vietnamerica: A Family's Journey (GB Tran, 2010)
We Were Soldiers Once . . . and Young (Joseph Galloway and Hal Moore, 1992)
When Heaven and Earth Changed Places: A Vietnamese Woman's Journey From War To Peace (Le Ly Hayslip, 1989)

Critical works

Edited collections

America and the Vietnam War: Re-Examining the Culture and History of a Generation (Andrew Wiest, Mary Kathryn Barbier and Glenn Robins, 2009)
America Rediscovered: Critical Essays on Literature and Film of the Vietnam War (Owen W. Gilman, Jr. and Lorrie Smith, 1990)
Historical Memory and Representations of the Vietnam War (Walter L. Hixson, 2000)
Inventing Vietnam: The War in Film and Television (Michael Anderegg, 1991)
The United States and Viet Nam From War to Peace: Papers From an Interdisciplinary Conference on Reconciliation (Robert M. Slabey, 1996)
The Vietnam War and American Culture (John Carlos Rowe and Rick Berg, 1991)

The Vietnam War and Postmodernity (Mark Bibby, 2000).
The Vietnam War: Its History, Literature, and Music (Kenton J. Clymer, 1998)
Walking Point: American Narratives of Vietnam (Thomas Myers, 1988)

Monographs

American Exceptionalism in the Age of Globalization: The Spector of Vietnam (William V. Spanos, 2008)
How the War Was Remembered: Hollywood and Vietnam (Albert Auster and Leonard Quart, 1988)
Prisoners of Culture: Representing the Vietnam POW (Elliott Gruner, 1993)
Receptions of War: Vietnam in American Culture (Andrew Martin, 1993)
The American War in Contemporary Vietnam: Transnational Remembrance and Representation (Christina Schwenkel, 2009)
Vietnam in American Literature (Philip H. Melling, 1990)
Writing After War: American War Fiction from Realism to Postmodernism (John Limon, 1994)

WORKS CITED

Adair, Lara. "A Girl's Flight to a Bright, Harsh Land." *San Francisco Chronicle*. May 18, 2003: M3. Print.
Aguilar-San Juan, Karin. *Little Saigons: Staying Vietnamese in America*. Minneapolis, MN: University of Minnesota Press, 2009. Print.
Allen, Esther. "No Man's Land by Duong Thu Huong; Nina McPherson; Pham Huy Duong (Review)." *World Literature Today* 80.5 (2006): 58–60. Print.
Anderegg, Michael, ed. *Inventing Vietnam: The War in Film and Television*. Philadelphia, PA: Temple UP, 1991. Print.
Appy, Christian. *Working Class War: American Combat Soldiers and Vietnam*. Chapel Hill, NC: University of North Carolina Press, 1993. Print.
Bacevich, Andrew. *Breach of Trust: How Americans Failed Their Soldiers and Their Country*. New York: Henry Holt, 2013. Print.
—. "I Lost My Son to a War I Oppose. We Were Both Doing Our Duty." *The Washington Post*. May 27, 2007. Web.
—. *The New American Militarism: How Americans are Seduced by War*. New York: Oxford University Press, 2005. Print.
Band of Brothers. Dir. David Frankel, Mikael Salomon, Tom Hanks, David Leland, Richard Loncraine, David Nutter, Ohil Alden Robinson, and Tony To Perf. Scott Grimes, Michael Leitch, and Damian Lewis. HBO. (2001). TV Mini-series.
Banerian, James. "Novel Without a Name by Duong Thu Huong; Phan Huy Duong; Nina McPherson (Review)." *World Literature Today* (1995): 653–654. Print.
Bảo Ninh. *Special Feature—Bao Ninh Interview*. Anh.ibo.org. September 2009. Web.
—. *The Sorrow of War (Nỗi buồn chiến tranh)*. Trans. Phan Thanh Hao. New York: Random House, 1993. Print.
Bates, Milton J. *The Wars We Took to Vietnam: Cultural Conflict and Storytelling*. Berkeley, CA: University of California Press, 1996. Print.
Beamish, Thomas D., Harvey Molotch, and Richard Flacks. "Who Supports the Troops? Vietnam, the Gulf War, and the Making of Collective Memory." *Social Problems* 42.3 (August 1995): 344–360. Print.

Beattie, Keith. *The Scar that Binds: American Culture and the Vietnam War*. New York: New York University Press, 1998. Print.
Beidler, Philip D. *American Literature and the Experience of Vietnam*. Athens, GA: The University of Georgia Press, 1982. Print.
—. "Thirty Years After: The Archaeologies." *Thirty Years After: New Essays on Vietnam War Literature, Film, and Art*. Ed. Mark Heberle, 10–27. Print.
Berlant, Lauren. *The Queen of America Goes to Washington City: Essays on Sex and Citizenship*. Durham, NC: Duke University Press, 2002. Print.
Blang, Eugenie M. *Allies At Odds: America, Europe, and Vietnam, 1961–1968*. Lanham, MD: Rowman & Littlefield, 2011. Print.
Blodgett, Harriet. "The Feminist Artistry of Vietnam's Duong Thu Huong." *World Literature Today* 75.3/4 (2001): 31–39. Print.
Boal, Mark. "The Real Cost of War." *Playboy* (March 2007): 53–54, 62, 128–134. Print.
Bonnet, Michele. "'To Take the Sin Out of Slicing Trees . . .': The Law of the Tree in *Beloved*." *African American Review* 31 (1997): 41–54. Print.
"Boston Manifesto." October 18, 2004. Web. November 29, 2013.
Bourke, Joanna. *An Intimate History of Killing: Face to Face Killing in 20th Century Warfare*. New York: Basic Books, 1999. Print.
Boyle, Brenda M. "At Home With the Unhomely: Vietnamese and Iraqi Narratives of Invasion, Occupation, and 'Resettlement'." *Representations of War, Migration and Refugeehood: Interdisciplinary Perspectives*. Ed. Daniel Rellstab and Christiane Schlote. New York: Routledge, forthcoming, 2014. Print.
—. *Masculinity in Vietnam War Narratives: A Critical Study of Fiction, Films and Nonfiction Writings*. Jefferson, NC: McFarland, 2009. Print.
—. "Rescuing Masculinity: Captivity, Rescue and Gender in American War Narratives." *The Journal of American Culture* 34.2 (June 2011): 149–160. Print.
Bradley, Mark Philip. *Imagining Vietnam and America: The Making of Postcolonial Vietnam, 1919–1950*. Chapel Hill, NC: University of North Carolina Press, 2000. Print.
—. *Vietnam At War*. New York: Oxford University Press, 2009. Print.
Bradley, Mark Philip and Marilyn B. Young, eds. *Making Sense of the Vietnam Wars: Local, National, and Transnational Perspectives*. New York: Oxford University Press, 2008. Print.
Brigham, Robert K. *Iraq, Vietnam, and the Limits of American Power*. New York: PublicAffairs, 2006. Print.
Britto, Karl Ashoka. *Disorientations: France, Vietnam, and the Ambivalence of Interculturality*. Hong Kong: Hong Kong University Press, 2004. Print.

Buchholz, Brad. "Tim O'Brien: On Life, Literature, and Peace." *Austin American-Statesman* 11 (November 2012): D1; D6; D7. Print.
Buckley, C. "The Wall." *Esquire* (September 1985): 61–73. Print.
Bùi Diễm. *In the Jaws of History*. New York: Houghton Mifflin Harcourt, 1987. Print.
Butler, Judith. *Gender Trouble: Feminism and the Subversion of Identity*, 2nd edn. New York: Routledge, 1999. Print.
—. *Precarious Life: The Powers of Mourning and Violence*. New York: Verso, 2006. Print.
Capote, Truman. *In Cold Blood*. New York: Random House, 1965. Print.
doCarmo, Stephen N. "Bombs from Coke Cans: Appropriating Mass Culture in Bobbie Ann Mason's *In Country*." *The Journal of Popular Culture* 36.3 (January 2002): 589–599. Print.
Cheung, King-Kok. *Articulate Silences: Hisaye Yamamoto, Maxine Hong Kingston, and Joy Kogawa*. Ithaca, NY: Cornell University Press, 1993. Print.
Christopher, Renny. *The Viet Nam War/The American War: Images and Representations in Euro-American and Vietnamese Exile Narratives*. Amherst, MA: University of Massachusetts Press, 1995. Print.
Cleland, Max. *Strong at the Broken Places: A Personal Story*. Lincoln, VA: Chosen Books, 1980. Print.
Coffey, Michael. "Tim O'Brien; Inventing a New Form Helps the Author Talk About War, Memory, and Storytelling." *Publishers Weekly* (February 16, 1990): 60–61. Print.
Combe, Kirk and Brenda Boyle. *Masculinity and Monstrosity in Contemporary Hollywood Films*. Global Masculinities. New York: Palgrave MacMillan, 2013. Print.
Connell, R. W. *Masculinities*. Berkeley, CA: University of California Press, 1995. Print.
—. "The Social Organization of Masculinity." *The Masculinities Reader*. Ed. S. Whitehead and F. Barrett. Cambridge: Polity, 2001, 30–50. Print.
Connell, R. W. and James W. Messerschmidt. "Hegemonic Masculinity: Rethinking the Concept." *Gender & Society* 19.6 (December 2005): 829–859. Print.
Connery, Thomas B., ed. *A Sourcebook of American Literary Journalism: Representative Writers in an Emerging Genre*. Westport, CN: Greenwood, 1992. Print.
Cooper, Nicola. *France in Indochina: Colonial Encounters*. New York: Berg, 2001. Print.
"Costs of War." 2011. http://www.costsofwar.org/article/who-we-are December 9, 2013. Web.
Cullen, Jim. *Born in the USA: Bruce Springsteen and the American Tradition*. Middletown, CT: Wesleyan University Press, 2005. Print.

Dang, Thuy Vo. "The Cultural Work of Anticommunism in the San Diego Vietnamese-American Community." *Amerasia* 31.2 (2005): 65–85. Print.
Del Vecchio, John. *The 13th Valley*. New York: Bantam Books, 1982. Print.
Department of Defense. "A Pocket Guide to Vietnam," revised edn. DoD PG-21 A. 1966. Print.
Didion, Joan. *Slouching Toward Bethlehem*. New York: Simon & Schuster, 1979. Print.
Dinh, Linh, ed. *Night, Again: Contemporary Fiction from Vietnam*. New York: 7 Stories Press, 1996. Print.
Dommen, Arthur J. *The Indochinese Experience of the French and the Americans: Nationalism and Communism in Cambodia, Laos, and Vietnam*. Bloomington, IN: Indiana University Press, 2001. Print.
Doyle, Jeff, Jeffrey Grey, and Peter Pierce, eds. *Australia's Vietnam War*. College Station, TX: Texas A&M Press, 2002. Print.
Dumbrell, John and David Ryan, eds. *Vietnam in Iraq: Tactics, Lessons, Legacies and Ghosts*. New York: Routledge, 2007. Print.
Duong, Lan. *Treacherous Subjects: Gender, Culture, and Trans-Vietnamese Feminism*. Philadelphia, PA: Temple University Press, 2012. Print.
Dương Thu Hương. *Novel Without a Name (Tiểu thuyết vô đề)*. Trans. Phan Huy Đường and Nina McPherson. New York: William Morrow, 1995. Print.
—. *Paradise of the Blind (Những thiên đường mù)*. Trans. Phan Huy Dường and Nina McPherson. New York: Penguin, 1993. Print.
Durkin, Anita. "Object Written, Written Object: Slavery, Scarring, and Complications of Authorship in *Beloved*." *African American Review* 41.3 (2007): 541–556. Print.
Elliott, David. "Parallel Wars? Can Lessons of Vietnam be Applied to Iraq?" Ed. Lloyd C. Gardner and Marilyn B. Young, 17–33. Print.
Elliott, Mai. *Sacred Willow: Four Generations in the Life of a Vietnamese Family*. New York: Oxford University Press, 2000. Print.
Espiritu, Yen Le. *Asian American Women and Men: Labor, Laws and Love*. Thousand Oaks, CA: Sage Publications, 1997. Print.
—. "The We-Win-Even-When-We-Lose Syndrome." *American Quarterly* 58.2 (2006): 329–352. Print.
Faas, Horst and Tim Page, eds. *Requiem: By the Photographers Who Died in Vietnam and Indochina*. New York: Random House, 1997. Print.
Faludi, Susan. *The Terror Dream: Fear and Fantasy in Post-9/11 America*. New York: Metropolitan, 2007. Print.
Faris, Wendy. "Devastation and Replenishment: New World Narratives of Love and Nature." *Studies in the Humanities* 19.2 (1992): 171–182. Print.

Flags of Our Fathers. Dir. Clint Eastwood. Perf. Ryan Phillippe, Barry Pepper, Joseph Cross, Jesse Bradford. Paramount, 2006. Film.

Franklin, H. Bruce. "Can Vietnam Awaken Us Again? Teaching the Literature of the Vietnam War." *Radical Teacher* 666 (2003): 28–31. Print.

—. "Kicking the Denial Syndrome: Tim O'Brien's *In The Lake of the Woods.*" *Novel History: Historians and Novelists Confront America's Past (and Each Other).* Ed. Mark C. Carnes. New York: Simon & Schuster, 2001, 332–343. Print.

—. *Vietnam and Other American Fantasies.* Amherst, MA: University of Massachusetts Press, 2000. Print.

Gardner, Lloyd C. and Marilyn B. Young, eds. *Iraq and the Lessons of Vietnam: Or How Not to Learn from the Past.* New York: The New Press, 2007. Print.

Geng, Veronica. "Capable of Anything." *The New Yorker* May 11, 1987: 111. Print.

Gibbons, Reginald. "*Paco's Story.*" *TriQuarterly* (Winter 1988): 221. Print.

Gibson, James William. *The Perfect War: Technowar in Vietnam.* Boston, MA: The Atlantic Monthly Press, 1986. Print.

Gilman, Owen. *Vietnam and the Southern Imagination.* Jackson, MS: University Press of Mississippi, 1992. Print.

Goellnicht, Donald. "'Ethnic Literature's Hot': Asian American Literature, Refugee Cosmopolitanism, and Nam Le's *The Boat.*" *Journal of Asian American Studies.* Vol. 15. 2 (June 2012): 197–224. Print.

Goldenburg, Suzanne. "Why Vietnam's best-known author has stayed silent." *The Guardian/The Observer*, November 18, 2006. Web.

Gourevitch, Philip and Errol Morris. *Standard Operating Procedure.* New York: Penguin, 2008. Print.

Greiff, Louis K. "In the Name of the Brother: Larry Heinemann's *Paco's Story* and Male America." *Critique* 41.4 (2000): 381–389. Print.

Hagopian, Patrick. "Voices from Vietnam: Veterans' Oral Histories in the Classroom." *The Journal of American History* 87.2 (September 2000): 593–601. Print.

—. *The Vietnam War in American Memory: Veterans, Memorials, and the Politics of Healing.* Amherst, MA: University of Massachusetts Press, 2009. Print.

Halberstam, Judith. *Female Masculinity.* Durham: Duke University Press, 1998. Print.

Hale, Dana S. *Races on Display: French Representations of Colonized Peoples, 1886–1940.* Bloomington, IN: Indiana University Press, 2008. Print.

Hall, Stuart. "Cultural Identity and Diaspora." *Colonial Discourse and Post-Colonial Theory: A Reader.* Ed. Patrick Williams and Laura Chrisman. London: Harvester Wheatsheaf, 1994, 392–401. Print.

Hammond, William M. *Reporting Vietnam: Media and Military at War.* Lawrence, KS: University Press of Kansas, 1998. Print.

Harpham, Geoffrey Galt. *The Humanities and the Dream of America.* Chicago: The University of Chicago Press, 2011. Print.

Hawkins, Ty. *Reading Vietnam Amid the War on Terror.* American Literature Readings in the 21st Century. New York: Palgrave Macmillan, 2012. Print.

Healy, Dana. "Literature in Transition: An Overview of Vietnamese Writing of the Renovation Period." *The Canon in Southeast Asian Literatures: Literatures of Burma, Cambodia, Indonesia, Laos, Malaysia, the Philippines, Thailand and Vietnam.* Ed. David Smyth. New York: Curzon Press, 2000, 41–50. Print.

Heberle, Mark, ed. *Thirty Years After: New Essays on Vietnam War Literature, Film, and Art.* Newcastle-Upon-Tyne, UK: Cambridge Scholars Publishing, 2009. Print.

Hedges, Chris. *War Is a Force That Gives Us Meaning.* New York: Anchor, 2002. Print.

Heinemann, Larry. *Paco's Story.* New York: Penguin, 1987. Print.

Hellmann, John. *American Myth and the Legacy of Vietnam.* New York: Columbia University Press, 1986. Print.

—. *Fables of Fact: The New Journalism as New Fiction.* Urbana, IL: University of Illinois Press, 1981. Print.

Hemingway, Ernest. *A Farewell to Arms.* 1929. New York: Scribner, 1995. Print.

Henke, Suzette. *Shattered Subjects: Women's Life-Writing and Narrative Recovery.* New York: Palgrave Macmillan, 1998. Print.

Herman, Judith. *Trauma and Recovery.* New York: Basic Books, 1992. Print.

Herman, Judith Lewis. *Trauma and Recovery: From Domestic Abuse to Political Terror.* London: Pandora-Rivers, 2001. Print.

Herr, Michael. "Conclusion at Khe Sanh." *Esquire* (October 1969): 118–123, 201–208. Print.

—. *Dispatches.* New York: Random House, 1977. Print.

—. "Hell Sucks." *Esquire* (August 1968): 66–69, 109–110. Print.

—. "High on War." *Esquire* (January 1977): 82–94. Print.

—. "Illumination Rounds." *New American Review* 7. New York: New American Library, 1969, 64–85. Print.

—. "Khe Sanh." *Esquire* (September 1969): 118–123, 148–156. Print.

—. "Lz Loon." *Rolling Stone* (November 3, 1977): 10–18. Print.

—. "The War Correspondent: A Reappraisal." *Esquire* (April 1970): 95–101, 160–185. Print.

Herzog, Tobey. *Vietnam War Stories: Innocence Lost.* New York: Routledge, 1992. Print.

Hess, Gary R. *Vietnam: Explaining America's Lost War*. Malden, MA: Blackwell Publishing, 2009. Print.
Hinrichsen, Lisa. "'I Can't Believe It Was Really Real': Violence, Vietnam, and Bringing War Home in Bobbie Ann Mason's 'In Country.'" *The Southern Literary Journal* 40.2 (Spring 2008): 232–248. Print.
Hirsch, Marianne. *Family Frames: Photography, Narrative and Postmemory*. Cambridge, MA: Harvard University Press, 2002. Print.
Hixson, Walter L. "Viet Nam and 'Vietnam' in American History and Memory." Ed. Laderman and Martini, 44–57. Print.
Holbling, Walter. "Literary Sense-Making: American Vietnam War Fiction." *Vietnam War Images: War and Representation*. Ed. Jeffrey Walsh and James Aulich. New York: Macmillan Press, 1989, 123–140. Print.
Homosexuality and the Military: A Sourcebook of Official, Uncensored U.S. Government Documents. Upland, PA: DIANE Publishing, 1993. Print.
Horvitz, Deborah. *Literary Trauma: Sadism, Memory, and Sexual Violence in American Women's Fiction*. New York: State University of New York Press, 2000. Print.
Huebner, Andrew J. *The Warrior Image: Soldiers in American Culture from the Second World War to the Vietnam Era*. Chapel Hill, NC: The University of North Carolina Press, 2008. Print.
Hune, Shirley and Gail M. Nomura, eds. *Asian/Pacific Islander American Women: A Historical Anthology*. New York: New York University Press, 2003. Print.
James, Evan. "A Vietnam Epic Uncovers Old Wounds: An Interview With Karl Marlantes." *Mother Jones* (April 30, 2010). Web.
Janette, Michele, ed. *My Viet: Vietnamese American Literature in English, 1962–Present*. Honolulu, HI: University of Hawai'I Press, 2011. Print.
Jason, Philip K., ed. *Fourteen Landing Zones: Approaches to Vietnam War Literature*. Iowa City, IA: University of Iowa Press, 1991. Print.
Jeffords, Susan. "Tattoos, Scars, Diaries, and Writing Masculinity." *The Vietnam War and American Culture*. Ed. John Carlos Rowe and Rick Berg. New York: Columbia University Press, 1991, 208–225. Print.
—. *The Remasculinization of America: Gender and the Vietnam War*. Bloomington, IN: Indiana University Press, 1989. Print.
Johnson, Denis. *Tree of Smoke: A Novel*. New York: Farrar, Strauss & Giroux, 2007. Print.
Kaiko, Takeshi. *Into a Black Sun*. 1968. Trans. Cecilia Segewa Seigle. New York: Kodansha International, 1980. Print.
Kakutani, Michiko. "Did *Paco's Story* Deserve its Award?" *The New York Times*. November 16, 1987. Web. October 20, 2013.

Kang, Laura Hyun Yi. *Compositional Subject: Enfiguring Asian/American Women*. Durham, NC: Duke University Press, 2002. Print.

Kibria, Nazli. *Family Tightrope: The Changing Lives of Vietnamese Americans*. Princeton, NJ: Princeton University Press, 1993. Print.

Kim, Elaine. "Asian Americans and American Popular Culture." *Asian American History Dictionary*. Ed. Robert H. Kim. New York: Greenwood Press, 1986. Print.

—. "'Bad Women': Asian American Visual Artists Hanh Thi Pham, Hung Liu, and Yong Soon Min." *Feminist Studies* 22.3 (Autumn 1996): 573–602. Print.

Kinney, Katherine. *Friendly Fire: American Images of the Vietnam War*. New York: Oxford University Press, 2000. Print.

Klinkowitz, Jerome and John Somer, eds. *Writing Under Fire: Stories of the Vietnam War*. New York: Dell Publishing, 1978. Print.

Kovic, Ron. *Born on the Fourth of July*. New York: Pocket Books, 1976. Print.

Krasteva, Yonka. "The South and the West in Bobbie Ann Mason's 'In Country'." *The Southern Literary Journal* 26.2 (Spring 1994): 77–90. Print.

Laderman, Scott. "Hollywood's Vietnam, 1929–1964: Scripting intervention, Spotlighting Injustice." *Pacific Historical Review* 78.4 (November 2009): 578–607. Print.

Laderman, Scott and Edwin Martini, eds. *Four Decades On: Vietnam, the United States, and the Legacies of the Second Indochina War*. Durham, NC: Duke University Press, 2013. Print.

Lembcke, Jerry. *The Spitting Image: Myth, Memory, and the Legacy of Vietnam*. New York: New York University Press, 1998. Print.

Lê Minh Khuê. *The Stars, The Earth, The River*. Willimantic: Curbstone, 1997. Print.

Le, Sonny. "Embedded in My Mind: A Vietnam War Survivor Reflects on Iraq." *AsianWeek* March 23, 2003. Web.

le, thi diem thuy. *The Gangster We Are All Looking For*. New York: Knopf, 2003. Print.

Lieu, Nhi T. *The American Dream in Vietnamese*. Minneapolis, MN: University of Minnesota Press, 2011. Print.

Lindaman, Dana and Kyle Ward, eds. *History Lessons: How Textbooks from Around The World Portray U.S. History*. New York: New Press, 2004. Print.

Liparulo, Steven P. "Beyond the American Canon: *Paradise of the Blind*, the Politics of Family, and the Economics of Affect." Ed. Mark Heberle, 215–223. Print.

—. "'Incense and Ashes': The Postmodern Work of Refutation in Three Vietnam War Novels." *War, Literature, and the Arts* 15.1/2 (2003): 71–94. Print.

Loewen, James W. *Lies My Teacher Told Me: Everything Your American History Textbook Got Wrong*, revised edn. New York: Simon & Schuster, 2007. Print.
Logevall, Fredrik. *Choosing War: The Lost Chance for Peace and the Escalation of War in Vietnam*. Berkeley, CA: University of California Press, 1999. Print.
—. *Embers of War: The Fall of an Empire and the Making of America's Vietnam*. New York: Random House, 2012. Print.
Lowe, Lisa. *Immigrant Acts: On Asian American Cultural Politics*. Durham, NC: Duke University Press, 1996. Print.
Luckhurst, Roger. "In War Times: Fictionalizing Iraq." *Contemporary Literature* 53.4 (2012): 713–737. Print.
—. *The Trauma Question*. New York: Routledge, 2008. Print.
Machida, Margo. *Unsettled Visions: Contemporary Asian American Artists and the Social Imaginary*. Durham, NC: Duke University Press, 2008. Print.
Maguen, Shira and Brett Litz. "Moral Injury in Veterans of War." *PTSD Research Quarterly* 23.1 (2012): 1–6. Print.
Mailer, Norman. *Miami and the Siege of Chicago*. New York: New American Library, 1968. Print.
—. *The Armies of the Night: History as a Novel, the Novel as History*. New York: New American Library, 1968. Print.
—. *The Executioner's Song*. Boston, MA: Little, Brown, 1979. Print.
—. *The Naked and the Dead*. New York: Rinehart, 1948. Print.
Marlantes, Karl. *Matterhorn: A Novel of the Vietnam War*. New York: Atlantic Monthly Press, 2010. Print.
Martini, Edwin A. *Invisible Enemies: The American War on Vietnam, 1975–2000*. Amherst, MA: University of Massachusetts Press, 2007. Print.
Marvin, Carolyn and David W. Ingle. *Blood Sacrifice and the Nation: Totem Rituals and the American Flag*. New York: Cambridge University Press, 1999. Print.
Mason, Bobbie Ann. *In Country*. 1985. London: Flamingo-Fontana, 1990. Print.
—. "P.S.: About the Book". *In Country*. 1985. New York: Harper Perennial-HarperCollins, 2005: 4–7. Print.
McDermott, Sinéad. "The Ethics of Postmemory in Bobbie Ann Mason's 'In Country.'" *The Journal of the Midwest Modern Language Association* 39.2 (Fall 2006): 5–21. Print.
McGrath, John J. *The Other End of the Spear: The Tooth-to-Tail Ratio (T3R) in Modern Military Operations*. The Long War Series. Occasional Paper 23. Fort Leavenworth, KS: Combat Studies Institute Press, 2007. Print.

McHale, Shawn. "Vietnamese Marxism, Dissent, and the Politics of Postcolonial Memory: Tran Duc Thao, 1946–1993." *Journal of Asian Studies* 61.1 (2002): 7–31. Print.
McNamara, Robert S. *In Retrospect: The Tragedy and Lessons of Vietnam*. New York: Vintage, 1996. Print.
McPherson, Nina. *Duong Thu Huong*. 2010. Web. October 25, 2013.
Miles, Jack. "In Defense of *Paco's Story*." *Los Angeles Times*. November 22, 1987. Web. October 20, 2013.
Miller, Edward and Tuong Vu. "The Vietnam War as a Vietnamese War: Agency and Society in the Study of the Second Indochinese War." *Journal of Vietnamese Studies* 4.3: 1–16 (2009). Print.
Morrison, Toni. "A Bench by the Road. Melcher Book Award acceptance speech. *World Magazine* January/February 1989. Web. October 20, 2013.
—. *Beloved*. New York: Vintage, 1987. Print.
Neilson, Jim. *Warring Fictions: Cultural Politics and the Vietnam War Narrative*. Jackson, Mississippi: University Press of Mississippi, 1998. Print.
Nguyen, Kim. "Without the Luxury of Historical Amnesia." *Amerasia* 31.2 (2005): 65–85. Print.
Nguyen, Lien-Han T. *Hanoi's War: An International History of the War for Peace in Vietnam*. Chapel Hill, NC: University of North Carolina Press, 2012. Print.
Nguyen, Nathalie Huynh Chau. "Images of Postwar Vietnam in Phan Huy Duong's 'Un Amour Métèque: nouvelles.'" *The French Review* (2004): 1206–1216. Print.
Nguyễn Thị Minh Hà, Nguyễn Thị Thanh Bình, and Lady Borton, eds. *The Defiant Muse: Vietnamese Feminist Poems from Antiquity to the Present*. New York: The Feminist Press at the City University of New York, 2007. Print.
Nguyen, Viet Thanh. "Grunts vs. Gooks: Vietnam War Literature and Marlantes' *Matterhorn*." *diaCRITICS* (June 6, 2010). Web.
—. "Remembering War, Dreaming Peace: On Cosmopolitanism, Compassion, and Literature." Ed. Scott Laderman and Edwin Martini, 132–154. Print.
—. "Speak of the Dead, Speak of Viet Nam: The Ethics and Aesthetics of Minority Discourse." *New Centennial Review* 6.2 (Fall 2006): 7–37. Print.
Nguyen-Vo Thu-Huong. "Forking Paths: How Shall We Mourn the Dead?" *Amerasia* 31.2 (2005): 157–175. Print.
Ninh, Erin Khuê. *Ingratitude: The Debt-Bound Daughter in Asian American Literature*. New York: New York University Press, 2011. Print.
Norindr, Panivong. *Phantasmatic Indochina: French Colonial Ideology in Architecture, Film, and Literature*. Durham, NC: Duke University Press, 1996. Print.

O'Brien, Tim. Breadloaf Writer's Conference Lecture. Undated. Tim O'Brien Manuscript Collection. Box 27, Folder 1. Harry Ransom Humanities Research Center, University of Texas at Austin. Print.
—. *Going After Cacciato*. 1978. New York: Broadway Books, 1999. Print.
—. *If I Die in a Combat Zone, Box Me Up and Ship Me Home*. 1973. New York: Broadway Books, 1999. Print.
—. *In the Lake of the Woods*. 1994. New York: Penguin Books, 1995. Print.
—. *July, July*. New York: Houghton Mifflin Company, 2002. Print.
—. *Northern Lights*. 1975. New York: Broadway Books, 1999. Print.
—. *The Nuclear Age*. 1985. New York: Penguin Books, 1996. Print.
—. *The Things They Carried*. 1990. New York: Broadway Books, 1998. Print.
—. "The Vietnam in Me." *New York Times Magazine* October 2, 1994: 48–57. Print.
—. *Tomcat in Love*. 1998. New York: Broadway Books, 1999. Print.
Olster, Stacey. "New Journalism and the Nonfiction Novel." *The Cambridge Companion to American Fiction After 1945*. Cambridge: Cambridge University Press, 2012. Print.
Palumbo-Liu, David. *Asian/American: Historical Crossing of a Racial Frontier*. Stanford, CA: Stanford University Press, 1999. Print.
Park, Jinim. *Narratives of the Vietnam War by Korean and American Writers*. New York: Peter Lang, 2007. Print.
Paul, Christopher and James J. Kim. *Reporters on the Battlefield: The Embedded Press System in Historical Context*. Santa Monica, CA: Rand, 2004. Print.
Pelaud, Isabelle Thuy. *This is All I Choose to Tell: History and Hybridity in Vietnamese American Literature*. Philadelphia, PA: Temple University Press, 2011. Print.
Phillips, Rufus. *Why Vietnam Matters: An Eyewitness Account of Lessons Not Learned*. Annapolis, MD: Naval Institute Press, 2008. Print.
Prados, John, ed. *In Country: Remembering the Vietnam War*. New York: Ivan R. Dee, 2011. Print.
PTSD: National Center for PTSD, November 12, 2013. Web. November 17, 2013.
Puar, Jasbir. *Terrorist Assemblages: Homonationalism in Queer Times*. Durham, NC: Duke University Press, 2007. Print.
Rejali, Darius. "A Long-Standing Trick of the Torturer's Art." *The Seattle Times* May 14, 2004. Web. June 6, 2013.
Rescue Dawn. Dir. Werner Herzog. Perf. Christian Bale, Marshall Bell, François Chau, Jeremy Davies et al. MGM, 2006. Film.
"Resign, Rumsfeld." *The Economist* May 8, 2004. Cover. Print.
Ringnalda, Don. *Fighting and Writing the Vietnam War*. Jackson, MI: University Press of Mississippi, 1994. Print.

Rody, Caroline. "Toni Morrison's *Beloved*: History, 'Rememory,' and a 'Clamor for a Kiss.'" *Understanding Toni Morrison's Beloved and Sula: Selected Criticisms of the Works by the Nobel Prize-Winning Author*. Ed. Solomon Iyasere and Marla Iyasere. Troy, NY: Whitson, 2000, 82–112. Print.

Rowe, John Carlos. *The New American Studies*. Minneapolis, MN: University of Minnesota Press, 2002. Print.

Ryan, Maureen. *The Other Side of Grief: The Home Front and the Aftermath in American Narratives of the Vietnam War*. Amherst, MA: University of Massachusetts Press, 2008. Print.

Rydstrøm, Helle. "Gendered Corporeality and Bare Lives: Local Sacrifices and Sufferings during the Vietnam War." *Signs* 37.2 (2012): 275–299. Print.

Sachs, Dana. "Small Tragedies and Distant Stars: Le Minh Khue's Language of Lost Ideals." *Crossroads* 13.1 (1999): 1–10. Print.

Sack, John. *M*. New York: New American Library, 1967. Print.

Savelsberg, Joachim J. and Ryan D. King. *American Memories: Atrocities and the Law*. Rose Series in Sociology. New York: Russell Sage Foundation, 2011. Print.

Saving Private Ryan. Dir. Steven Spielberg. Perf. Tom Hanks, Matt Damon, Tom Sizemore, Edward Burns. Dreamworks, 1998. Film.

Schafer, John C. "The Collective and the Individual in Two Post-War Vietnamese Novels." *Crossroads* 14.2 (2000): 13–48. Print.

—. "The Vietnamese Land Reform Program as Literary Theme." Ed. Mark Heberle, 180–213. Print.

Schiller, Nina Glick, Linda Bash, and Cristina Blanc-Szanton, eds. "Towards a Definition of Transnationalism: Introductory Remarks and Research Questions." *Towards a Transnational Perspective on Migration: Race, Class, Ethnicity, and Nationalism Reconsidered*. New York: Annals of the New York Academy of Sciences, 1992, ix–xiv. Print.

Schroeder, Eric James. "Herr, Michael. 'We've All Been There.'" *Vietnam, We've All Been There: Interviews with American Writers*. Westport, CN: Praeger, 1992, 32–49. Print.

Scott, Grant. "*Paco's Story* and the Ethics of Violence." *Critique* 36.1 (1994): 69–80. Print.

Scott, Wilbur J. and Sandra Carson Stanley. *Gays and Lesbians in the Military: Issues, Concerns, and Contrasts*. Social Problems and Social Issues. New York: Aldine de Gruyter, 1994. Print.

Searle, William J. "Dissident Voices: The NVA Experience in Novels by Vietnamese." *War, Literature, and the Arts* 10.2 (1998): 224–238. Print.

Shah, Sonia, ed. *Dragon Ladies: Asian American Feminists Breath Fire*. Boston, MA: South End Press, 1997. Print.
Shay, Jonathan. *Achilles in Vietnam: Combat Trauma and the Undoing of Character*. New York: Touchstone, 1994. Print.
—. *Odysseus in America: Combat Trauma and the Trials of Homecoming*. New York: Scribner, 2002. Print.
Sheehan, Neil. *A Bright Shining Lie: John Paul Vann and America in Vietnam*. New York: Random House, 1988. Print.
Shilts, Randy. *Conduct Unbecoming: Lesbians and Gays in the U.S. Military, Vietnam To the Persian Gulf*. New York: St. Martin's Press, 1993. Print.
Silesky, Barry. "Larry Heinemann: A Conversation." *Another Chicago Magazine* 25 (1993): 179–96. Print.
Smith, Lorrie. "'The Things Men Do': The Gendered Subtext in Tim O'Brien's *Esquire* Stories." *Critique: Studies in Contemporary Fiction* 36.1 (Fall 1994): 16–40. Print.
Solis, Tatjana. *The Lotus Eaters*. New York: St. Martin's Griffin, 2011. Print.
Standard Operating Procedure. Dir. Errol Morris. Sony Pictures Classics, 2008. Film.
Statler, Kathryn C. *Replacing France: The Origins of American Intervention in Vietnam*. Lexington, KY: University Press of Kentucky, 2007. Print.
Steigerwald, David. *The Sixties and the End of Modern America*. New York: St. Martin's Press, 1995. Print.
Stolorow, Robert. *Trauma and Human Existence: Autobiographical, Psychoanalytic, and Philosophical Reflections*. New York: Routledge, 2007. Print.
Stur, Heather Marie. *Beyond Combat: Women and Gender in the Vietnam War Era*. New York: Cambridge University Press, 2011. Print.
Sturken, Marita. *Tangled Memories: The Vietnam War, The AIDS Epidemic, and the Politics of Remembering*. Berkeley, CA: University of California Press, 1997. Print.
Sullivan, Richard. "The Recreation of Vietnam: The War in American Fiction, Poetry, and Drama." *The Legacy: The Vietnam War in the American Imagination*. Ed. D. Michael Shafer. Boston, MA: Beacon Press, 1990, 179–181. Print.
Tái, Huệ Tam Hồ. "Dương Thu Hương and the Literature of Disenchantment." *Việt Nam Forum* 14 (1993): 82–91. Print.
—. *The Country of Memory: Remaking the Past in Late Socialist Vietnam*. Berkeley, CA: University of California Press, 2001. Print.

Tal, Kalí. "Speaking the Language of Pain: Vietnam War Literature in the Context of a Literature of Trauma." Ed. Philip K. Jason, 217–250. Print.

—. *Worlds of Hurt: Reading the Literatures of Trauma*. New York: Cambridge University Press, 1996. Print.

Taylor, Mark. *The Vietnam War in History, Literature and Film*. Tuscaloosa, AL: The University of Alabama Press, 2003. Print.

Thien, Madeleine. *Photocopies of Photocopies: On Bao Ninh*. May 31, 2011. Web. October 8, 2013.

Thompson, Hunter S. *Fear and Loathing in Las Vegas: A Savage Journey to the Heart of the American Dream*. New York: Random House, 1971. Print.

—. *Hell's Angels: A Strange and Terrible Saga*. New York: Random House, 1966. Print.

—. "The Kentucky Derby is Decadent and Depraved." *Scanlan's Monthly* (June 1970). Print.

Timmerman, John H. "Tim O'Brien and the Art of the True War Story: 'Night March' and 'Speaking of Courage.'" *Twentieth Century Literature* 46.1 (2000): 100–114. Print.

Tran, Barbara, Monique T. D. Truong, and Luu Truong Khoi, eds. *Watermark: Vietnamese American Poetry and Prose*. New York: Asian American Writers; Workshop, 1998. Print.

Trần Mạnh Hảo. *Separation (Ly Thân)*. Ho Chi Minh City: Đồng Na, 1989. Print.

Tran, Nhung Tuyet and Anthony J. S. Reid, eds. *Viet Nam: Borderless Histories*. Madison, WI: The University of Wisconsin Press, 2006. Print.

Tran, Thy. "Modern Woman: An Exclusive Interview with Novelist le thi diem thuy." *Nha Magazine* (September/October 2003): 80–88. Print.

Tritle, Lawrence. *From Melos to My Lai: War and Survival*. New York: Routledge, 2000. Print.

Tropic Thunder. Dir. Ben Stiller. Perf. Ben Stiller, Robert Downey, Jr. Dreamworks, 2008. Film.

Trương Như Táng. *A Viet Cong Memoir*. New York: Vintage, 1986. Print.

Turse, Nick. *Kill Anything That Moves: The Real War in Vietnam*. New York: Henry Holt, 2013. Print.

US Government Printing Office. "Why Vietnam." House Document No. 311. Washington, DC. October 1965. Web.

Văn Tiến Dũng. *Our Great Spring Victory*. New York: Monthly Review Press, 1977. Print.

Vickroy, Laurie. *Trauma and Survival in Contemporary Fiction*. Charlottesville, VA: University of Virginia Press, 2002. Print.

Vietnam Veterans to Correct the Myths. *Our "Pre-Sponse": A Supplement to the TTU-NARA Conference on Vietnam in the Year 1963*. Houston, TX: Radix Press, 2013. Print.

Weaver, Gina Marie. *Ideologies of Forgetting: Rape in the Vietnam War*. Albany, NY: State University of New York Press, 2010. Print.

Webb, James. *Fields of Fire*. New York: Bantam Books, 1978. Print.

Weingarten, Marc. *The Gang that Wouldn't Write Straight: Wolfe, Thompson, Didion, and the New Journalism Revolution*. New York: Crown, 2006. Print.

We Were Soldiers. Dir. Randall Wallace. Perf. Mel Gibson, Madeleine Stowe, Greg Kinnear, and Sam Elliott. Paramount and Icon, 2002. Film.

Wiest, Andrew and Michael J. Doidge, eds. *Triumph Revisited: Historians Battle for the Vietnam War*. New York: Routledge, 2010. Print.

Wolfe, Tom. *The Electric Kool-Aid Acid Test*. New York: Farrar, Straus, & Giroux, 1968. Print.

—. *The Kandy-Kolored Tangerine-Flake Streamline Baby*. New York: Farrar, Straus, & Giroux, 1965. Print.

Wolfe, Tom and E. W. Johnson, eds. *The New Journalism: With an Anthology*. New York: Harper & Row, 1973. Print.

Young, Marilyn. "Human Sacrifices." *The Women's Review of Books* (1993): 24–25. Print.

INDEX

Abu Ghraib scandal 153–6
American military advisors 3–4
Appy, Christian 62, 69n. 15
atrocity 9, 143

Bacevich, Andrew 160, 162, 179
Bảo Ninh 47–70 see also *The Sorrow of War*
Bates, Milton 16
Beidler, Philip D. 13–14
Beloved 137–58 see also Morrison, Toni
Berlant, Lauren 72, 89, 92
"blood sacrifice" 168–78
Boyle, Brenda 17, 159–82
Bradley, Mark Philip 2–3
Butler, Judith 91–3, 164

Christopher, Renny 10
Connell, R. W. 164–5
critical theory 21

Dispatches 27–45, 165
see also Herr, Michael
Đởi Mới 50
Duong, Lan 47, 49, 56, 60, 61, 98, 102, 112
Dương Thu Hương 47–70
see also *Novel Without A Name, Paradise of the Blind*

Espiritu, Yen Le 68, 109

femininity/ies 80, 119–30
France in Viet Nam 2–3, 5, 27–8, 55
Franklin, H. Bruce 47, 134–5, 181n. 22

gender 80–2, 95–114, 117–19
see also femininity/ies, masculinity/ies
geography 29–30, 65–8
Going After Cacciato 119–24
see also O'Brien, Tim

Halberstam, Judith 166
Hawkins, Ty 15
Hedges, Chris 4
Heinemann, Larry 137–58
see also *Paco's Story*
Hellmann, John 15, 62
Herman, Judith (Lewis) 78, 139
Herr, Michael 27–45, 165
see also *Dispatches*
Herzog, Tobey 14–15, 115
Hirsch, Marianne 76

Ingle, David W. 168–78
In Country 71–94 see also Mason, Bobbie Ann
In the Lake of the Woods 130–6
see also O'Brien, Tim

Jeffords, Susan 15–16, 81, 151
Johnson, Denis 159–82
see also *Tree of Smoke*

INDEX

Kinney, Katherine 16, 22, 115–16

le thi diem thuy 95–114
  see also *The Gangster We Are All Looking For*
Luckhurst, Roger 78, 158n. 6

Marlantes, Karl 159–82
  see also *Matterhorn: A Novel of the Vietnam War*
Marvin, Carolyn 168–78
masculinity/ies 81, 86, 119–30, 151, 163–82
Mason, Bobbie Ann 71–94
  see also *In Country*
Matterhorn: A Novel of the Vietnam War 170–4
  see also Marlantes, Karl
memory 100
"postmemory" 75–7, 105
morality of war 117
Morris, Errol 154, 155
Morrison, Toni 137–58
  see also *Beloved*

Neilson, Jim 16
New Journalism 31–5, 35–40
Nguyen, Viet Thanh 17
"compulsory empathy" 17
Nguyen-Vo Thu-Huong 48
Novel Without A Name 47–70
  see also Dương Thu Hương

O'Brien, Tim 115–36
  see also *Going After Cacciato, In the Lake of the Woods, The Things They Carried*

Paco's Story 137–58
  see also Heinemann, Larry
Paradise of the Blind 47–70
  see also Dương Thu Hương
Park, Jinim 17

Pelaud, Isabelle Thuy 17
Post-Traumatic Stress Disorder (PTSD) 11, 18, 78–9

race 95–114, 171, 181n. 18
Ringnalda, Don 15
Ryan, Maureen 10–11
Rydstrøm, Helle 61, 62

sacrifice 57–62
Schafer, John C. 48–51, 54, 55
Shay, Jonathan 138–9
Solis, Tatjana 159–82 see also *The Lotus Eaters*
Sturken, Marita 72, 81, 88, 91
"Support the Troops" Syndrome 162–3, 168

Tal, Kalí 79, 122, 153
Taylor, Mark 16–17
The Gangster We Are All Looking For 95–114 see also le thi diem thuy
The Lotus Eaters 174–8
  see also Solis, Tatjana
The Sorrow of War 47–70
  see also Bảo Ninh
The Things They Carried 124–30
  see also O'Brien, Tim
Thompson, Hunter S. 32–8
trauma 18, 27–45, 85, 100, 104, 137–58
Tree of Smoke 166–70
  see also Johnson, Denis
Turse, Nick 9–10

Vietnamese American literature 109–13
Vietnamese diaspora/displacement 96, 104, 110
Vietnamese literature 47–70
"disillusionment" literature 49–57
Renovation Literature 53–4

Vietnam Syndrome 95
Vietnam Veterans Memorial
  (VVM) 71, 87–91
Vietnam War,
  American literature 7–12
  films 1–2, 31, 161
  and Iraq War 160–1
  Korean literature 17
  veterans 72, 77
  veteran authors 12–17

Wolfe, Tom 32–8

www.ingramcontent.com/pod-product-compliance
Lightning Source LLC
Chambersburg PA
CBHW050138240426
43673CB00043B/1719